362.2086 BOBROW
Bobrow, Joseph.
Waking up from war :a better way home
for veterans and nations /

Advance Praise

———— •◦• ————

"'The costs of war are so great that we just have to find ways to resolve our differences that do not involve killing one another.' The speaker is not the Dalai Lama or the Pope or Dr. King. He is Major General Mike Myatt, USMC, speaking over the serried graves of 30,000 American warriors in the San Francisco National Cemetery. He is speaking the truth as only a warrior can understand it. In *Waking Up from War*, Joseph Bobrow stuns us with that truth revealed, often through the words of warriors, in ways we cannot fail to grasp, to grieve over, and to lament our failure to deal with. Read this book and begin to understand a great deal about how we are neglecting our men and women veterans, about what is wrong today in America, and most vitally, about how to change for the better both situations."

—*Lawrence Wilkerson, Colonel (Ret.), U.S. Army; former Chief of Staff for Gen. Colin Powell*

"Dr. Joe Bobrow is a true American hero. He's worked tirelessly to support our community through the hardest times and the toughest spots. He overflows with wisdom and has been a real leader. His dedication, innovative approach, and compassion serve as an example and an inspiration to people worldwide. His words should be a wake-up call for anyone who cares about the future of our country."

—*Paul Rieckhoff, Founder and CEO, Iraq and Afghanistan Veterans of America; author of* Chasing Ghosts

"*Waking Up from War* is a 'must read' not only for mental health professionals treating our veterans and their families, but for all of us. Bobrow's emphasis on the need for an accepting and compassionate culture that will truly listen to the moral suffering of our veterans is profoundly important."

—*Judith Broder, MD, Founder, The Soldier's Project*

"Joseph Bobrow has captured the soul of the young Americans who go to war to defend our freedoms. His book tells the story of the Coming Home Project as it shepherds our veterans back into their communities and families, and goes beyond usual approaches to support and nourish their deepest experience."

—*Stephen N. Xenakis, MD, Brigadier General (Ret.)*

WAKING UP FROM WAR

WAKING UP FROM WAR

A Better Way Home for Veterans and Nations

Joseph Bobrow

Foreword by H. H. The Dalai Lama

PITCHSTONE PUBLISHING
Durham, North Carolina

Pitchstone Publishing
Durham, North Carolina
www.pitchstonepublishing.com

10 9 8 7 6 5 4 3 2 1

Library of Congress Cataloging-in-Publication Data

Bobrow, Joseph.
 Waking up from war : a better way home for veterans and nations / Joseph Bobrow ; foreword by H. H. The 14th Dalai Lama.
   pages cm
 Includes bibliographical references.
 ISBN 978-1-63431-032-1 (hardcover : alk. paper)
  1. Veterans—Mental health services—United States. 2. Veterans families—United States—Psychology. 3. Post-traumatic stress disorder—United States. 4. Coming Home Project (Organization) 5. Iraq War, 2003-2011—Veterans—Mental health—United States. 6. Afghan War, 2001—Veterans—Mental health—United States. I. Title.
 UH629.3.B63 2015
 362.2086'970973—dc23
                                    2015015108

Cover image description and credit: Sgt. 1st Class Justin Hathaway, United States Forces–Iraq Provost Marshal Office operations noncommissioned officer in charge, braves a sandstorm after leaving the 9th Air and Space Expeditionary Task Force–Iraq and U.S. Forces–Iraq Provost Marshal Office at Al Asad Air Base, Iraq, September 27, 2011. U.S. Air Forces Central, Baghdad Media Outreach Team Photo by Master Sgt. Cecilio Ricardo.

For all the veterans, service members, and their families, children,
and care providers with whom I have had the privilege
of learning and growing.

For my son Aaron, and for all sons and daughters everywhere: Pacem.

In loving memory of Jean Sanville and Hedda Bolgar.

Contents

Foreword

I have always believed that Gandhi's way of using nonviolence to achieve political goals is the best way to solve international problems. Almost every conflict can be solved by sincere negotiations. We know all too well how many lives were lost and how much destruction was wrought during two world wars and the conflicts that followed them in the last century.

Wars are fought to achieve a desired goal. But war's results are unpredictable and almost always detrimental. This has been especially true with the wars fought in recent memory. When war breaks out, nations send their young men and women to face off with the intention of protecting civilians and defending the nation. But soldiers are also human beings and also wish for safety. Can't we realize how great is the suffering they undergo as a result of wars?

The suffering war creates is universal. Veterans leave the battlefield with physical, moral, and emotional injuries that can last a lifetime. When one combatant is killed or maimed, five or ten others—relatives and friends—suffer also. We should be horrified by this tragedy.

I am deeply happy to learn that since 2007, Joseph Bobrow and the interdisciplinary team at Coming Home Project have made the inner peace of veterans and their families their priority and have dedicated themselves to helping them. They are now bringing out a book titled *Waking Up from War: A Better Way Home for Veterans and Nations*, based on the findings of their research on the psychological, social, family, and moral traumas of veterans and how best to help them.

I congratulate Joseph and his team for their altruism and dedication and wish them success.

With prayers,
Tenzin Gyatso
The 14th Dalai Lama

Introduction

Call

"Pay no attention to the man behind the curtain!" With these words, the Wizard of Oz gave a direct order: *Do not be aware. Don't see what is before your eyes.* Our nation's leader and commander-in-chief gave essentially the same message at the outset of the Iraq War. *Don't worry about war, costs, or consequences. Exercise your freedom; go shopping.* Too many of us were glad to comply. The Great Disconnect had begun, and from there it only got worse.

Pay no attention to what's going on in the war zone. Ignore the coffins of American service members arriving at Dover Air Force Base. Do not look at their body parts, which have been scattered hither and yon. Pay no attention to the thousands of veterans and service members falling through the cracks of an unprepared healthcare system. Don't notice those systems as dysfunction and corruption worsen. Don't listen, learn, connect, reflect, and respond to what's going on, its impacts, or its costs.

Thus was born the collective trance of America, and it continues to the present day. If the United States were a psychiatric patient, we would diagnose this as dissociative identity disorder. *Cheer up, keep spending, and don't let the terrorists get the better of you. Wars are for your safety and the security of the homeland. Danger is lurking; there's no time to lose. If you ask too many questions or wait for a smoking gun, it could come in the form of a mushroom cloud. Disavow your mind and unhitch your sensibilities. No draft, no skin in the game for the general public: Leave the driving to us.*

Since 2007, my colleagues and I have had the honor of helping American service members and veterans—as well as their families and children—reintegrate into civilian life. We need to start by *integrating*, reclaiming our wholeness through paying attention. Modern medicine has done wonders with physical injuries and amputations, but modern society has abdicated its own critical faculties. It's time to shake free of forgetting, to register what we see and know, and to act in accord.

This fog of war envelops not only service members and veterans, but also families, caregivers, service providers, veteran service organizations, and government entities like the Department of Veterans Affairs, the Department of Defense, Congress, and the White House. What will it take to wake our nation up from its collective trance? We have compartmentalized the experience of years of war and put it out of our mind's eye. Until we can face the truth of war and its dreadful costs, we will not provide the best care for our veterans.

I have written *Waking Up from War* to remind us all to pay attention, to wake up together, and to rediscover our fundamental responsibility and connectedness. As individuals and as a nation, we must face the havoc wreaked by war and do everything we can to repair the damage. Only when we face the suffering with patience, courage, and love will we be able to reclaim our humanity, connect the dissociated pieces, and heal. Only by facing these realities that are so difficult to bear can we learn from the past and stop making the same mistakes over and over again.

Response

It's January 2007, the first moments of our first Coming Home Project retreat, an opportunity for veterans and families from around the country to come together to share stories and support one another. We gather for our first circle, thirty-three veterans and family members from seven states, with four facilitators. In the opening moment of silence, as we remember those unable to be with us, Ben, Stefanie and Michael's three-year-old son, is playing with Isaiah, also three, around the edges of our circle. Amid the reverent quiet, we hear Ben say, "My daddy died in Iraq." We learn later from Stephanie that Michael actually committed suicide six months after returning home. Out of the mouth of babes, the first words spoken at a retreat have their own truth: something inside Michael did die in Iraq.

As I reflect on Ben's words, I see the roots of what would blossom over the following six years: In a safe space, short on judgment and filled with compassion, an environment where trust and belonging prevail, veterans and families would express their truth, their experience of war. Toddler Ben spoke to everyone and we heard him loud and clear. He laid the groundwork for a weekend of truth-telling and a reliable path to healing the traumas of war.

Given the chance, veterans and their families want to reconnect and heal. It begins as they come together with one another as fellow veterans, spouses and partners, children and teenagers, parents and grandparents, siblings, uncles and aunties, finding and creating affinity. In an atmosphere of safety it spreads; family members rebuild bridges, and everyone begins to connect with something inside that has gone untended.

Ken Sargent, a Marine master sergeant, and Rory Dunn, an Army specialist, are Iraq veterans who both sustained severe traumatic brain injuries that required life-saving and massive reconstructive surgery. Ken was shot in the head, Rory was hit by an improvised explosive device. Both also suffer from post-traumatic stress. As people mill around, Rory and Ken meet for the first time, up close and personal. Since neither can see very well, they touch each other's wounds, comparing scars and injuries. They are long-lost brothers. The process of making emotional connections palpable has begun.

Rory was angry and bitter. It wasn't just the open head injury that cost him the sight of his left eye and that resulted in a brain composed partially of plastic filler. He was also upset about the buddies in his unit who died in the massive IED (improvised explosive device) attack on his twenty-second birthday, and about the associated failures in leadership. "No one but a vet can understand another vet" are his first words. But at the end of the day, he says to a civilian volunteer, "You're alright." As he is leaving, I notice a scrap of paper on the floor near his seat, pick it up, and ask if it's his. He says, "Yeah, it's nothing." I look at it and see a note, with three family trees. I ask him about it: "It's all the people back home blown away by my buddies' dying." I look and see the words: "girlfriend," "baby," "church members," "mother," "father," "sister," and so on—three little stories, three little family trees. Radiating impacts that eat at him. Although Rory sustained a severe traumatic brain injury and post-traumatic stress, given the chance, he reclaims not just the piece of paper, but an important part of his emotional life. He is able to leave with a measure of hope and trust.

War trauma is like an IED blast. The sonic waves radiate out on multiple levels simultaneously, fragmenting the intrinsic connections within the warrior, his body, brain, mind, and soul, fragmenting his family, social supports, relationship with his community, the organizations charged with his care, the institutions and leaders responsible for protecting the country, and the entire culture. Repairing this pervasive fracturing means regenerating capacities for connectivity at every level, waking up from the dissociative fog of war that enshrouds all the players in this devastating cycle, transforming the traumatic residues, and learning from experience. In this book, I demonstrate how this healing and awakening can be accomplished and where and why it often fails.

Visible injuries, including amputations and disfigurements, are today being remedied with astonishing medical advances. Not so the unseen wounds, including closed-head mild and moderate traumatic brain injury, post-traumatic stress, and pervasive moral and spiritual injuries. One service member per day takes his or her own life. The rate is 18 per day for veterans. More service members have died over the past two years at their own hands than on the battlefield. For every service member killed in the war zone, 25 veterans are dying by their own hands.[1]

Post-9/11 veterans are not a breed apart. They reside in our neighborhoods. They toil alongside us in the workplace. Their children are our children's schoolmates; their wives and husbands, mothers and fathers, wait with us in the checkout lines at the grocery store. They fill our community and state colleges and universities right alongside the sons and daughters of civilians. Veterans are in our prisons, our courts, our public health clinics. They live on our streets, show up in homeless shelters, and participate in substance abuse and domestic violence programs. Their rates of homelessness, unemployment, and suicide are significantly higher than the national average, and they are keeping our law enforcement rapid response units busy. Nearly 40 percent of veterans suffer some mental health impacts of service or traumatic brain injury. Many are also superbly qualified leaders and civic resources who must overcome multiple obstacles to find opportunities to serve in the civilian world.

Throughout history, warriors have returned bearing both visible and unseen scars. But today—after the longest wars in U.S. history—our entire country is shell-shocked and benumbed. As veterans navigate the road home, they see few signs of shared sacrifice on the home front and often feel alienated and misunderstood. The burden of these wars has been dramatically uneven: less than 1% of our population, about 2.8 million people, have served in Iraq and Afghanistan. When we factor in extended family and close friends, the number of those directly touched by these two wars is closer to forty million, still only about 12% of Americans. The majority has not been asked to sacrifice for these war efforts.Ordinary people throughout the country, however, do bear great good will toward our service members and veterans and many have a compelling desire to do right by them.

In my experience most civilians are keenly interested in communicating with veterans and their families—in both learning from them and sharing with them. Veterans and their families are surprised and buoyed to experience the genuine concern of civilians. With opportunities to bridge the military-civilian chasm, veterans feel less isolated from the rest of society. Our first weekend workshop was preceded by a community gathering of 250 people at First Congregational Church in Berkeley. Presenters were military officers, Buddhist teachers, veterans, spouses, and poets. Although a few attended to see whether a fight would break out among incompatible presenters, it didn't. To the contrary, the diversity made for an inspiring, heartwarming, and heartwrenching evening. The next day, workshop participants who had been in the audience said they were surprised so many people cared enough to come out to hear what they had gone through. One said he woke up the next morning "with the wind at my back."

The two undeclared but very real wars we have all been enduring have fostered a numbing sense of unreality. Until a few years ago, the country was prohibited from seeing the coffins of the fallen arrive back home. Body parts of those killed were discarded or destroyed and not included in burials. Media coverage of American and civilian losses was tightly managed. Now we are coming face to face with the costs, including alarmingly high suicide rates, high rates of substance abuse, violent episodes at home, and atrocities in the war zone.

A *New York Times* article reported that an attack by American helicopters that left 23 Afghan civilians dead was found to be a mistake caused by an undigested "swirl of data."[2] The nature of war has changed, with a growing emphasis on "surgical" and tactical strikes and the use of drones. More and more American Air Force pilots go to war by sitting in front of a series of screens, right here in Nevada, New Mexico, and California. Not surprisingly, some service members have great trouble focusing—and even more importantly, some become desensitized and prone to glaze over—a modern variant of the old "thousand-yard stare," a phrase popularized when *Life* magazine published a painting by World War II artist and correspondent Tom Lea portraying a marine at the Battle of Peleliu.[3]

For airmen who operate drones thousands of miles away, the stress lingers when the shift is over. Anthony, an airman first class, says his "brain hurts each night" when he returns home. He tries working out but what actually helps the tension ebb is "just being able to enjoy a nice bowl of cereal with almond milk." Video games, the activity of choice for many veterans, don't do the trick. "I need something real," Anthony says.[4]

That *something real*, I have learned, is actuated by reconnecting in a safe community of veterans and families. For seven years my colleagues and I have been working with thousands of returning troops and their family members, helping create just such a community. Community grows a connective social tissue where the unseen injuries such as post-traumatic stress and traumatic brain injury can be safely addressed. "Something real" is discovered by coming alive to the beauty in the great outdoors, hiking the Sierras, journaling in a grove of old-growth Redwoods, or rafting down a river. It is coming back to one's body, to the present moment, through wellness practices like meditation and qigong. It is learning to laugh again with buddies, with partners and children. Much of the primary material in the book is drawn from a unique source: nationally recognized, research-proven reintegration retreats that create trust, belonging, and camaraderie, where veterans feel safe enough to open up with one another about experiences they have rarely if ever shared with anyone else.

As a psychoanalyst (and as a patient), I had experienced the transformative power of the emotional connections that develop in the consulting room. My intuition told me they could be cultivated in a non-psychiatric, community-building setting characterized by unconditional acceptance. But I did not anticipate being moved to tears in the moments before our first retreat when I saw Kenny and Rory come up to within inches of the other, straining to see, and then spontaneously trace with their fingers the contours of one another's scars. They wanted to make contact, and we were providing the opportunity for them to do just that.

My friend, psychoanalyst Jean Sanville, called this "reparative intent" and said we all have it. We are wired to connect. She liked to quote child psychiatrist Rene Spitz, "Life begins in dialogue and all psychopathology can be seen as derailment of dialogue."[5] War represents just such an unraveling of natural connections *and* the capacity to make them. But this ability can be restored, when the right ingredients are present. That is what I set out to do with colleagues in 2006 when we founded the Coming Home Project.

I write this book through the eyes of a Zen master, clinical psychologist, and psychoanalyst. But my personal and professional trajectory has taken me off the beaten path. For the past four decades, I have been integrating western psychology and Buddhist mindfulness to create non-denominational learning and healing environments that bring together the best of East and West. While a freshman at City College of New York, I worked in recreation programs for disadvantaged youth at East Side House Settlement in the South Bronx, traversed Harlem photographing children, and created after-school enrichment programs for minority youth in the suburbs of Paris. I brought young parents together for tea while their toddlers played and made art in a daycare center in working class London, and founded a cooperative nursery school in culturally diverse rural Hawai'i. While training in Zen Buddhism, my teacher and I led a meditation group for incarcerated adults before mindfulness became popular. Much later I began an educational and support program for high-conflict divorcing families at a large urban medical center, created mentoring and meditation groups for incarcerated teenagers, and residential learning workshops for mental health practitioners on spirituality and emotional growth. As I look back, the thread that runs through all of these endeavors is a profound conviction in the transformative power of community. I see now that I have been a community activator, helping catalyze the connectedness and healing that lie latent within and among us, waiting to be unleashed.

Six months into working on Coming Home Project, I recognized that I had what is sometimes called "the passion" for this work. As I thought about how this came to be, I was gazing at the cover of a book that had a famous *Life* magazine photo of a G.I., with a shell-shocked, glazed-over look on his face. Suddenly, I "remembered" that my father loved this photo, and that he himself had served in the infantry in World War II, and lost his two brothers. They had been like fathers to him, given the traumatic loss of his father from a heart attack when he was two years old. "Broken," was the word that floated up. I understood, as if for the first time, that, on returning home, he, like so many war veterans, was looking to lose and heal himself at the same time. He became involved with my mother, and I was the result of their passionate union. A wave of sadness and shame rolled through me. He had left when I was a baby, unable to sustain the marriage. For years, I wasn't sure who my father was, but when I was 24, I found him. After four years of coming to know each other, he died of leukemia the day after Father's Day, at age 60. I wished my entry into this world had been more conscious; with a father and mother who both wanted a child, and wanted to raise that child together.

I took the risk of sharing this experience with my friend Steve Robinson, a former Army Ranger, veteran of the first Gulf War, and a tireless veteran advocate. Steve died recently, working at his desk—a tragic loss. I was grateful to him for listening, and relieved to learn that his story was much the same as mine: a war veteran father, in his case Vietnam era, who, in his brokenness conceived a child but was unable to commit to his new family due to profound unaddressed emotional injuries. When I was able to write a poem, "Day of Atonement," my sense of shame receded. I realized what I already knew: I was implicated. I was a military kid.

September 11, 2001 left me reeling. Like so many people, I felt helpless thinking about the great damage a war would inflict, not only on this generation, but on many generations to come. Rather than stew in this state, given my experience with meditation, healing communities, and trauma, I realized that I could join with others and try to make a difference. I responded by organizing programs to support fellow psychotherapists whom I knew would be tested as they helped their patients process this collective tragedy. It was life-giving to gather together, share our experiences in a safe setting, and use expressive arts to represent what could not yet be put into words. Writing a poem, "The First Casualties," also helped.

I knew the perpetrators of 9/11 needed to be brought to justice, but I was concerned as the drumbeats to war in Iraq became louder. I attended a number of panels where veterans spoke about their experiences in the war zone and how it was after they returned to civilian life. I could not abide the moral outrage of letting brave women and men and their families and children languish after sacrificing so much.

It was 2006 and troops were returning stateside in droves. They and their family members were falling through the cracks of the unprepared, overtaxed, and outmoded healthcare systems of the Veterans Administration (VA) and the Department of Defense (DoD). If we waited for the government to fulfill these basic responsibilities, anguish would only intensify and tens of thousands would fail to receive the care they desperately needed and had fully earned. While I couldn't change the course of our response as a nation, I didn't have to stew in indignation and frustration. I could do something.

Most service members who needed treatment, especially for unseen injuries such as post-traumatic stress and mild to moderate closed head TBIs were loathe to come forward—afraid of losing their security clearances, their promotions, the respect of their comrades, and opportunity to continue to serve alongside their battle buddies. I had the sense that an unconditionally welcoming non-judgmental community that included veterans' families could be an inviting and healing resource.

Initially I envisioned offering two tracks: one, confidential, pro-bono psychological treatment with a cadre of psychotherapists trained not only in trauma but in military culture, working collaboratively to augment the stretched VA and DoD mental health services. In tandem with providing accessible treatment, I conceived a second track: a welcoming and therapeutic environment that would diminish the sense of stigma, because it was not seen as therapy. We could tap into, mobilize and leverage peer support, provide an atmosphere of unconditional acceptance, instruction in stress management and wellness practices, a range of expressive arts, and vigorous outdoor recreation in teams that drew on war experiences, but adapted to a civilian setting. I imagined that those in psychological treatment could partake in the family-based retreats, and some attending the retreats might see the need for further care and, given the long wait times at VA and DoD facilities, be able to conveniently access a trusted, confidential, and free local resource.

Later that year, with colleagues—volunteer psychotherapists, chaplains, seasoned veterans and family members—we began offering retreats for veterans and their families. The retreats provided small peer support groups, expressive arts, wellness practices such as meditation, and vigorous outdoor activities. After the first few retreats, we added secular rituals into the program. I enjoyed the dawning realization that these elements were not a new "quick fix," but have been utilized since time immemorial to transform trauma. These five activities came together organically and added value to one another: sharing stories in a safe environment (healing dialogue), wellness practices such as meditation, yoga, and qigong (spiritual practice), expressive arts, being active in beautiful places (the healing power of nature), and secular ritual (adapted from reverent religious experience). Four core human capacities emerged from these retreats—aliveness, bonding and closeness, self-regulation, and a sense of meaning and purpose—elements of a life worth living. A marine's exclamation helped me grasp the importance of aliveness.

Jeremy Williams and his wife were struggling. After two long tours, he was drinking, shouting at the kids, and taking his exasperation out on his wife. The couple had broken up and gotten back together twice. They came to a retreat to improve their relationship and get help with Jeremy's post-traumatic stress. Retreat participants could elect to spend an afternoon kayaking on beautiful Tomales Bay. Jeremy and his wife won the impromptu family race back from Heart's Desire Beach. When they hit shore back in Marshall, Jeremy exclaimed, "Joe, I'm so high!" His and his wife's faces showed the natural high of being connected within themselves, between one another, among other veteran families, and with the sheer beauty of the great outdoors. Aliveness is our birthright, but Jeremy had been unable to reclaim this quality after the adrenaline-fueled surges of the war zone. On the beautiful, rushing waters of Tomales Bay, together with his wife and children and other supportive military and veteran families and civilian volunteers, he found a way once again to enjoy life-giving exhilaration and share nourishing connection.   For many veterans, the stigma of needing help is a huge obstacle, but we witnessed stigma evaporate by the end of the retreats, as isolation lifted, replaced by a sense of belonging, being in the soup together. We knew we were on to something when, during the closing circles, participants' comments began to echo across retreats. They said they'd never experienced an environment this safe, this trusting, where they could be real and reconnect with their fellow vets, their families, and themselves—where they could risk letting their guards down, experience the belonging and camaraderie of service again, and feel free to open up as much or as little as they wanted. At the end of a retreat, as we were saying our goodbyes, one veteran said, "This is how church should feel."

Since 2007 Coming Home Project's interdisciplinary team has provided both psychological treatment and multidisciplinary retreats and other programs that help veterans, their families, and their caregivers transform the traumas of war and enjoy genuine well-being. Coming Home is a non-profit organization committed to alleviating the unseen injuries of war faced by Iraq and Afghanistan veterans, service members, and their families and caregivers. Combining early intervention, prevention, and treatment elements, it addresses the whole person with an integrative, bio-psycho-social/family-spiritual approach. It helps veterans and families experience a sense of safety and community that supports them in rebuilding the connections among body, mind, heart, and soul that often come unraveled as a result of military service. It provides opportunities to renew relationships with family members, create and sustain protective peer support networks, eliminate the stigma that interferes with exploring further support, and connect with needed care. Coming Home has served 3,000 people from all fifty states, in four regions around the country, without government funding.

In 2012, the Defense Centers of Excellence for Psychological Health and TBI (DCoE), a joint DoD and VA agency mandated to identify, evaluate, and disseminate best practices, issued its comprehensive *Review of Post-Deployment Reintegration Programs*.[6] Coming Home was recognized as among the top eight programs nationally, and the only one that met their fourteen recommendations while also having significant positive outcome data. Research published in a peer-reviewed professional journal demonstrated the benefit of Coming Home's community-building approach in enhancing post-traumatic growth. Stigma was reduced and participants reported highly significant reductions in stress, exhaustion, burnout, anxiety, isolation, hopelessness, and emotional "numbness." Furthermore, they reported significant increases in happiness, relaxation, energy, sense of support, and ability to care for and calm themselves. In follow-up studies four to eight weeks post-retreat, these positive results remained strongly significant, consistent, and reliable.

Getting Up to Speed

When I began this work in 2006, I was an experienced clinical psychologist, psychoanalyst, and Zen teacher and had worked for decades with survivors of various kinds of trauma including some Vietnam veterans. But I knew nothing about contemporary military culture, the spoken acronyms and lingo and the unspoken protocols and procedures, the values and contradictions, and the place of veterans and military personnel in culture and society. My learning curve was steep. I met with a trauma therapist who had worked with sailors and marines. Over a long cup of coffee, he gave me a crash course in military cultural competency and agreed to help facilitate our first weekend workshop. He said Coming Home Project had one chance: If participants—service members, veterans and their families from around the country—felt that we treated them with respect and understanding, were sincere and did not pretend or go through the motions. If we did that, our program would be launched, he said, with a cadre of loyal supporters who would spread the word. If not, no one would return and the word would go out to steer clear. After the second successful retreat, and an emotional spouses group which he facilitated, my co-facilitator said dryly, "Whoa, I don't think I'd want to be in your shoes. You don't know what you've opened up here."

Building a Team

He introduced me to a friend of his, an active duty officer who was trying, despite an oppressive and antagonistic system, to create the first transition program for returning members in his branch as well as for families. He helped many retreat participants, especially Rory. Soon I met David Rabb, clinical social worker, a Colonel in the Army Reserve, and commander of a combat stress unit in Iraq; he had recently returned from his first deployment to Iraq. We visited in his new office at the Palo Alto VA where he served as DoD-VA liason for the "Seamless Transition" program, doing everything within the confines of the dysfunctional system to help injured service members as they moved from DoD to VA care. We discovered a shared passion for building community. David wanted to see for himself, and asked if he could come to a retreat. I said there were no observers, only participants. After volunteering as a facilitator he told me that he had witnessed more change in five days than in a year of therapy and became part of our facilitator team and a trusted advisor.

Later I met Lt Col Steve Torgerson, a Seventh Day Adventist minister and Air Force chaplain, at a DoD Suicide Prevention conference in San Antonio. We each were enthusiastic about the other's presentations on the spiritual dimension of war and healing. Steve had been the Deputy Command Chaplain for the Multi-National Force in Iraq from 2006-2007. We got to know one another well when he became the Wing Chaplain at Travis Air Force Base in the Bay Area. He also directed Travis' Community Action and Information Board. The next time we met was at the coffee house he'd set up at Travis as a user-friendly, supportive environment. Steve became a facilitator and close collaborator whose inspiring, down-to-earth, non-doctrinaire talks on spirituality left few unmoved.

Early on I brainstormed about my vision with Loren Krane, a psychologist, trauma therapist, teacher, and supervisor at San Francisco General Hospital. Loren, who had extensive experience with refugees who were victims of torture, many also veterans in their own countries, became the clinical coordinator of our therapist cohort. I also met Keith Armstrong, head of family therapy at the San Francisco VA, and his colleague, Chad Peterson, a psychiatry fellow and the Medical Director of their PTSD team. Chad looks like a marine and, with the skills of an experienced therapist, he soon became a stalwart, trusted partner at retreats. Chad introduced me to Therese Garrett, a child psychiatry fellow who would later become the leader of our child team. Mary Dudum, nurse and Marine mother, volunteered at our first retreat at First Congregational Church in Berkeley, bringing her two daughters and a nursing colleague to help with the children. Mary became a community advocate for Coming Home and veteran families.

Nathan Johnson was a young Iraq Marine veteran who came to our first retreat while working as a readjustment counselor at the Concord Vet Center. He had returned to UC Berkeley for his Masters in Social Work. Nathan and I co-facilitated many men's veterans groups. Bob Bradley, a retired National Guard officer with a bellowing baritone voice, taught us about logistics. Catherine Morris, also a retired officer in the National Guard, was a pioneer in helping student veterans. Ed Dieden was a Marine platoon leader in Vietnam and a retired contractor. Dave Walker, a retired navy seabee and police chaplain, had developed a substance abuse problem during his second tour in Vietnam. Ed and Dave's solid character helped them connect with the post-9/11 vets whom Coming Home served. Ed and Mary Dudum co-founded the East Bay Collaborative to bring together community organizations to coordinate and share information. Ed's wife, Kathy Dieden, educated and mobilized the faith community about the impacts of war. Carrie Knowles, who joined our team in 2010, went through several careers; first as a research and clinical psychologist, then an attorney, a chaplain, and "finally" a Unitarian Universalist minister. She brought invaluable professional and life experience.

We went through a number of dedicated if inexperienced planners. One unintentionally routed the bus bringing participants from San Francisco International Airport to Moscone Center, in downtown San Francisco, rather than Marconi Center, on the shore of Tomales Bay two hours further north. Finally we found Nicolette Oliaro, our event planner extraordinaire, who recruited, brought together, and trained logistics team volunteers, ordinary citizens from around the country who would become integral parts of our retreat contingent.

Walking the Walk

If we were going to invite retreat participants to reconnect, we needed to demonstrate connectedness amongst ourselves and, of course, with them. Diversity and collaboration ran like red threads through all we did. We were completely "purple," welcoming participants from all branches. Our facilitation team was interdisciplinary, composed of veterans, family members, therapists, and chaplains. Our first yoga instructor came from the Marines, and Nancy Saum, a cardiac nurse and our qigong instructor, had done multiple deployments and had a son who had served in Iraq. These and other Coming Home staff, almost entirely volunteers, were quite simply the best, the brightest, most experienced, and devoted team imaginable, a "dream team" if ever there was one. In their inclusiveness and diversity, they were a microcosm of the wider community, whose true welcome was exactly what veterans and their families needed. Although our staff included skilled and seasoned professionals from the fields of psychotherapy, chaplaincy, and wellness, degrees, ranks, and honors were left at the door in an egalitarian ethos: asymmetrical but equal. We came to know one another by what we did: Nancy led qigong and co-facilitated the women vets' group, Chad co-facilitated the men's vet group, Steve gave a brief on spirituality, Jim was the cook.

After our first two successful retreats, colleagues asked what made the retreats work so well. Were we using mindfulness? Other complementary and alternative methods? I was at a loss. There was no singular technique, not even my personal favorite, meditation practice. I found myself mentioning safety, the importance of a safe space. Not very snazzy, I thought. But if the fear of one's own death or the death of a buddy, and the mistrust generated by crises of betrayal and meaning were as pivotal as we were observing, then safety and trust were indeed critical ingredients. Coming Home Project did provide meditation instruction and practice, but that component alone certainly didn't explain our success. I think it was how we deployed our own attention and intention to build a mindful, responsive, diverse, and collaborative, environment. We learned to pay attention to logistics, a central factor in military life. We provided more than child care; we created a child team composed of a child psychiatrist, expressive arts therapists, and seasoned parents. Retreat leaders met twice a day to discuss the group and any individuals or families who needed more support to ensure that no one fell through the cracks. We cultivated a strong team where everyone's input—that of leaders, instructors, facilitators, and logistics team members—was valued. Participants could see and feel the cohesiveness, humanity, and expertise of our team, and they came to feel they were in good hands, enabling some measure of hypervigilance to dissipate.

There's a story about group of blind men (or in some versions men in the dark) who touch an elephant to learn what it is like. Each one feels a different part, but only a single part, such as the side or the tusk. Their versions of what it is they are touching are completely discrepant, of course. Since war trauma sponsors fragmentation and compartmentalized thinking, everyone's shared perspectives in meetings proved incredibly valuable. Twice-a-day facilitator meetings were the time to voice and hear multiple perspectives, as we tried to forge a composite working understanding together.

This approach also helped sidestep the streetlight effect: A policeman sees a drunk man (or someone who's very stressed out) searching for something under a streetlight and asks what the person has lost. He says he lost his keys and they both look under the streetlight together. After a few minutes the policeman asks if he is sure he lost them here, and the person replies, no, he lost them in the park. When the policeman asks why he is searching here, the man replies, "Because this is where the light is." Integrating multiple perspectives mitigates tunnel vision and group think, bringing to bear the wisdom of all. It helps reestablish the interconnectedness that war trauma unravels.

We learned how important it was to keep participants "in mind." When challenging circumstances arose, such as indications of possible child abuse in one family, we searched to piece together a working understanding that permitted us to be of support and to do what was necessary. Not just at the retreat but moving forward. And in the process, we discovered we were leveraging an ethic participants knew well, but which in their experience had been betrayed too often: Leave no one behind, never forget. At the end of an emotionally moving retreat, the sharing around the closing circle was especially poignant. After everyone had spoken, one could feel the love and closeness in the room; nobody moved or seemed to want to. Then a woman vet rose and said, "Yeah, things were pretty good, no, really good. But I keep thinking, 'When are you going to break out the Kool Aid?'" Everyone roared with laughter, recognizing that she spoke the lingering skepticism of many who were not used to trusting that the civilian community really cared about and understood them.

Here are two examples, one a participant whom our team realized needed more support than the scheduled events could provide, and one that illustrates how the facilitators supported one another. Rory was about to boil over, not wanting to act out yet struggling with rage at being blown up and losing his buddies. He felt betrayed by the government's lack of responsiveness and accountability. His anger, rather than being transformative, amplified in escalating loops. The more angry he became, the more the energy of the group intensified, which in turn amplified his emotions. Two people left the room—one took issue with Rory's facts, another felt his comments were too polarizing. Rory, of course, had every right to express his outrage and sense of betrayal, but as his complaints became increasingly politicized, he was alienating himself from his fellow vets. Our team thought his traumatic brain injury might be part of what made it difficult for him to regulate the strong emotions that were rising up.

Over the course of two retreats, Rory began to shift in a way I'd never seen where there was such grievous physiologic and functional damage. Through frequent, long conversations with a member of the facilitation team, an active duty officer, who accompanied and was available to him throughout the day, gradually Rory became noticeably lighter, more open to hearing others' stories. He began to share his own experiences with a sense of measure, calibrating the impact, modulating his tone, and bringing his accounts to a close. The validation and containment his fellow vets provided him was deeply moving to witness.

In 2008, my friend Keith Armstrong and I shared a powerful moment. I had been invited to join Keith and a few other therapists providing support at a workshop of Gold Star families, those who had lost a child or parent in the post 9/11 wars. I was looking through memorabilia of their lost loved ones, arranged shrine-like on tables. Pictures, baseballs and gloves, clothing, poems, each table more personal and moving than the last. I was reading a letter in which a soldier wrote about what really mattered to him, what life was all about, and what he hoped to do with his, and a sob of grief knifed through me. When I turned around, I saw Keith. We each placed our hand on the other's shoulder and walked to sit together in another room. The grief that gripped my gut as I surveyed the lives on display in remarkably vivid particulars was accompanied by a question similar to one vets often asked, "What have we got to show for it?" For me it was, "For what?"

If "it takes a village" (and we learned anew at each retreat that it does), then all of us—facilitators, participants, volunteers, veterans, and civilians—became that village. We were the connective tissue that formed a safety net, providing the conditions for healing.

Throughout the Coming Home Project, we tried to cultivate collaborative relationships with all the major players. So we were glad that after receiving an invitation to use VA facilities to hold an educational training for our growing therapist cohort, we learned that there was one condition: VA employees had to be able to attend. We built bridges wherever we could. In retrospect it is possible to see that, without our conscious intent, we were modeling organizationally the repairing and reconnecting of broken connections that plague veterans and families. What did veterans want? To be respected, to receive what they had earned, to be treated like human beings, to be heard and seen, to become whole. Not to be "fixed."

After a few years, Coming Home Project's constituency expanded. While visiting a longtime county veteran service officer, I was describing how veterans were responding to our retreats, and I noticed her eyes growing round as saucers. When I was finished, she said, "What about us?" Yes, I thought, what about the providers who work with war trauma? In the literature what they experienced is referred to as secondary or vicarious trauma. But such concepts are wholly inadequate to describe how war trauma perniciously impacts not only service members, but families, children, caregivers, and professional providers. Within a year we received support from the Bob Woodruff Foundation to provide retreats for therapists, physicians, care managers, case mangers, nurses, and many others providing care on the frontlines at VA and DoD facilities around the world. At the outset, Coming Home Project was funded by a few small grants from local Bay Area foundations and modest seed monies from Deep Streams Institute. Deep Streams is a nonprofit religious organization whose mission includes Zen Buddhist practice, developing interdisciplinary models of healing, and implementing those models in service to the community to build peace. Coming Home Project was a non-denominational program of Deep Streams. In 2008 we were fortunate to receive a three-year grant from the Iraq and Afghanistan Deployment Impact Fund, developed by Nancy Berglass and funded by David and Monica Gelbaum, the largest privately endowed fund for veterans in U.S. history. Weekend retreats became four- and five-day residential-living experiences for up to 150 people, and we expanded from northern to southern California, and to Texas and Virginia.

As we expanded the groups we served, I began to understand the traumatic impacts of war literally as shockwaves, like the concussive sonic waves from an IED blast. They radiate in all directions on multiple levels instantaneously, reflecting and dismantling the connectivity of human life. In a time-release manner, they wait for the right conditions to surface and last for generations and centuries. The impacts of war don't stop at service members and providers. Their effects compromise institutions, administrators, policy makers, government officials, and leaders in the halls of the Congress and the White House.

On June 12, 2014, Richard Engel, NBC News chief foreign correspondent, speaking of the chaotic fragmentation in "post-war" Iraq, said: "*The sectarian fight never ended. This was a time bomb that exploded with the US invasion. It just ticked away in a low gear for a little while the US was here. Then the US left, and now it's back with abandon*" [italics added].[7] A bomb that explodes once and continues exploding unpredictably, over time; a kind of time-release bomb. How ironic, since "ticking time bomb" is a phrase sometimes used apprehensively to describe some returning veterans.

A "bomb" can be devastating even when the hit is "indirect," as this story illustrates. Romeo Dallaire, a General in the Canadian Armed Forces and now a Senator, was the commander of NATO peacekeeping forces in Rwanda during the genocide that took place there in 1994. Members of the Hutu ethnic majority murdered 800,000 people, mostly from the Tutsi minority. Lt Col Stephane Grenier was his second-in-command. Grenier spoke after me at a conference in Los Angeles and chided me for my use of the term "combat veteran." He was vociferous in pointing out that a service member need not have been in a fire fight to have experienced the impacts of the war zone. I knew that but I took the hit. He only mentioned tangentially the heart wrenching story of how he and his boss were commanding the peace-keeping forces in Rwanda at the time of the mass slaughter. It was not what Grenier and Dallaire had done that caused their massive post-war anguish, but what they were not able to do. Upon returning to Canada, having been unable to prevent the genocide, they collapsed. Only after long treatment were they able to pull their lives together again.

War trauma affects everyone who serves, whether or not he or she has been in firefights. And the impacts don't stop at the borders of the war zone: the shockwaves continue to radiate out across individual, family, community, and culture. Repeated trauma unravels veterans' connections with their families, their peers, and their communities—as well as within themselves. There is a saying in military families, "When a service member deploys, the whole family deploys." What I came to see is that this "family" is not limited to the veteran's immediate and extended kin. We are *all* that family. Veterans are *our* veterans. Their families and children are our families and children.

Mark, a Marine helicopter pilot during the first Gulf War, a Buddhist priest, a father, a photographer, and a graduate student in fine arts, described how, while facilitating the teen break-out group, he began with a moment of silence, then asked "How are you doing?" Kenny's daughter Tasha was quick to respond, "Do you really want to know?" and she immediately started crying. Her sister Alishiya said she was "'fine" and told Tasha not to open things up. Alishiya looked to be "strong" like her mom, Tonia, but was holding a lot inside. Neither wanted to upset their parents. Jesse's daughter, Brittney, was also feeling isolated: no one could understand, there was no one to talk to, and she didn't want to burden her parents with her own feelings. Brittney said that her wounded and blinded father can't see her face and doesn't know if she is sad or happy. She uses that to hide her emotions and feels bad about it. She wants to talk to him but is afraid that she will make things worse. Mark made suggestions for communicating with him. The girls bonded and developed a sense of trust. For Mark it was his most emotionally powerful experience since leaving the Marines.

After the breakout groups, Tasha and Alishiya shared their drawings in the big circle and haltingly spoke about how isolated they felt and how difficult it was to tell their parents what they were thinking and feeling. Ken and Tonia were able, with some difficulty, to listen and take it in, allowing their daughters this freedom of expression and learning from what they heard.

Crossing the Great Divide

Due in part to the impacts of war on my own development, I became sensitized to attitudes about the men and women who fight our wars and their family members. I realized that there is an unconscionably wide chasm between the nearly three million people who served in the Iraq and Afghanistan wars and the rest of us. While civilians today are able, for the most part, to distinguish between the wars and the warriors, unlike during the Vietnam era, many veterans still feel alienated when they return stateside. At first I didn't understand why. But think about it: you come home and look around you, and the country does not appear to be at war. There are few if any signs of the sacrifices that usually accompany war. Civilians don't seem genuinely interested in what it was really like for you. Remember that these wars were undeclared and unpaid for. Taxes were cut, not raised. There was no draft. War front news was mostly managed. The sight of returning caskets was hidden from view. What war?

The vast majority of civilians have no "skin in the game." Many, encouraged by our commander-in-chief's directive to go to the mall, turned on cruise control. A classic scene from the film *The Hurt Locker* conveys the irony that on returning stateside, some of the most disorienting, disturbing places for service members are large stores and malls.

As a young man I was moved by the lyrics of a song written by Chet Powers and made famous by the Youngbloods, "You hold the key to love and fear / All in your trembling hand / Just one key unlocks them both / It's there at your command."[8] Our conscious and unconscious reactions to trauma hold the key to waking up and healing. Individually and collectively, veteran, family member, or civilian, we are what we make of the cards we are dealt. Veterans' struggles with post-war stress and anguish—*making the peace with war*—cannot be addressed without facing this pervasive divide between the veteran and military community, on the one hand, and civilians, on the other. Why? *Troops come home to a community, not a set of isolated institutions. It takes a strong community to welcome the warrior home.* We are a chronically divided nation with profound ambivalence about recent wars and even about our veterans.

We don't have to look far for examples of this ambivalence. While contemporary veterans are referred to by some today as "The next greatest generation," the stereotype of war veterans as "Ticking time bombs" plays out beneath the surface in fields as diverse as media, employment, education, healthcare, corrections, even law enforcement. Politicians and business leaders often wrap themselves in the veteran flag for self-promotion, rather than taking the time and effort to get to know the real problems and explore substantive and sustainable solutions. "Thank you for your service" is heard wide and far, but it can take nine months to get a doctor's appointment at the VA. Jack Nicholson, as Colonel Nathan Jessup in *A Few Good Men*, captured elements of the ambivalence during his cross examination by Tom Cruise, playing a navy lawyer, Daniel Kaffee. When Nicholson says, "You want answers?!" Cruise says, "I want the truth!" Nicholson replies with this memorable retort, "You can't *handle* the truth!" He continues, "Son, we live in a world that has walls, and those walls have to be guarded by men with guns. Who's gonna do it? You? You? . . . I have a greater responsibility than you can possibly fathom. . . . And my existence, while grotesque and incomprehensible to you, saves lives! You don't want the truth, because deep down in places you don't talk about at parties, you *want* me on that wall. You *need* me on that wall."[9]

Veterans know that talk is cheap. Our collective ambivalence plays itself out in action. It can function subtly and in a counterintuitive manner. I've been struck by the rush in the military to "stand up" programs, to "fix the problem," as if service members' and veterans' hearts and minds were reducible to a math question on the SAT. Urgency is a good thing, right? But military strategy on suicide prevention can be best described as a whack-a-mole approach. In testimony to Congress by the Pentagon's Defense Suicide Prevention Office, Jackie Garrick, acting director, and Lt. Gen. Howard Bromberg, Army deputy chief of staff for personnel, predicted increasing rates despite 900 prevention programs.[10] The strategies utilized are commonly one-dimensional, symptom-driven, one-size-fits-all, and, despite the rhetoric about "gold standard," "top shelf," and "evidence-based effectiveness," unproven. Programs like Comprehensive Soldier Fitness that cost hundreds of millions of taxpayer dollars are re-upped without reliable evidence. Planners and leaders can't, don't, or won't stop to think about what vets really need and want. Here, too, the press of trauma and our maladaptive reactions on the one hand, and concealed self-interest coated with unctuous honorific talk on the other, seem to rule the day.

It's not just the military that until recently has stigmatized war trauma as weakness and punished it. As a culture, we are allergic to emotional pain. How does this play out in the recent epidemic of military suicides? Pulitzer Prize-winning journalist Tom Ricks recently wrote in *Foreign Policy* about two researchers who did something novel: They actually listened to marines, who in turn described in detail their experiences of war.[11] What did the researchers learn? They found that crises of meaning were central. Some marines were able to bounce back from these moral injuries by forgiving themselves for perceived errors on the battlefield. Others judged themselves harshly for perceived failures. Yet others remain plagued by doubts. The researchers observed real people describing their struggles to make sense of things they'd done, not done, or witnessed. Their results followed on the heels of an earlier study that revealed a critical factor in military suicides: overwhelming emotional pain. The need for meaning and overwhelming emotional pain are quintessential features of our humanity that, sadly, we need to be reminded of by the social sciences. The model that currently drives most veteran mental health care sees war trauma as a psychiatric anxiety disorder, informed by a view of the veteran in isolation, like someone who has contracted an exotic illness in a strange country, the cure for which we must urgently find. This approach misses the point. When we mistake the register on which the basic issues lie, we miss the veteran and our programs tend to be of limited or no benefit—if not actually harmful. Why are we so eager to see veterans' mental health problems through the narrow blinders of an infectious disease model? When the anguish of veterans and their families becomes like a strain of bacteria for which we try to discover a new miracle cure, the flesh and bones of the matter are lost. This protects us from seeing the true and multidimensional nature of the damage. We forfeit the possibility of coming together to redeem the moral impacts for which veterans shoulder a disproportionate burden.

Amid the hundreds of millions of dollars being spent to identify specific biomarkers to distinguish who is more or less predisposed to war stress and to bypass traumatic memory entirely through medical means, the following headline appeared, "New Obama plan calls for implanted computer chips to help U.S. troops heal." Program representatives said, "The goal is to develop a technology that could help people heal more quickly through the use of biosensors and electromagnetic devices that control human organs."[12] Technology will proceed apace and may bring some benefits. But how quick we are to leapfrog over proven low tech, high (relational) "touch" and community approaches that cost far less. Connection may be harder to implant, but it is how our species heals.

Torterello and Marcellino, whose study Ricks cited, ask, "On what scientific basis are quantifiable bio-phenomena substituted for what a marine says in describing his or her stress?" Only if we assume that biology *causes* certain social meanings can we ignore whole people in favor solely of their biology or their psychology. It is difficult to face the stark limits of a primarily biologic approach that characterizes the best funded DoD and VA projects, with their endless streams of data points that are analyzed and broken down into discrete variables with the goal of locating and isolating the holy grail: the biological marker, the smoking gun of "PTSD" or military suicide. This is a futile and costly search. It misses the veteran-person right here shopping alongside us or pushing his or her child on the swing in the park. It misses the human being struggling to regain wholeness.

Restoring Justice and Integrity
Acclaimed war journalist and documentarian Sebastian Junger says veterans today have to bear a starkly uneven share of the "moral burden" of recent wars.[13] The story of our war veterans is part and parcel of our collective story. In fact it is our story. How could it be otherwise, since we are all so intimately connected? Unless we wake up and see, hear, and recognize the story of our veterans, and their families, children, and caregivers as our story, we will surely repeat those past errors, with similar or more grievous costs.

Caring for veterans inevitably involves restorative justice; setting right what has been torn asunder, physically, emotionally, and spiritually. This is not meant in a moralistic or religious sense, but rather as an ethical "turning" or course correction. When troops are sent to war, an unstated but powerful covenant is forged, a compact hidden in plain sight. The service members agree, "We will help our country, even, if necessary giving our lives. If we return, we expect to receive the care and services we have earned." When this covenant is broken, as it has been so often during the past fourteen years, it is an ethical betrayal. Real reintegration addresses this wounding and restores trust.

The most entrenched, profound, and treatment-resistant problems my colleagues and I encountered related to sense of purpose, meaning found and meaning lost. Veterans do not want all that they and their loved ones have gone through, all they have lost, to have been in vain. They want it to mean something. In one veterans' small group the theme became, "What have we got to show for it?" The inner conflict was so profound that even broaching the topic made some of the participants testy and defensive, as though others were blaming them just by bringing it up. Today we see this dynamic emerging in many Iraq war veterans. As the country they fought to save falls apart, many are experiencing a resurgence of emotional pain linked with a sense of meaninglessness.

Feeling like it was all for nothing is a terrible blow. When we factor in the element of betrayal—by a leader, a government, or a healthcare system—we have a potent mix. Add the emotional and moral reverberations of having killed, of having witnessed death and grave injury, of having acted in a way that is at odds with one's sense of right and wrong and the mix is turbocharged. Shame, guilt, and self-loathing stoke the fires.

A New Framework for PTSD

The experience of war veterans cannot be captured by an isolated formula. War trauma is of a piece. Coming Home Project has tried to capture this unity by using a framework which sees human beings as complex and interconnected. A bio-psycho-social/family-spiritual mode includes body and brain (biological), cognition and a range of adaptive functions needed for everyday functioning (psychological), our belonging to and participation in multiple intersecting contexts (social/family), and the registers of identity, existence, the meaning and purpose of life and death, and the deeper strata of connectedness we share with all creatures (spiritual). Each dimension influences the others in a dynamic balance that shifts moment to moment. But try as we may to "*get* it all together," we can't. Because it *is* together.

I suggest that there are two kinds of "PTSD," neither of which is exactly like the aggregate of symptom clusters and temporal criteria in the *Diagnostic and Statistical Manual of Mental Disorders* universally used by mental health professionals and institutions including VA and DoD. Although we can't capture in an image or a theoretical model something so human that it inevitably slips through such a net, there is practical value in making this distinction. In order to mobilize the right tools to solve a problem, we need to understand the problem.

One form of post-traumatic stress, which I call PTsxD, represents a cluster of debilitating anxiety symptoms with roots in a nervous system dysregulated by cumulative exposure to war-related trauma. Lower case "sx," a medical abbreviation for "symptoms," here refers to psycho-neurobiological symptoms that reflect shifts in arousal and reactivity such as increased irritability and anger, reckless behavior, hypervigilance, exaggerated startle response, concentration problems, and sleep disturbances. It draws on the biological (brain) and psychological dimensions of the bio-psycho-social/family-spiritual model that characterizes our overall approach. The "D" in PTsxD does not refer to a disorder, though lived and felt experience can certainly become disordered. It also does not refer to a psychiatric disturbance, although experience can become terribly disturbed and disturbing to others. Rather it relates to *dysregulation*, the body and brain's way of adapting to overwhelming traumatic experience in order to survive.

The second form I call PTspD. The "sp" here refers to the spiritual register in our integrative model. It also draws on elements of the social and psychological registers. The injury here, the "D," does not refer to a psychiatric disorder or disturbance. Rather it speaks to the *dismantling* of the natural connectedness among all registers. There is a cluster of other "D" words that it encompasses: *disabling* of native capacities for reflecting on and processing trauma; *dispirited*, the evaporation of basic aliveness, l'élan vital; *disbelief*, as in the crises of faith that are generated when one's entire assumptive world, often though not always including religious beliefs, comes tumbling down with disastrous effects on one's sense of meaning, purpose, and direction; *dissed*, as in not being recognized or respected; *despair*, a loss of hope, a sense of being helpless to remedy the situation, and *disaster*, with its existential angst. There are also the *deprecation* and *disparagement* that unfold from the moral injuries of war.

In any honest discussion of what is therapeutic for returning veterans, there is no way to avoid ethics and spirituality. There is an implicit ethical element of fairness and justice that runs through the "D" elements of PTspD. Since spirituality also speaks to expanding registers of human connectedness, PTspD also encompasses the cultural dimensions of veterans' experience, how their communities respond to and hold them, consciously and unconsciously.

Moral injuries include betrayals, which can be every bit as painful as physical injuries, and self-reproach or shame for actions or inactions that clash sharply with one's internal compass of right and wrong, how things should be, and how one should act. Betrayal and shame generate a shearing moral dissonance that wreaks havoc with one's sense of identity, accompanied by disabling guilt— and self-loathing. We can summarize the experiences that come under the "D" umbrella of PTspD with *damage,* soul damage.

Veterans' experiences contain elements of each kind of post-traumatic stress in "proportions." The image of a double helix captures something of their dynamic relationship. Each strand is discrete, yet each intersects the other and in so doing, changes the other and is itself changed. This can help us think about what constitutes the most suitable approaches to healing. PTsxD is responsive to a variety of ancient and modern practices. Such approaches, helpful as they are when skillfully utilized, often don't touch the register of PTspD. To ignore the latter or reduce it to the former can be ineffective, and in some cases can even amplify the suffering.

The hope for permanent elimination of the symptoms of PTsxD drives much of the funding and research. I think that focusing solely on PTsxD is misguided. Relief, yes—a more functional, meaningful and vibrant life, indeed—but literal and permanent elimination of the symptoms of suffering is neither possible nor desirable. Reintegration means integrating and reclaiming dissociated elements that were involuntarily sequestered away, usually in the interest of survival in the face of death. As traumatic ghosts are transformed, the haunting, debilitating traumas of war gradually become usable memories that link past and present and make a future possible.

Paying Attention
When a Zen master was asked about the meaning of the most profound sacred teachings, he responded by drawing the Chinese character for "Attention." That which we attend to deeply and genuinely grows. This kind of attention is like sunshine, an expression of love. When I tell participants how small breakout groups work, I say that listening is an act of love: they support one another by listening and speaking from the heart when they are moved to. There's a funny and sad story from my clinical practice. A mother brought her son to see me. She said he had an attention disorder, indicating Attention Deficit with Hyperactivity. When I asked her for more information, she spoke a while and then said, "He just wants more and more attention." She was stretched to the limit by a series of life challenges and her son's understandable need for his mother's engaged attention put her over the top. When it comes to our veterans and their families, the capacity of our country for responsive, skillful attentiveness seems to have gone south during these recent long wars. A speaker at Maya Angelou's memorial last year eloquently captured the importance of this nourishing human quality.

The thing that struck me about [her book *I Know Why the Caged Bird Sings*] even more than the horrible abuse she endured and the five years of silence that followed, was that this little kid, the whole time this was going on, was paying attention. She may have stopped talking, but she never stopped looking. She was paying attention. And absorbing the people she saw, the patterns of life, the experience, and trying to make sense of it. She had enough experiences for five lifetimes. . . . And by the time she started writing her books and poetry, what she was basically doing was calling our attention to the things she'd been paying attention to. And she did it with the clarity and power that will wash over people as long as there's a written and spoken word. . . . She just kept calling our attention to things. I often thought of her gigantic figure as like the little fireflies we used to catch in the summertime and put in jars. They just come on at unpredictable times and they'd make you see something that you otherwise would have missed. Something right before your nose you'd been overlooking. Something in your mind you'd been burying. Something in your heart you afraid to face. She called our attention in thousands of ways to her belief that life is a gift, manifest in each new day. She called our attention to the fact that things that really matter—dignity, work, love and kindness—are things we can all share and don't cost anything. . . . So, my friend, we thank you for calling our attention to the things you paid attention to. We thank you for helping to organize our scale so that we give heavy weight to the most important things.[14]

Giving sufficient weight to the things that matter; like paying attention to the details and the extensive costs of war and the well-being of those who sacrificed so much by their service.

You may be asking yourself if this will be a political book. The answer is no, not in a partisan squabbling sense of Democrats vs. Republicans or Republicans vs. Tea Party. But it is in the sense that the word comes from the Greek *politikos* meaning "of, for, or relating to citizens"—in other words, "we the people." Since veterans and their families are *our* family, that makes it political. We cannot separate the condition of veterans from the condition of our nation, our leaders, our congress, our federal, state, and local governments, just as we cannot separate veterans from their families, and family caregivers from professional providers. We also can't separate civilians from the military and veterans. We unhitch these key players at our peril, perpetuating in our approach the very fragmentation of war trauma itself. In this book I weigh in not only on the diagnoses used for veterans, but I also offer informed diagnoses of these other component parts of society as a whole whose impacts redound directly to the detriment or the well-being of veterans.

Focusing on What's Really Real

Turning a blind eye, even with good intentions, saves us from seeing that the antidote for war trauma is less a cure—quarantining and eliminating an isolated strain of illness brought back from a foreign land—than a *restorative environment* that carries with it an element of adjudication. Such an environment does not simply renew health, wellness, and wholeness; in so doing, it restores justice, redresses the ethical burdens and imbalances, and redeems the many transgressions. It is by nature redemptive. It feels real.

When vets gather to face, process, and heal war's injuries, it is not a sterile or surgical affair. You cannot cut out the parts that hurt. Veterans were trained to complete their mission no matter what the cost; the price is often their own emotional and spiritual wholeness. I remember a service member in a small group meeting who asked why he couldn't just will away his inner anguish relating to incidents that were already over. Others echoed his frustration. I paused, uncertain how to respond. "Because you have a beating heart," I finally said, "because you're human."

Most veterans have an exquisitely developed bullshit detector; many are constantly reading peoples' motives, identifying, assessing, evaluating, on alert for potential danger, for deception and betrayal. But there is another motive; they are also searching for something straight, trustworthy, and real. In the fog of war, where dissociation, pretense, hypocrisy, and false sentimentality prevail, real is rare, real is gold. Real restores trust, and hope for making a life worth living.

When the workshop ends, Tonia and Ken renew their wedding vows. Her eyes reach out for Ken's, while Ken strains to respond and make eye contact with Tonia, in spite of being unable to see much. It is heart-wrenching and heart-warming at once. After the ceremony, outside the room in the hallway, their older daughter Tasha begins to weep. As Mary Ellen, a family friend, volunteer, and Marine mom holds her, Tasha sobs and cries without restraint. What is striking is that no one interrupts the pair; everyone recognizes the outpouring of feeling and lets it be.

I. Community Heals and Isolation Kills

In 2008, my friend Keith Armstrong arranged a meeting with his boss, Charles Marmar, chief of psychiatry at the San Francisco VA, one of the elite VA hospitals and medical centers in the country. Dr. Marmar began, "Joe, patients come in to our clinics but they don't stay. What have you learned that might shed some light on this?" His posing the question seemed to convey an openness that brought me up short. I replied, "There needs to be a 'there' there." An awkward silence ensued, which I soon filled with a superfluous explanation, "Something to connect to. Troops come home to a community, not a set of isolated services."

Sayings from many traditions covey this "there" that is always right here with us. In the Bible, "The whole creation groans and labors together."[1] John Muir wrote, "When we try to pick out anything by itself, we find it hitched to everything else in the universe."[2] My Zen teacher, Robert Aitken Roshi, always said, "Time is short and we are all in this together." No one knows this better than troops in the war zone, who frequently say, "We fight for the guy to our right and the guy to our left."

We share with one another and with all creatures a profound inter-connectedness that is vaster and more fundamental than any one of us individually. My friend and Coming Home Project collaborator, retired Air Force chaplain Steve Torgerson, likes to quote the writer G. K. Chesterton, "We are all in the same boat in a stormy sea, and we owe each other a terrible loyalty." My friend Col. David Rabb often reminds us, "Community heals, isolation kills."

Service members understand this implicitly because it is their on-the-ground reality in the face of death. Military families get it without being told that their well-being is inextricably intertwined with the well-being of others. The fate of others is intimately tied to our fate. When the Buddha experienced enlightenment under the bodhi tree, he is reported to have said, "At this moment all beings and I awaken together." Pediatrician and psychoanalyst Donald Winnicott wrote of a particularly vulnerable stage of infant development where we cannot say the word "baby" without saying "mother" (and I like to add "father"). The Buddha expressed it with deceptive simplicity, "This is because that is." We *interare*.

Cultures in Tatters

The institutions responsible for caring for our veterans and their families have not, alas, incorporated this fundamental reality.

As I came to see how veterans, family members, children, and providers were all impacted by war trauma, I also began to understand that the institutions responsible for their care were also affected. During the last year of our major grant, I began to travel extensively to forge contacts at VA, DoD, Congress, the White House, corporations, and large foundations, searching for long-term funding for our program. By then we had more than anecdotal accounts and personal testimonials to prove its effectiveness; we had data.

Crisscrossing the country, I learned some important lessons. First, organizations did not communicate with one another, especially VA and DoD. Relationships, when they existed at all, were fragmented and compartmentalized. Everyone I met with would ask me the same questions: "Where have you been? Who have you met with? What did they have to say?" Relatively naive and guileless, I tried to respond to their questions. Then it dawned on me: these people and the institutions they represented did not actually talk with one another or share information, much less coordinate their efforts to benefit service members and veterans. In questioning me, they wanted to gather some intel, and I sensed another motivation as well. They seemed genuinely curious about their colleagues in other organizations and what they were up to. As an outsider, I found myself in the role of connector. Like veterans and others who are facing overwhelming circumstances, employees compartmentalize in order to survive in dysfunctional systems. Yet when given the opportunity, they wanted to learn what was happening on "the outside."

I came to see first-hand how hunkered down and compromised our institutions are; how "tribal" identifications override the collaboration and coordination that could bring clear benefit to veterans and families. This was the case not just among different organizations. Within the same system, say a military branch, the disconnects were equally startling. The left hands did not know what the right hands were doing. One leader I met with genuinely thanked me when I asked him for more information about a major grant specifically designed for those his department served. He had not even heard about it. How could our institutions help veterans repair damaged connectivity when these institutions themselves were so fractured and their staffs so overwhelmed?

During a discussion with a senior military chaplain, I learned about a new program he was directing with the mission of harnessing spirituality to help fellow chaplains. We explored how Coming Home might help support the alarming number of chaplains buckling under impossible workloads. Due to staffing shortages, they were serving multiple tours and helping thousands of service members. It's not commonly known that military chaplains are the only helping professionals in the military required to maintain strict confidentiality. They therefore had no one with whom to share the horrific stories they were hearing from service members.

I thought it would be supportive to have a dedicated retreat for chaplains from this particular branch. The director asked me how many breakout groups there were at a Coming Home retreat. I said about six to twelve groups, and asked him how many chaplains he was considering sending. He repeated my words, "six to twelve." I didn't understand at first, but then I caught on. Constant trauma and threat without support had bred an organizational culture of paranoia and a fear of retribution so pronounced that there could only be one unit chaplain per group. The organizational dynamics were so toxic that a chaplain couldn't trust his colleagues to maintain confidentiality. The director confirmed that the esprit de corps was so compromised that offering a retreat just for chaplains would actually be counterproductive.

Troop camaraderie and morale, unit cohesion, and esprit de corps are military analogues of community. Community in the broadest sense is each of us, inasmuch as we constitute the sectors of civic life that veterans interact with on a daily basis: employment, education, housing, legal, law enforcement, health, and the government institutions responsible for implementing policy and caring for our veterans and families. Community also encompasses the leaders we elect and send to Congress and the White House to represent us, the leaders responsible for formulating policy, funding programs, and overseeing their operation, effectiveness, and integrity.

Why is community so critical for us to grasp? Because the effects of an absent or dysfunctional community compound and exacerbate the injuries veterans sustain in theater. Moreover, at the national level, the lack of community "buy-in" to war decisions and policies (having "skin in the game") disenfranchises ordinary citizens and deprives policy makers of vital feedback. This can contribute to a slippery slope that leads to further ill-advised wars that create additional loss, devastation, and more injured and killed veterans—wars from which we have to continuously dig ourselves out at enormous expense.

The knee-jerk reasons often given for this generalized institutional dysfunction are: "That's how bureaucracies work, especially in the federal government, especially inside the Beltway." I challenge this response. It has become clear to me that the role of war trauma and our conscious and unconscious reactions to it cannot be overlooked. These are potent factors—hidden in plain sight—contributing to the spate of scandals that have plagued our veteran-care systems and the institutions responsible for their policies and performance. I am convinced that the way war trauma is actually transmitted—along multiple dimensions at once—contributes mightily to individual, collective, and institutional dysfunction, extending all the way to the highest levels of leadership. Our leaders are not exempt: in function of their response to war trauma, their capacities can also become compromised.

On May 15, 2014, I watched the lengthy hearings of the Senate Veterans Affairs Committee. Then VA Secretary Eric Shinseki was grilled about reports that some clinics had "cooked the books" on wait times and covered up secret waiting lists containing the real data while publicly substituting made-up lists that falsely reflected exemplary performance. A number of veterans may have died while waiting for an appointment. Shinseki said he was "mad as hell," and the others who testified—government officials, leaders of congressionally chartered veteran service organizations (VSOs), and well-established community-based veterans organizations (CBOs)—seemed concerned if not outraged.[3] It turns out that the problem that was now creating a media firestorm had actually been festering for up to fifteen years. And it was only one of many scandals over the years regarding timely adjudication of veteran benefits claims, quality of services, accuracy of data reported, access to care, and other problems. While senators and others routinely used the word "systemic" to describe the problems at VA, they seemed to not have a clue, as they minimized and misunderstood the degree and the type of problems they were investigating.

It was eerie listening to Shinseki respond to questions. If the secretary was so passionate, why was he using life-sucking bureaucratic doublespeak, referring to possible related deaths as "adverse events," rather than speaking plainly? We could give him the benefit of the doubt, even chalk it up to personality style, were he not to describe himself soon after as "shocked" to learn that whistleblowers' allegations had been confirmed by the VA inspector general's investigation. Shocked? Wouldn't such a distinguished military man get the intel he needed before initiating a critical mission? Did Shinseki's recon fail to reveal the chronic brokenness of VA systems? David Wood, the esteemed *Huffington Post* journalist, called him "too trusting," which I found perplexing, given the general's decorated military career.

I was also struck during the hearing by how easily everyone, savvy devoted veteran advocates included, fell prey to oversimplifying the extent of the problem, reducing it to a simple concern over "access," while touting the quality of VA health care. As if "access" and "quality," two of many elements that constitute the "system" of care, could be unhitched. I thought, "Tell the family of a veteran who died while on the secret waiting list that this was 'just an access problem.'"

One after another, those who gave testimony agreed with this incorrect assessment. I thought they sounded like sheep in an echo chamber, repeating the meme that "VA health care is terrific and access is the real problem." The brilliant and indefatigable Tom Tarantino of Iraq and Afghanistan Veterans of America (IAVA) observed that veterans' *experience* with the VA was problematic, before he too joined the chorus. The sudden spell of amnesia was startling; certainly many knew of the reports by Aaron Glantz and others regarding suicides, over-prescription of opiates, inept pain management, ineffective veteran outreach, insufficient programs for families. In 2008, McClatchy News Service reported that a U.S. senator had charged the VA with lying about the number of veterans who had attempted suicide, citing internal e-mails that put the number at 12,000 a year, when the department was publicly saying it was fewer than 800.[4] This discrepancy created quite a furor, but it was short-lived, like our sputtering memories.

During this scandal and Senate hearing, the terms used by investigators, government officials, and journalists to characterize VA culture ranged from dysfunctional and corrupt to broken, corrosive, and punitive. A June 15, 2014 article in the *New York Times* details how VA administrators routinely punished employees who spoke out in the interest of improving patient care. The article provides pictures and names and interviews with real VA employees who, after speaking up on behalf of patient-care issues, were punished and made to feel as if they were "crazy," and in an "alternate universe."[5] I had heard scores of similar stories during Coming Home Project retreats adapted to serve overworked service providers in VA, DoD, and CBOs. I found this exposé an important step in breaking the iron grip of a pervasive culture of silence and intimidation. Recent assurances of governmental protection for VA whistleblowers may also be cause for cautious optimism. This stagnant closed system may be opening itself to new information and real feedback about its functioning.

While on the road fundraising and networking, I had my own close encounters with dysfunction. In 2007 I gave testimony at California State Senate hearings in Sacramento, California. Bucking the anti-VA tide of most speakers and legislators, I testified that there are some in VA who were working collaboratively with CBOs to explore innovative ways to effectively serve large number of veterans. Within two weeks the leader at the VA with whom I had initiated discussions, and whose name I did not publicly reveal, was nearly fired and cut off all discussions in fear for his job. This was not simply dysfunctional; this was a paranoid system in action.

In 2012, a newly appointed national-level VA lead in DC expressed enthusiasm about collaborating with Coming Home Project and instructed me to speak with a respected VISN (Veterans Integrated Service Network) employee who could explore details. I happened to know this person and we collaborated to draw up a very modest proposal, which was submitted for review. After months with no word, I finally received a call back and learned that for the first time during this employee's long tenure, a proposal had been rebuffed. No clear reason was provided, only scant details about the likelihood of "getting into trouble" with Congress.

At the time I had also been meeting with congressional leaders who expressed their frustration with, not surprisingly, the VA. As I pieced things together, I realized that this person's boss was afraid of repercussions from a powerful legislator whom they feared would cause funding trouble for their VISN if they worked with an out-of-state, though more established, group. It was suggested that I contact the head of their unit in DC again. After doing so I was shocked to receive an e-mail saying that they too could not help, "due to the same reasons" given at the VISN level. I was aghast: a national-level VA lead was confirming that the fear of "getting in trouble" was the reason they would not be able to support exactly the kind of evidence-based CBO the VA claimed to want as a partner.

It reminded me of my meeting at the Pentagon with a chaplain and administrators from DoD's controversial Comprehensive Soldier Fitness (CSF) resilience program, who were interested in learning about Coming Home Project retreats and their suitability for CSF and the woefully neglected Wounded Warrior Transition Units. The meeting seemed promising, until I used the phrase "spouses and partners," rather than just "spouses." This was in the "Don't ask, don't tell" era. Later I received an email from CSF that I keep to this day. "It was great to meet you and hear about your program. After discussions, however, we cannot work together because our program does not do direct service for people but rather is a training platform."

The beat continued. In 2013 the VA offered several $10 million grants for CBOs to provide innovative programming to a large underserved and high-priority segment of the veteran population. Complex grant proposals involving numerous community partnerships with entities such as local and state government entities, Reserve and National Guard units, and institutions of higher learning were submitted by ninety organizations. Five awardees were selected and the results sent to the secretary's office for final review. There they languished for a year past the VA's own deadline. If processing veterans' benefit claims can take a year and more, why should implementing innovations in services be exempt? I recently received from VA an invitation to apply for another grant. I contacted the senior advisor to the secretary for public-private partnerships to suggest that before offering a new grant it would be a good idea to tie up outstanding grant proposals that were stalled. He said it was "not in his lane." I wrote back saying this attitude and his fobbing off of well-qualified VA partners represented exactly the problem that was at the root of the past and recent VA malfeasance.

So it did not come as a surprise to read the candid transcript of an e-mail written by VA telehealth coordinator David Newman describing how patients at the Cheyenne VA Medical Center should always be listed as getting appointments within a 14-day window, no matter when the appointment was first requested, and no matter how long the patient's wait time actually was. The memo said, "Yes, this is gaming the system a bit . . ." because "when we exceed the 14 day measure, the front office gets very upset, which doesn't help us." He instructs staff on how to "get off the bad boys list" by "cancelling the visit (by clinic) and then rescheduling it with a desired date within that 14 day window."[6]

Such examples of institutional dysfunction do not simply reflect a lack of connection and community. Reading the statements of VA whistleblowers, or listening, as we at Coming Home Project have, to hundreds of providers delivering care at these institutions, reveal the effects of a toxic culture. Comedian Jon Stewart euphemistically used the term: "post-bureaucratic stress disorder." While VA has the dubious distinction of leading the way in this department, DoD is certainly not exempt. The reporting of Mark Benjamin, Daniel Zwerdling, and others have drawn our attention to issues such as the hundreds of wounded soldiers arriving by design under cover of darkness back in the United States, the squalid living conditions of injured soldiers at Walter Reed Army Medical Center, and the systemic military discharges made on the basis of a preexisting condition, a "personality disorder." These types of discharges generally left the service member ineligible for the VA benefits and follow-on care they would have been entitled to had they been discharged with post-traumatic stress, the condition they were likely suffering from, as a result of their service in the war zone.

Steve Robinson was an Army Ranger and injured veteran of the first Gulf War, a brilliant, courageous, and tireless veterans advocate. He first made headlines when he worked with soldiers at Fort Carson, Colorado, who had been pushed out of the military with these "personality disorders," rather than war trauma. A personality discharge is administrative, which means a soldier receives no health benefits. Post-traumatic stress disorder, if it causes a soldier to be unable to work, requires a medical retirement hearing. Robinson, who worked as director of Veterans for America at the time, testified about the problem before Congress, which then brought in the Government Accountability Office to investigate.[7] He kept applying pressure with Andrew Pogany, also a former soldier. When the discharges changed from "personality disorder" to "adjustment disorder" to "pattern of misconduct," the pair argued that each category amounted to kicking out combat-wounded service members without benefits.

Inequitable, dysfunctional, and toxic cultural dynamics were not the only issues; competence was also questionable. A recent study by the prestigious, independent, nonprofit Institute of Medicine (IOM) reported that DoD and VA are unable to say if they are successfully treating hundreds of thousands of troops and veterans with PTSD because neither agency is adequately tracking long-term patient outcomes. The two departments have a combined budget of $3.3 billion annually for therapies addressing PTSD. Clinicians at DoD and VA also did not share with one another information on the medical hits or misses they've documented from their differing attempts to ease post-traumatic stress symptoms. Dr. Sondro Galea was chair of the IOM committee that carried out the congressionally-mandated assessment of post-traumatic stress programs at the two departments. According to him, "We are hoping [our report] serves as a clarion call and blueprint to guide where we should be."[8]

The IOM urged the two agencies to begin collaborating on the health progress of all current and former military members diagnosed with PTSD— "regardless of where they receive treatment." They also found that the Defense Department's PTSD programs "appear to be local, ad hoc, incremental, and crisis-driven, with little planning devoted to the development of a long-range approach; leaders within DoD and the service branches at all levels are not consistently held accountable for failing to implement programs meant to effectively manage post-traumatic stress in troops. It is also unclear whether VA hospital administrators around the country follow the agency's minimum-care requirements for veterans suffering from war trauma."

Parallels and Ironies

I spoke recently with a well-informed friend and colleague about how crushing the effects of toxic bureaucracies can be; he added, "and isolating." If there is a sequence it would be isolation and disempowerment by means of stigmatizing and ostracizing, then crushing. But that skips an important step: gas-lighting. Gas-lighting is a term that comes from the play *Gas Light* (and its film adaptations). It means making someone doubt their sanity and feel crazy. More than one report of this phenomenon has emerged among whistleblowers during recent VA scandals about deaths possibly related to deception and secret wait lists. "I felt completely crazy," said one whistleblower. "It was as if I was in an alternate universe," a doctor reported. Such systems are, in the truest sense of the word, toxic; they generate states akin to psychopathology. But this pathology is iatrogenic, the effects of pathological care systems.

In one of many ironic but not surprising parallels, many veterans, like the employees cited above, feel that they are somehow different, that their experience is crazy, and that they will be greeted by scorn and derision or worse, even by their fellow vets. Part of this is attributable to cultural norms and fear of being stigmatized as soft, weak, and unable to handle their problems like a true warrior. But one result of fragmentation, internal and institutional, is the experience of the center not holding, of coming apart at the seams and somehow being painfully isolated, feeling like the only one who is going through this. It follows suit then that it would be like pouring gasoline on the fire when veterans seek assistance at institutions that, rather than providing help, turn around and indirectly or directly blame them for their own "preexisting conditions." How can veterans, whose own psyches have become fragmented in the service of survival, find care in broken systems plagued by endemic institutional "linkage problems" and worse, conditions that parallel their own individual struggles to cope emotionally with the aftershocks of war trauma?

It is difficult to convey the relief experienced by hundreds of veterans, family members, and their caregivers and service providers with whom we've worked when they realize that everyone in the room, indeed everyone returning from the war zone, is wrestling with one challenge or another from their service. When they grasp that they are not alone, that as anguished and broken as they feel, they are with sisters and brothers who share a common experience. Then they realize that they are not "wrong" and they are not "crazy," despite crazy-making and infuriating experiences of "personality disorder" discharges, institutional gas-lighting, and women veterans at VA who routinely had their claims of injuries sustained in combat invalidated.

The health of an organism at whatever level of complexity— individual, family, community, nation, or planet—depends on the ability to adapt to changing circumstances and challenges by responding appropriately, robustly, and flexibly. Greg Friccione's comprehensive interdisciplinary research strongly indicates the added survival value of systems that utilize a collectively informed ethic that favors cooperative behavior.[9] This cannot be accomplished if disinformation or lies rule the day as means of motivation, intimidation, and control.

It is interesting to consider some additional ironies and parallels. First, how "shock and awe," the name given to our initial bombing campaign in Iraq, has come home, with the epidemic of veteran suicides and behavioral health, family, homelessness, substance abuse, and other issues. With the eruption of egregious malfeasance in our caregiving institutions, with the disintegration of Iraq, the country we invaded in order to save it. Second, it can be said that our government, with the cooperation of much of the media, sleepwalked American citizens into a needless and costly war, based on false premises, while preying on our most basic fears about survival. Terror was a motivational lever used to compel our silence and compliance and to ensure we would dissociate our natural connectedness, disable our attentive engagement and mutual concern, and instead go shopping at the mall. How ironic in an awful sense to learn of the thousands of VA employees living in work environments characterized by paranoia bordering on terror, feeling like they're being driven crazy. In some cases, they feel like they are literally "in an alternate universe," doubting their own sanity.

War trauma is indeed a time-release bomb whose continuing and unpredictable shockwaves shatter links, a metaphor alluded to earlier in a quote by war correspondent Richard Engel describing the original invasion of Iraq. In the film *The Bourne Supremacy*, CIA supervisor Pamela Landy is speaking with Ward Abbott, former head of the covert Operation Treadstone, about wanting to bring in Jason Bourne, a black ops operative on the loose. For Abbott, Bourne is a danger and should be eliminated. He thinks Landy is underestimating him and tries to convince her. She doesn't budge and finally Abbott says, in frustration tinged with truth, "His mind is broken, Pam. We broke it."

Given our intricately interconnected humanity, the impacts of war trauma radiate out on multiple levels simultaneously and keep exploding and imploding in ways we never anticipated long after we think they should be done with. You don't have to be a Democrat or a Republican to consider this: when we rain terror on a country that is not responsible for our traumatic anguish, when we terrorize (torture) those we capture, when our citizens are deceived and manipulated using terror to disable discernment and engagement, it should not be surprising to find that our veterans are not the only ones plagued by the terrors of PTsxD and PTspD. We should not be surprised that family members, employees, and caregivers find themselves not just shined on but terrorized and driven crazy by the very institutions mandated to provide care. We should not be surprised that veterans are made to feel crazy and retraumatized by having their lived war experience invalidated through reference to "preexisting conditions"—by delaying and denying them the care, support, and benefits they have earned. When terror, deception, and dissociative unreality are the coins of the realm, it should not surprise us that their impacts spread insidiously across boundaries and barriers that common sense tells us should keep them contained, but don't.

Colin Powell said about Iraq, "If you break it, you own it."[10] Although we pay unctuous lip service to our responsibility to care for our returning veterans, we do not follow through with sustained action and purpose. Motivation matters. It's not what you say but who you are as revealed by your actions and their effects. The road to hell is paved with good intentions. How many righteous intentions rolled glibly off the tongue at the beginning of the Iraq War? Like our veterans, most civilians have very good bullshit detectors, otherwise known as intuition. In Buddhism it's not just your actions but the true intent behind the actions that determines whether they will be beneficial or not. The rolling reverberations of damaging, misguided, or ill-intended endeavors continue today.

Growing Connective Tissue

A genuine community offers a simple yet rare ingredient: integrity. Certainly skilled staff, well-thought-out proven strategies, experienced instructors, solid methods, and practices and programs count. But when a fundamental lack of integrity is such a pivotal and grave concern, we get nowhere without restoring it. Without integrity, PTsxD becomes inflamed and chronic and brings in its wake PTspD.

Peace is not a partisan policy, the province of hippies, liberals, and antiwar proponents. My colleagues and I have yet to meet a veteran or family member who does not want peace of mind. For that to occur, terror must be recognized, faced, and ended. Peace has to break out by making the peace after the war. Terror recedes in healing environments and cultures of integrity, like those Coming Home Project creates for returning veterans and their families. Photo ops, poster children, Band-Aids, and quick fixes won't do; thoroughgoing cultural change is needed. And it is here that, as a country, we have repeatedly come up short.

These and numerous other examples of chronic dysfunction give credence to the saying, "Been down so long don't know what up looks like." So what would a healthy culture look like? One with a "there" there?

Malcolm Gladwell begins his 2008 book, *Outliers*, with just such a description.[11] That he uses this example to convey the meaning of the word itself speaks volumes to the rarity of genuine community. The town of Roseto, Pennsylvania, was, he writes, unknown in the surrounding regions and might have stayed that way but for the experience of a physician named Stewart Wolf, who was intrigued by accounts of the relative absence of heart disease. This was the 1950s, and heart attacks were the leading cause of death in men under the age sixty-five.

With students and colleagues Wolf gathered residents' death certificates from as far back as possible and scrutinized physicians' records. He took medical histories and developed family genealogies. He brought in sociologist John Bruhn, who, with medical and sociology graduate students, talked to every person aged twenty-one and over.

Years later, Bruhn was still amazed at what they discovered. "There was no suicide, no alcoholism, no drug addiction, and very little crime. They didn't have anyone on welfare. Then we looked at peptic ulcers. They didn't have any of those either. These people were dying of old age. That's it." In Roseto, virtually no one under fifty-five had died of a heart attack or showed any signs of heart disease. For men over sixty-five, the death rate from heart disease was half that of the country as a whole. The death rate from all causes in Roseto was 30 to 35 percent lower than expected.

When analyses showed that the usual factors—genetics, diet, exercise, and location—were not at play, Wolf and Bruhn puzzled over what factors might be responsible. They turned their attention to the details of everyday life in Roseto and came to see how residents "visited one another, stopping to chat in Italian on the street, say, or cooking for one another in their backyards. They learned about the extended family clans that underlay the town's social structure. They saw how many homes had three generations living under one roof, and how much respect grandparents commanded." They observed the unifying and containing effect of the church and the "egalitarian ethic" of the community, which "discouraged the wealthy from flaunting their success and helped the unsuccessful obscure their failures."

Wolf began to see that the secret lay hidden in plain sight: the townspeople had created "a powerful, protective social structure capable of insulating them from the pressures of the modern world. They were healthy . . . because of the world they had created for themselves in their tiny little town in the hills."

Bruhn and Wolf faced skepticism from the medical field. At conferences where other researchers presented "long rows of data arrayed in complex charts and referring to this kind of gene or that kind of physiological process . . . they talked instead about the mysterious and magical benefits of people stopping to talk to each other on the street and having three generations living under one roof." Nobody "was used to thinking about health in terms of community." Nobody was paying attention to the life-giving "there" there. As in the earlier story of the "spotlight effect," they were not looking in the right place. When it comes to policy making and planning for the health of our returning service members and veterans, together with their families and children, the situation has not changed much in sixty years. Planners are so focused on short-term, quick-fix techniques that the life-giving power of community is almost entirely ignored.

* * *

Let's look at examples of community in the service of healing. After the initial moment of silence, and toddler Ben's spontaneous words, "My Daddy died in Iraq," we begin to go around the circle, introducing ourselves. Stephanie, Ben's mom, felt isolated in Houston, where she lived with the heavy legacy of her husband Michael's suicide. The group's reaction is palpable; Tonia, Ken's wife, puts her arms around Stephanie as she weeps. During break, Stephanie is taken in like family by a swarm of other spouses and parents. I learn later that the web of support is radiating out. Three full-time caregivers—Stefanie, Tonia, and Cynthia, Rory's mother—gather to be with one another in Seattle for renewal. Stephanie comes to join them, visiting Tonia in Oceanside beforehand and traveling up to Seattle together.

That evening over dinner I saw and felt a togetherness and outpouring of nonsentimental love as pronounced as any I had experienced. People were taking good care of one another without prompting; the atmosphere was relaxed, congenial, and permeated with non-self-conscious compassion. Christianity and Buddhism might feature love and compassion as cornerstones of their teachings but neither they nor any other religion had a monopoly on the real thing.

An active duty officer and his wife looked out for Nancy, whose marriage was in crisis, and whose husband had finally entered in-patient substance-abuse treatment. Marine mother Mary Ellen listened as Tonia spoke over dinner about feelings that came up after the renewal of vows ceremony with husband Ken. Lisa, sister of a veteran, reached out later that week and the same officer responded to assist her and her brother Matt. Jeremy and Christina relocated shortly afterward from Camp Pendleton to Texas, near Stephanie and Ben. With children of similar ages, they stayed in close touch, just as Stephanie did with Cynthia and Tonia on the West Coast after the first weekend.

Now giving, now receiving. No passing the buck, no "stay in my lane." And no one left behind, no one forgotten.

Rather than paranoia, intimidation, disinformation, and gas-lighting, a healthy community encourages transparency, spontaneity, and humor. These blossom in a culture of safety, trust, and belonging—characterized by affirmation and respect for the worth of each unique individual as part of the bigger whole. These qualities are invaluable when processing the tough stuff. It takes experiences of nonsuffering to be able to productively face and transform acute suffering.

Mauricio, an active duty injured Marine noncommissioned officer said at one retreat, "When we meet together, the tears come; when we break, we're all laughing. We meet again and I'm crying, and we hang out and we're cracking up.

Laughing and crying." He provided comic relief, challenging his fellow marine Kenny by claiming that, of the two master sergeants, he was on top of Kenny. Mauricio got everyone laughing about who was on top and who was on bottom. When he kidded the whole group about status and rank, we laughed even harder. It buoyed our spirits.

In the small vets group, however, he was quiet. Gradually he began to talk about how difficult it was to no longer feel like himself in body and mind. Due to several TBIs, he couldn't remember important parts of his childhood. Given that he had many marines under his command, it was tough not to be able to function like he used to. He spoke slowly, with an undercurrent of deep emotion, a slight crack in his voice. "I'm not myself; I don't know if I can do my job anymore."

Jessie, formerly an Army master sergeant, blinded while serving in Iraq, shared his deep sense of betrayal with a sense of gravity and conviction. After all he had endured, offered, and sacrificed, it felt like a broken covenant. He had to do it all himself, become his own advocate, and find his way through the disconnected maze of services to locate and access those he needed. We had just had lunch and were about to begin a period of writing. I went over and asked Jessie if he wanted someone to act as a scribe, maybe a vet or a family member. So he and Colin, a Marine vet now a Buddhist priest, went into the library. Jessie asked if I would request that people say their names before speaking; it helped him orient and recognize people. I suggested he make the request himself.

He spoke simply and with dignity. Afterward, when people began to speak, they would stop, remember his request, and say, "Sergeant Major, this is so and so," addressing Jessie by his title. In Coming Home retreats we leave rank and degrees at the door, but this was different: it was an expression of deep respect. When people forgot to identify themselves, Jessie would gently remind them. Once, later on, when he had just begun to say something, a participant said, "You forgot to say your name." Jessie laughed and, taking his lead, everyone broke out laughing, the role reversal incongruous, funny, and poignant all at once. There were times during the day where we laughed till we cried, and laughed and cried both, sometimes not knowing which was which. Our laughter also helped us bear the pain and so was good for the soul.

Everyone present in the room knew that by asking fellow participants to say their names Jessie wanted to communicate and feel part of the group, to hear and recognize everyone, and in turn be recognized by us. While he could not see, he did not want to feel invisible, like he felt to the institutions entrusted with his care that were not responsive. It was the desire for mutual recognition that came across loud and clear, a crucial element of healing that I recognized from the consulting room, now as clear as day in this new context. A provision of a healthy community. He was seen.

There's a saying attributed to Tolstoy, "Happy families are alike; unhappy families are all unhappy in their own ways." But in my experience of community, which is after all a kind of family, well-being and joy find far more nuanced and diverse expressions than does the misery of toxic cultures.

The symptoms of war-zone trauma are real and can become disabling: withdrawal, freezing over, hyperarousal and high anxiety, insomnia, eruptions of anger and other emotions, flashbacks, depression. I refer to these as PTsxD, symptoms of nervous system dysregulation. But as painful as these symptoms are, often they are just the tip of the iceberg. We have learned time and again that, as veterans and service members come to trust the community setting, one another, and themselves, we get to hear what radio commentator Paul Harvey would call "the rest of the story." This includes but isn't limited to pervasive meaninglessness, terrifying night visitations, shattered worldviews, inescapable guilt, overwhelming grief, helpless rage, despair and hopelessness, unbearable shame, and deeply buried self-loathing—what I am calling PTspD. If we just focus solely on symptoms, we often miss the deeper layers of anguish.

Safety is the core relational condition necessary for addressing these injuries: a nonjudgmental atmosphere of acceptance, a warm compassionate welcome, without qualification. I will call it by its name: *unconditional love.* I am not talking organized religion, though all religions speak about it in their own manner. I am talking about providing spiritual nourishment. It is not esoteric or otherworldly. People feel supported and nourished when this type of love is present—the ice begins to melt, the turbulence starts to subside, the heart begins to open. Deep listening in the company of a trusted companion is the activity of unconditional love. It promotes speaking from the heart, another gift, as veterans' fears are disconfirmed and they discover to their surprise that what they have to say is actually encouraging to others.

The group that provides this elusive and overlooked ingredient is, in the Judeo-Christian tradition, sometimes called the "beloved community." In Buddhism, it is the "sangha." In the Native American tradition, it is "all my relations." With the provision of such an emotional atmosphere, people find their own way to reconnect within themselves, with their peers, with their families, and with their various circles of belonging.

Reconnection takes patience. Veterans test the waters to see how real and how deep they are before venturing in; they want to verify how genuine the environment is, how devoted and skilled the people. Suspicion runs deep. No one wants to be retraumatized. But once veterans feel safe, a process is set in motion that takes on a life of its own: the natural urge to become whole. The words healing and religion both refer to binding together something that has become frayed or broken. The path to our wholeness takes us, as my friend Steve Torgerson often says, through experiencing and accepting our brokenness.

Lest the idea of unconditional love as the key provision of community, and central in the transformation of trauma, seem too warm and fuzzy for some readers, I recommend Greg Fricchione's book, *Compassion and Medicine in Healing and Society*. He presents copious scientific documentation of what most of us intuitively know to be true: personal connections make us feel better. Fricchione demonstrates that we all "benefit from genuine expressions of selfless love." Moreover, he convincingly shows that our very evolution as a species depends on it. The voluminous research on the power of social supports in healing confirms this.

Although the benefits of a sense of community are salutary, they are not magical or esoterically mysterious as the excited descriptions by Wolf and Bruhn in *Outliers* might lead some to think. Googling "benefits of social supports" brings up 3,600 scholarly articles. If feeling safe, understood, accepted, and listened to without judgment are pivotal elements of community, another is a sense of belonging. David Kahn, an authority on suicide prevention, wrote in 2008, "Connection and a feeling of social belonging is, I think, the most important initial step in preventing suicide." It can also help reduce stigma: "Once the person feels that sense of trust in belonging to the community, they may be more receptive to suggestions that they seek help, if they haven't sought it already."[12] Unit cohesion has been linked in the war zone with lower stress levels and lower incidence of suicide. Here's another secret we have discovered that is hidden in plain sight: community is the unit cohesion of civilian life. Although not a panacea, it helps heal and prevent, strengthen and inoculate, all at the same time.

On May 7, 2012, there was a gala Veterans Summit aboard the USS *Intrepid*, the foundation of the Intrepid Sea, Air & Space Museum in New York City. The highlight for me was an interview with Salvatore Giunta, veteran of the war in Afghanistan and Medal of Honor recipient, conducted by Jon Stewart. Stewart asked whether veterans are hesitant to receive attention and help. Giunta responded, "The military is not an 'I' organization; it is a 'We' organization. The few times you hear someone in the military say 'I' it usually goes something to the tune of, 'I screwed up.' That's when 'I' is used, when you're taking personal accountability for your actions." Stewart, ever the wisecracker, commented, "It's so interesting, because many of the people [here] are in the financial industry, and it's the same ethos, in many regards . . ." As the audience laughed, Stewart added, "Maybe we should just hire you guys." More laughter and applause, as Giunta responded, "Absolutely."

Let's delve further into what community actually is. I'm using the word primarily to express a distinctive set of group characteristics and interactions, rather than to indicate a particular group itself, be it a circle of friends, a community of one's peers, a church community, a workplace, an institution, or a town, state, country, or international community of nations. The term *communitas* is sometimes used to distinguish the modality of social relationship from an area of common living.[13] The word conveys an intense community spirit characterized by social equality, solidarity, and togetherness. It is intriguing to note that it also can refer to characteristics of people experiencing liminality together, in other words, people inhabiting a kind of in-between zone, rather than being positioned squarely within the dominant culture. How ironic and apropos given the transitional state of being and the marginalization that returning veterans and families know only too well.

Every community has its own culture, an intertwining set of written and unwritten mores and operational rules of engagement or conduct. But culture refers primarily to what does not stand out, and is not or cannot be questioned. Culture embodies a kind of implicit transactional guidebook that we take for granted and relegate to the background of our attention, once we're socialized or acculturated (like language).

Let's look now at the origins of community—the sense of solidarity, communion, and camaraderie—in human development. I once had a friend who liked to have the radio on when she was home alone, even though she wasn't listening to it. A relative used to describe how she didn't mind but actually liked the traffic noises and the sounds of neighbors in her apartment building. I've lived in a number of places that overlooked schoolyards and realized how much I enjoyed the sounds of children playing. In early psychoanalytic research on "the sound object," findings show that the infant in utero is already responding to the sound of the parents' voices, gravitating some think to the father's voice. We want and need to know that we are not alone, that someone is there.

In the old film, *The Amazing Newborn*, we see the breathtaking way in which many newborns reach out with their just-opened eyes to meet the gaze of their mother. Research on developing primary attachments demonstrates that it is not traumas themselves that necessarily jeopardize our sense of security but rather the inability to reflect on them and organize them into a cohesive and meaningful narrative. Parents ideally create an environment for the baby that is stimulating but within tolerable limits, avoiding "overwhelm" whenever possible. But when baby is overwhelmed, the parent responds using instinctual empathic understanding to help transform the entire situation and assist the baby in regulating the overwhelm. This kind of relational give-and-take develops within the baby the capacity to manage the inevitable ups and downs of emotional life. From the beginning baby and caregivers *interare*, drawing on a finely choreographed mutuality that is emblematic of communion. Sigmund Freud wrote that the first ego, or sense of self-cohesion, is a body ego. How we physically hold our baby and child and respond to its physical needs means a lot. How we hold their emotions and overall well-being, providing safety, guidelines, acceptance without judgment, and empathic responsiveness, is just as critical.

In focusing so much on post-traumatic stress as an anxiety disorder, we have neglected the impacts of war trauma on veterans' and families' capacity to negotiate meaningful and satisfying relationships. At Coming Home Project, we've learned from experience the importance of attentiveness to the minutiae of logistics, the provision and felt experience of care that functional systems convey—simple things like returning calls and e-mails promptly, providing reminders and lists for those with memory problems stemming from traumatic brain injury, maintaining a comfortable temperature in rooms, arranging for parking, bringing in cots so young children could sleep in their parents' room while teens slept in an adjacent room. We've come to see that we are taking care of our participants. When they feel well taken care of, participants immerse into their direct experience, less wary and vigilant.

At Coming Home retreats, the large and small group cohorts help participants regulate their internal affective ups and downs. The natural beauty all around us also plays an important role. Many a "rough and tough and hard to bluff" service member can be found sitting in a gazebo, or down by a stream, or in a rose garden. They commonly say it helps them "ramp down," using a metaphor that unintentionally speaks to regulatory function. It's not just a single technique or method—including ancient practices like yoga, meditation, and qigong—that helps develop these regulatory capacities. It's the entire setting, and the quality of relationships among and within all retreat groups. That is the foundation. It is rooted in being part of an environment that is unconditionally welcoming, containing, and responsive. Bigger than yourself and yet recognizing, respecting, and valuing your distinctive experience. "There's a place for me here." Community provides a togetherness that enables aloneness to be fruitful, which in turn enriches the collective and generates harmony, a palpable force that lifts all boats in a benevolent circle of effects. We've learned over and over that this is not a liberal ideologue's dream; it operates with a robustness and reliability that stun many who attend in person or read our data.

The communitas of Coming Home Project's retreat culture enriches and strengthens participants' inner life—their inner culture, if you will—which is commonly fragmented, compartmentalized, and dissociated by emotional shrapnel, the shearing impacts of war trauma that unhitch body and mind, heart and soul. We've come to call this setting an optimal healing environment. Such a setting is also optimal, we learned, for new learning. However skeptical they may be at first, veterans are thirsty for experiences of community that provide them the opportunity to diversify their emotional and behavioral repertoire by disconfirming, with peers, the need for automatic defensive reactions that have become seared into neurobiological, emotional, and relational circuitry. It's become a commonplace of contemporary neuroscience that "circuits that fire together wire together," and continue to, even without the original stimulus. Among the common examples is a quick startle response, as when the backfire of a car generalizes, echoes as gunfire, and triggers a response suited for the war zone but not a city street—or when the car parked under a bridge becomes a car bomb requiring immediate evasive action.

Transitioning into civilian life means understanding experientially that these once-adaptive responses, hardwired in by war-zone experience, are not suited to the new environment. Alternative pathways and frameworks are created in an environment of safety, and they are nourished and experientially tested. They provide new experiences of trust, rather than a 24/7 360-degree threat. Experiences of nonsuffering provide alternative patterning that comes to exist alongside the trauma-induced circuits. With practice, the latter loosen their grip on us.

Mike was a well-educated and articulate vet who, along with holding down his day job, helped his wife with a nonprofit they'd founded to assist vets with post-traumatic stress. In our small group he opened up about the intense hatred he felt for anyone who looked Iraqi, or of Middle Eastern origin. He got quite a few "Amen to that" responses from the group, which turbocharged and prolonged his accounts. He "knew" he was generalizing, knew that even if someone he saw in a mall was Iraqi, the person most likely had nothing to do with attacks on his unit or deaths of his buddies. But this conceptual knowledge was disconnected from the emotional circuitry of rage, based on traumatic loss, that kept circling back on itself and fanning the fires. He felt well heard, but the feedback did not seem to help. After quite a while, there was a pause in the storm, and he half-whispered that this rage had not served him well. A vet said something about his own experience of the trouble that such automatic reactions had gotten him into. In the silence that followed we could almost see the emotions rise in Mike. For a little while, a sob of loss and vulnerability replaced the steady stream of rage that had kept him feeling pumped up and powerful rather than utterly helpless to alter traumatic circumstances. Later, he and his wife both wrote to tell us how meaningful that moment had been and how it enriched their educational work with post-traumatic stress.

Integrity is the cornerstone of this interconnected and coordinated community that holds vets and family in its attentive, responsive embrace. Along with unconditional love, it is the operative principle of an environment that permits veterans to relinquish hypervigilance. Community builds a culture that facilitates integration because it embodies integrity. When disparate parts that have been torn asunder come back together, reintegration is no longer the buzzword of the month; it becomes real. The biological, the psychological, the social-family, and the spiritual elements of our model each deepen, complement one another, and fall together naturally in a sense of profound well-being. In our closing circle, a chaplain who had been working for four years at the major receiving hospital for seriously wounded Iraq and Afghanistan veterans confessed that the retreat had been the first time he had let himself relax in four years.

As we saw with both Rory, whose traumatic brain injury and post-traumatic emotional pain made it nearly impossible to modulate his outrage, and his relationship with the active duty officer who shadowed and supported him through two retreats, new psychological and neurobiological capacities can develop even in brains and bodies that are massively compromised. Rory participated in a series of interconnected relational settings that helped him regulate his emotions. The overall retreat cohort, the small vets group, the presence of his parents, and primarily the intensive connection with the active duty officer set in motion a series of effects that allowed Rory to derive more from the bio-psycho-social/family-spiritual capacities at his disposal, to function at a demonstrably higher level, and to derive more from his inner and social experiences. Perhaps most important to him, it facilitated his ability to contribute to the well-being of his fellow vets, which enhanced his sense of self-efficacy and meaning. Post-traumatic growth (which I abbreviate as PTgr) is a much-ballyhooed notion in this era of resilience on the quick and dirty. But our experience with Rory shows how it just might operate, how hard-won it is, and the primacy of relational ingredients in its evolution.

For successful reintegration of our service members and veterans, we need integration to be activated at multiple levels, including in our care and support settings. In order to help veterans learn to rebuild connectivity, our methods and systems of care need to embody the basic ingredient, integrity.

Living and Learning

Operationally, community is characterized by solidarity, equal relations, a tendency toward closeness, and connection rather than isolation. "Talk therapy" gets a bad rap these days. The psychoanalyst Donald Winnicott thought the relationship between patient and therapist did not just involve talking but rather "living a bit of life together." Retreat participants live a chunk of life together. In the war zone this is amplified a hundred fold and more. The staying power of communal bonds cannot be overestimated, as revealed in the following excerpt from an interview with veterans.

> Interviewer [Kevin Reeder]: "How many of you would go back to a deployed environment with your branch of service right now if that opportunity was available? Lotta hands up. Real quick, why are your hands going up so much?"
>
> Gable Darbonne: "You miss it in a way. You miss everything about how hard it . . . how bitter you got, how angry and emotional, the things you saw and you missed that camaraderie, that brotherhood, sense of purpose, the struggling with things. Man, you . . . it's everything, but you miss it. You mourn that, it's weird. It's that intimacy. It's . . . you don't . . . I will never get that back. None of us will ever get that back."[14]

In Darbonne's case, proximity, common dangers, and a sense of brotherhood, sameness, contributed to the power of the emotional bond with his buddies. In addition to learning new ways to manage powerful emotions and stress and opening up to states of nonsuffering that help in encountering pain productively, there is another kind of learning that we've observed, one based on encountering difference rather than similarity.

During retreats, as part of looking out for one another, when we gather in the morning after breakfast and again after lunch, we check to see that everyone is present. If someone's missing, we go check on them. Once, a veteran had holed up in his room, refusing to come to plenary or small group meetings, or to any activities for that matter, including meals. I went to his room to talk with him. He was quite anxious and wanted to leave. He felt this wasn't the right place for him, that he shouldn't have come. While we explored what might be disturbing him, he was not forthcoming with details. Normally participants are required to attend all meetings and select among free-time activities. This vet felt positively hopeless about being able to be in the men's veterans group. I said that of course he could leave, but suggested he consider doing some writing while in his room alone. I returned with food during lunch and we talked some more. His anxiety was still quite generalized and, while he still wanted to leave, he was more communicative. Intuition told me he was afraid of not being accepted by the fraternity of male veterans, so I explored this with him. At first he was reluctant to talk but then agreed. By my next visit, he let me encourage him to come to group. We were missing him, I said.

By now I had a good sense of what might be going on, but I wasn't prepared for what unfolded after lunch in the men's vet group of about fifteen. I assured him that, like everyone in this support setting, he was free to speak or not as he wished. But toward the end of our meeting he ventured forth and spoke of how worried he had been of not being accepted, of being judged for being different, of becoming an outcast. After a while he said he was gay and had felt certain he'd be harshly judged and shamed. The reaction of the men was striking. They listened with rapt attention. A few spoke, one expressing appreciation, another respect, and a third admiration for the courage it took to share something so potentially explosive.

This occurred in the "Don't ask, don't tell" days, when "telling" could easily get you kicked out of the service. While I imagine that, on this occasion, some men may have kept less accepting feelings to themselves, the overall sense was one of having witnessed something remarkable and brave, a leap of faith that entrusted the group with a most personal and, in this setting, distinctively different part of him.

With a safe community as the lived context, participants are more likely to try to learn new things, sometimes on their own, sometimes because they see their peers or even their children doing them. Otherwise resistant male partners might not agree to attend a couples communication workshop. Quite a few adults have come to qigong on the invite of their teenager, or to meditation encouraged by their injured buddy. I was stunned at an early retreat to see a heterogeneous group of ten to fifteen male and female adult vets and family members sitting quietly at a table outside, beading, which then became the rage.

As a primarily volunteer staff, we have learned over the years to practice what we preach about community and embody it among our retreat team members. Really listening to one another makes things go: inviting and taking seriously multiple perspectives. Our facilitator group meets twice a day, after lunch and at the conclusion of the evening programs. Such is our need and desire to connect and process that evening meetings can go on for several hours. First and foremost, we share information from our respective small groups, and our overall observations and impressions. But we are also giving and receiving emotional support for the gratifying and demanding task of working sixteen hours a day during a five-day retreat. Our retreat planners and volunteers, too, are part and parcel of our intentional community and their observations are valued. All of us are absorbing and metabolizing the multifaceted and intense daily experiences of 40–150 people. The strategic and programmatic adjustments that unfold are certainly important. Ultimately it's the act of going through this as a team that reverberates silently yet powerfully, through the invisible yet palpable matrices of our community culture. Participants know and feel the "there" there; they know themselves to be in good hands, never far from our hearts and minds.

At the outset in 2007 we purposefully created a nonpsychiatric setting that was therapeutic without officially being psychotherapy. We wanted participants to feel at ease and unconcerned that they would be diagnosed or stigmatized. Given our concern about not "shrinking peoples' heads," we were surprised and delighted when participants themselves began to seek out staff, pick their brains, and engage them in discussions around life issues, strategies for managing anger, or resources for better parenting or information about child development. This led us to incorporate other kinds of educational and theme-focused groups to the schedule. But the added support that one-to-one connections provided, without being seen as formal psychotherapy, revealed to us, again, the power of a safe, trusting, and egalitarian, if asymmetric, community of belonging. This is a culture with firm guidelines but sans judgment, characterized by unconditional acceptance. In a setting where vigilance can recede, participants seek out the help they really need from those staff they have come to respect based on direct observation and interaction. This would occur despite the fact that many participants initially didn't know what they didn't know or what they might need. Some had let their arms be twisted into coming by family members or commanders; initially they were vociferous about not wanting or needing anything.

People frequently ask, "Okay, you don't do a traditional psychological screening; so what are your selection criteria? Who gets to be a member of the club?" Once I stopped to think about the implicit system we used, it was clear. There were three criteria. You had to want it, need it, and be able to benefit from it. A new office volunteer said she wasn't sure whether a new applicant was suitable. The veteran had written that she was suffering from "heavy PTSD." I read on and let the volunteer know this veteran fit our criteria to a tee. To supplement the written application form information, we talked individually with every adult applicant, an informal five to ten minute chat, to get a sense of who they were. We brought this information to a weekly meeting, went over every application, and decided who to invite. What were the criteria for having to leave "the club"? We developed clear and strictly enforced guidelines that contributed initially to a sense of skepticism and then to a sense of protection. Nearly all involved safety in one form or another, physical and emotional. Weapons were not infrequently brought along and we asked that they be turned in and safely stored until the end of the retreat. We learned the hard way about alcohol and drugs, and abuse of prescription pain and sleep medication. It simply was best for participants not to drink or use and rather let the support of the community and the activities and practices carry them through the retreat.

In an earlier era, a leader was trying to help divided factions reintegrate after a brutal protracted war. The qualities he outlined in his passionate call for reconciliation echo those that characterize the kind of healing community we have been discussing: "With malice toward none; with charity for all . . . let us strive to finish the work we are in; to bind up the nation's wounds; to care for him who shall have borne the battle, and for his widow and his orphan—to do all which may achieve and cherish a just and a lasting peace, among ourselves, and with all nations."[15]

Abraham Lincoln's phrase ". . . to care for him who shall have borne the battle, and for his widow, and his orphan . . ." became in 1959 the motto of the VA, and today a pair of metal plaques bearing those words flank the entrance to the Washington, DC headquarters of the Department of Veterans Affairs.[16] Embodying this profound purpose has been at best a work in progress for the troubled agency.

Today we know it is women and men both who bear the burdens of war. We know too that, in addition to the families who have lost sons and daughters, husbands, wives, and partners, fathers and mothers, there are thousands of families whose loved ones have returned markedly changed: injured physically, emotionally, or spiritually, or different in unmistakable ways.

The elements Lincoln urged us to cultivate 150 years ago—nonjudging, nonrecrimination, inclusiveness, charity, binding wounds, care, justice, and peace—are among the key ingredients for transforming trauma. They are not flashes in the pan but perennial healing qualities, which may explain why we came to understand that they underlie Coming Home Project reintegration efforts. Compassion (underlying charity) is at the heart. Inclusiveness and acceptance without condition or reproach are key, and there is an implied ethical responsibility or covenant. For peace, inner or collective, to be durable we must become able to learn from our experience, a rare ability.

Drawing from the Bible, Lincoln added, ". . . let us judge not, that we be not judged," and highlighted reconciliation and forgiveness. Reconciling parallels reintegration; both begin with taking stock. At Coming Home retreats veterans are often reconciling a chaotic inner world or a set of family relationships that have irrevocably changed after multiple deployments. Without "binding" their unseen wounds, they often feel both unbound (unbridled) and bound (imprisoned internally). A community such as I have been describing helps veterans learn to engage their war experience with more compassion and less self-blame and to understand and forgive themselves for actions committed or unable to be completed. This activity of reconciling the terrible costs of war, which often meets with strong internal and cultural resistance, is something that goes on throughout our country on multiple intersecting dimensions, even if it is muted, denied, or minimized.

We can see the power of community at play in the struggles of VA providers to transform the malfesance in their workplaces. In June 2015 it was reported that Deputy Inspector General Richard Griffin, the chief watchdog of the VA, was retiring after mounting criticism of his investigations and oversight.[17] The announcement came after whistle-blowers from VA facilities around the country, who had organized and formed a working support and advocacy network, urged President Obama to fire Griffin, saying "his office has gone after whistle-blowers rather than the problems they uncovered, failed to cooperate with lawmakers' oversight and in some cases [failed] to conduct thorough investigations, in a 'horrifying pattern of whitewashing and deceit.'"

Community is the foundation that facilitates the transforming of war trauma. This transformative human process is not a newfangled methodology cooked up in a sterile lab. We learned by doing and drew on perennial qualities and motivations from diverse spiritual and religious traditions, rooted in unconditional love and compassion, kindness, mutuality, skillful conduct, and not turning away or forgetting. Our approach also drew from Western psychology, and, as we went along, from military culture as well. While not eradicating war-related pain forever, it helps it find its rightful place while no longer torturing us. The safety and trust of community permits participants to represent and reexperience the shards of trauma within a new environment, and have them reencoded in their hearts and minds in a different way. And it requires mustering up something really tough: self-compassion. We turn our attention now to the ghosts of war and the alchemy by which they are transformed.

II. Turning Ghosts into Ancestors

"What's the matter? The war's over," someone said to a veteran. "Yeah," she replied, "over and over and over."

War trauma brings in its wake a collapse of time. The present is engulfed; the past colonizes moment-to-moment experience; and the future is collapsed. Severe PTsxD and all variants of PTspD are characterized by an experience of haunting. I am not referring to religious "demons" but rather to unprocessed experiences that have been sequestered away and frozen in time in the interest of survival. Their impacts are potent and fearfully unpredictable, but they cannot be easily identified and contained, not to mention explored and transformed.

Ghosts

In mythology, ghosts have no roots, and their restless wandering does not cease—and does not cease to disturb the living—until they are properly honored. Veterans and other trauma survivors can feel *as if* they were possessed, as if something were clamoring or silently exploding or imploding.

There is a way a ghost becomes an ancestor, and traumatic experiences become memories. The community provides the connective emotional tissue that holds. The fear of falling through the cracks abates; we stop holding our breaths in traumatic reaction and anticipation, and finally exhale. We hold ourselves less tightly wrapped and come to trust that we are supported. As this trust deepens, we allow ourselves to engage again in the moment. The community provides a bigger container in which unrepresented anguish can be represented, reexperienced in a new key, and transformed from a haunting ghost into a memory. The integrative and dynamic process I call turning ghosts into ancestors depends both on consciously cultivated attentiveness and unconscious emotional activity in the relational field. This transformative activity was originally named by the psychoanalyst Hans Loewald. Although he was not referring to dissociated traumatic residues such as war generates but to the unconscious byproducts that ensue when we repress sexual and aggressive drives, his words speak directly to the struggles we have been discussing.

"Those who know ghosts tell us that they long to be released from their ghost life and led to rest as ancestors. As ancestors they live forth in the present generation, while as ghosts they are compelled to haunt the present generation with their shadow life."[1]

Robert was remote and suspicious, and one could palpably feel just how depressed he was. A heavyset Iraq veteran, he came with his wife, who stayed close at all times. But he was not responsive to her, or to anyone for that matter.

Arnold had a gruesome tour in Afghanistan, witnessing things he could barely acknowledge. After returning he alternately withdrew and exploded. After blowing up at his son for being "soft," something Arnold of course could never let himself feel, Arnold flew into a rage and shoved his son against the wall. But he said he really felt like killing him. Ashamed, alarmed, and afraid, he fled his own house and did not return. The retreat was the first time he had been in the same room with his son for two months. In the group of fifteen fellow male veterans, he spoke little and often sat with his head near his lap, his face covered. Once, after beginning to speak, he bolted from the room.

In the introduction we met drone pilot Anthony, who said his brain hurt each night after returning home. Working out and video games, activities of choice for many veterans, didn't work for him. "*I need something real,*" he said. This experience of hearts and brains hurting, of "going out of my head," is also represented in a poem by Zen master Thich Nhat Hanh.

For Warmth

I hold my face in my two hands
My hands, hollowed to catch what might fall from within me
Deeper than crying
I am not crying
I hold my face in my two hands
To keep my loneliness warm
To cradle my hunger
Shelter my heart, from the rain and the thunder
Preventing my soul from flying in anger[2]

Writing from his own struggles, Nhat Hanh wrote also for the thousands of his fellow Vietnamese being shattered by destruction and loss during what the Vietnamese call the American war. In the poem he cradles his head in his two hands to prevent his soul, or his humanity, from fleeing in anger. *The Scream*, a renowned work of Norwegian painter Edvard Munch, captures the agony, the shock, and the helpless despair of severe trauma. The figure in the painting, who seems to both have seen and to be a ghost, has his hands over his ears, blocking out sounds, but could just as well be holding his head, preventing it from exploding with terror, leaving a vacant shell of a man.

Despite the surges of adrenaline and the profound bonding of going through hell together in the war zone, the sense of being real is often a major casualty of war trauma. Paradoxically, dissociation can also protect hidden corners of humanity from further damage. Chunks of lived experience retreat into a kind of witness protection program. "Can I get a witness?" becomes more than an old R & B song; it is one of the deepest desires of veterans and their families.

Army wife Angela Ricketts was going through a particularly bad time during one of her husband's many deployments. Her friends advised her to channel her "black soul," a phrase they used to mean going numb. Angela's words for this experience, to "hover above," clearly reflect dissociation, in service of making it through in one piece. Being in multiple pieces paradoxically helped her feel intact. Only when it was likely that her husband would not be deployed again could she "step back and really feel," a precursor to a more durable inner peace than "pieces" can provide. By dissociating potentially overwhelming emotion, Angela stayed psychologically alive until a time when she felt her husband would be reliably there to listen, when they could face things together. I think her appraisal of when that time was had both conscious and unconscious elements, much like participants' appraisals of safety during retreats.

Turning

Bearing witness is not a passive impersonal affair. The *something real* that drone pilot Anthony, other service members, and veterans need is kindled by reconnecting in a safe community of veterans and families. This helps make real what has become numb and lifeless by rendering unprocessed traumatic residues digestible—by making use of healing relational conditions to develop the capacities necessary to transform splintered parts into thinkable, feel-able, dream-able and narrate-able experiences and memories.

The five elements that comprise Coming Home retreats are not a new quick fix, but rather are rooted in how humans have, since time immemorial, worked to transform overwhelming trauma. They include sharing stories in a safe environment (healing dialogue), wellness exercises (spiritual practice), expressive arts, being active in the wild (the healing power of nature and beauty), and secular ritual (adapted from reverent religious experience). The veterans, family members, and providers we have worked with uniformly do not want their own suffering and the suffering of those they hold dear to have been in vain. They want it to mean something. "What have we got to show for it?" one service member asked about a certain campaign. He'd make any sacrifice, including the ultimate one, for a mission that to him made sense. Driven by the reparative instinct and the need for meaning, veterans commonly endeavor to "make something" of war-related trauma, to "redeem" it.

What we cannot acknowledge we cannot process. What we cannot process, we cannot transform. What we cannot transform haunts us. It takes other minds and hearts to help us heal our own, to help us grow the capacities we need to transform suffering. This is done in concert, reweaving the web of connective emotional, relational, and spiritual tissue that cumulative trauma tears asunder. With an informed, responsive culture, it is possible to transform ghosts into ancestors, to make what haunts us into elements we can hold and properly remember. This opens up the present once again, and the future as well.

Coming Home Project retreats provide optimal conditions for processing war trauma in a relational field bigger than ourselves, in the presence of others, breathing, listening, witnessing, and sharing our humanity with us. Transforming trauma asks that we recreate and reauthor it, rather than solely experience it as lodged within, a kind of foreign invasive element, inflicted on us, inscribed and burned into our neural and relational circuitry by the profound helplessness to change it. Without working it over and making it our own, overwhelming trauma remains a ghost, what some experience as an "inner demon."

A ghost gradually becomes an ancestor, and traumatic experiences become memories, by a most human alchemy. The community holds us as trust grows, and we learn to return our attentiveness to body, breath, peers, family, and surroundings. It provides the buoyancy that genuinely lifts all boats. The military chaplain whom we met earlier said that on the final day at a retreat he was able "to exhale" for the first time in three years of working continuously in a large military receiving hospital. In an unconditionally accepting environment veterans come to feel they belong, feel understood, and become less on the defensive and more open. Wellness practices that reconnect them to ignored and undeveloped inner resources can become internalized. Optimal environments for connecting and healing are also optimal for learning and relearning.

When the environmental conditions are right, participants feel safe enough to *represent* their experience. In Coming Home retreats this happens spontaneously among peers and family members, in small support groups, and through expressive arts. The fear of shame, humiliation, and other crushing reactions is disconfirmed and replaced by a loving response. Buoyed, they are freer to venture in and share, according to their own rhythm. The content and pacing of what they reveal is at the direction of the participant, modulated according to his or her degree of felt safety so that rarely, if ever, does it retraumatize. They are supported, as they are ready, in *reexperiencing* their anguish in a new key.

On the third evening of the retreat, Robert, the profoundly depressed Iraq vet whom we met earlier, watched a film on grief, one of several programs offered. Two-thirds of the way in, I looked over and saw him begin to emerge from his deep freeze. First his eyes began to water, then a few tears ran down his cheeks. When the film ended, he stood up. The color had returned to his face. His arm was around his wife. A few more tears trickled down. He made no effort to conceal or wipe them away. As we approached through the crowd, he began to talk in a low voice about his losses during the war, how unbearable they had been, how he hadn't told anyone. There were more hugs with his wife, conversation, and, during the large group the next morning, he leaned over and gave her a kiss. Everyone took this in.

He began talking with his fellow vets. He was alive again. In a men's veterans group he described how desperate he'd felt and revealed for the first time how he had tried unsuccessfully to kill himself. During the large closing circle he surprised everyone by actually speaking and expressing genuine gratitude to all gathered. It was visible that the numbing freeze had lifted, at least for the moment. He seemed to have come back from the dead. Then he said something that stopped me: he looked forward to seeing everyone again next year, if he was still here.

Note that Robert was *already* in psychological treatment, and on quite a few medications. After the retreat, a fellow spouse whom his wife had befriended contacted us to say his house was being foreclosed on. This had brought him spiraling back down, and he'd become suicidal. The support and resources he and his wife received from fellow vets and spouses they had connected with at the retreat helped him make it through the crisis and regain a measure of his aliveness.

Not only is this a huge relief, but repeated instances of this benevolent cycle regrow our capacity to encounter and integrate the "ghosts." The power of the community support and the inner capacities developed and practiced in this optimal relational setting work in concert to animate and bolster us through this process. Gradually the fear of being retraumatized abates and the traumatic shards reintegrate and take their place as memories. Our sense of meaning becomes renewed. Traumatic experiences thus represented and reexperienced, gradually become *reencoded* into a transformed, more cohesive worldview. Although painful, they are now memories rather than haunting ghosts. As they recede to the background, we can paradoxically remember them, think about and dream them.

They trigger us less because they've become more integrated, and when they do rear their heads, the community and our wellness practices are available to help us meet the surging tides of powerful emotion. We accept ourselves and our broken elements more, we breathe into, rather than react to the pain, and tame and regulate it better. Not perfectly—the wounds of war do not disappear—but we go forward with reduced anguish, increased hope, aliveness, emotional stability, and connectedness.

Safety, trust, and belonging are the alpha and omega and grow throughout this process. Let's expand the series of R words at play to unpack a sequence that, although operationally more interconnected than strictly sequential, we have seen repeated scores of times. It begins with the community invisibly helping *regulate* affect, as well as arousal and energy levels, in a relationally attuned field. Veterans *recognize* themselves in one anothers' stories, with a resulting destigmatizing and normalizing effect, and in turn feel recognized. They become more able to manage the anxieties of becoming visible and to *risk* sharing their story. As they *represent* their experience through expressive arts or verbally in a large or small group or one-to-one setting, they *reexperience* traumatic events that had been haunting them, but in a new setting, where fears of falling to pieces, leaving themselves open to physical harm, being painfully shamed, rejected, and ostracized are disconfirmed by the unconditionally loving response of the community. Through repeated mini-cycles of this process, traumatic experience is *reencoded* in a new key. Regulate, recognize, risk, represent, reexperience, reencode is not a conscious process. It occurs in varying sequences, each element supporting the others, as it is "practiced" in retreat and off-campus settings.

At Coming Home Project we knew we were onto something after our second retreat, in 2007, which confirmed and amplified the good results of the first and showed they weren't a fluke. But it took time for us to develop an instrument to effectively measure the changes. Initial program evaluations and anecdotal impressions were strong and consistent but did not "data" make. We overcame our reluctance to "studying" veterans and began to use traditional PTSD and some newer quality-of-life scales. We got some positive results, particularly in participants' ability to modulate anger, but the number of subjects was not high enough to make our results significant. I felt that the measures did not capture the effects because they were not tailored to do so.

The Rand Corporation was interested in studying the effects of the retreat, as was the Samueli Institute, but we couldn't find the necessary funding. So we brought together for several meetings a representative group of retreat participants, small-group facilitators, retreat leaders, and logistics team members that included veterans, family members, and staff and providers, all of whom had experienced the powerful but seemingly ineffable transformative results. We took turns describing the kernel of our and others' experience, recalling comments made during the retreats' closing circles. These feelings and impressions repeated common themes, time and again, from event to event. Yet they were expressed differently by new people. We developed a working list of participants' impressions and feelings, and developed scales based on these, fine-tuning as we went. We plugged along and after a series of five more retreats between 2010 and 2011 we had enough data. In 2012, Coming Home Project, an independent CBO unaffiliated with and not funded by a government or academic institution, published its results in a peer-reviewed journal of the American Psychological Association.

We had learned that turning ghosts into ancestors is a remarkably robust and consistent process, given the right ingredients, and its impacts are reliable and predictable. It enhances PTgr (post-traumatic growth) whether or not specific symptoms of PTsxD are altered. Stigma was reduced and participants reported highly significant reductions in stress, exhaustion, burnout, anxiety, isolation, hopelessness, and emotional "numbness." Furthermore, they reported significant increases in happiness, relaxation, energy, sense of support, and ability to care for and calm themselves. In follow-up studies four to eight weeks out, these positive results remained strongly significant, consistent, and reliable. While our article was being peer-reviewed for publication, I discussed our research trajectory with two of the leading researchers in DoD and VA; each said, of course, develop your own scales to tap what you're actually doing.

Finally, after three days, Arnold, who had blown up at his son and bolted from the family home for three months, felt safe enough to describe how ashamed he felt for what he had done. The warm response of comrades-in-arms melted his heart and he cried for a long time. On the final morning of the retreat, with eighty-five veterans and family members sitting in a large circle, participants shared their experience of being together and said their good-byes. After such profound alienation from his family, Arnold approached his shy son and gave him a hug that brought both tears and cheers from the group. The pain of isolation had receded, replaced by the warmth and acceptance of a healing community. Reconciliation takes many forms.

An optimal environment for connecting, transforming trauma, and learning helps regenerate four qualities that distilled out across many retreats: aliveness, bonding, emotional regulation, and meaning. Participants attended because the retreats were "not therapy," but they stayed and benefitted because the retreats were therapeutic and rebuilt eroded trust, alleviated isolation, and engendered feelings of belonging and being understood.

Reconnection takes patience. Veterans and family members test the waters to see how real and deep they are before venturing in; they want to verify whether the environment is genuine, and how devoted and skilled the staff is. Suspicion runs deep and is adaptive when you've spent fifteen months in a setting where, as many veterans recount, "people are trying to kill you." No one wants to be retraumatized, as illustrated by the story noted earlier, when, at the end of a particularly moving closing circle, there was a silence. I waited, remembering that a voice would often pipe up just when I thought the group was talked out. As I was about to draw things to a close, a woman veteran cleared her throat and began, half in jest, "So when are you guys gonna break out the Kool-Aid?" The entire room cracked up, aware of the residual skepticism.

Let's review: War trauma is like the shockwaves of an IED, splintering connections on multiple levels and disabling intrinsic capacities to process the trauma itself. An unconditionally accepting and compassionate culture is the engine for a process of transmuting war trauma that promotes a repair of these capacities and a transformation (not elimination) of the trauma reflected in PTgr. What does the operational implementation of this approach look like?

We've discussed the benefits of humor that flowers naturally as safety becomes a given, trust and belonging develop, and wariness and vigilance recede. To compassion and empathic responsiveness we can add the ingredients of mutual respect, clear boundaries, deep listening, and speaking from the heart. No one, however, is forced to "spill their guts." Participants are required to attend small group cohort meetings (male veterans, women veterans, spouses and partners, parents, children, teens, and so on) but nobody is required to speak. They can just listen, for as long as they like. This kind of freedom and the absence of coercion are critical. Transforming traumatic residues rests upon a (mostly unconscious) assessment by each participant of the relational conditions at play. Participants must be convinced that the emotional environment is safe enough. Although group facilitators regularly ask if there is anyone else who'd like to speak, a few participants wait until the last minutes of the last meeting. A striking example occurred at our first retreat for women veterans in 2009, an event that drew six hundred applications for sixty spaces.

Five minutes before the end of the final small group meeting of the four-day retreat, a woman who until this moment had been supportive of others but mum about herself was no longer able to hold things back. She described with a flood of emotion how she was sexually assaulted by her commanding officer. We all remained past the time allotted even though the closing circle was convening and return flight time margins were tight. During a pause in her account, the group went to finish packing and a facilitator remained with her for the next hour to help her work through and consolidate all that had emerged and discuss strategies for addressing it going forward.

I think three elements contributed to this veteran's decision to risk disclosing this rape for the very first time. One was the lack of coercion; since she knew nobody was going to "make her talk" or "force it out of her," she didn't want to return home without having herself taken advantage of the opportunity. Two was the fact that we spoke about her in our facilitator meetings, felt that she might need additional support, and one of us volunteered to connect with her over some meals. Three was the silently growing inner sense that she had the emotional hardiness to withstand the impacts sharing this experience would surely bring. This had been cultivated not only by practices like qigong and meditation; it had also been buoyed by having quietly internalized the examples of her sister veterans. Not only did she (mostly unconsciously) conclude that her immediate cultural environment, her sister veterans and the staff, would not harm, reject, or punish her, but she also discovered that her "processing power" (aka emotional or meditative muscle) was strong enough to venture forth.

This experience stirred up tremendous emotional turmoil for this veteran that needed further attention. But she also felt more peaceful. Dissociated pieces afford us a transitional resting place of sorts and can temporarily ensure our physical and psychological survival. But genuine peace only emerges as pieces reconnect.

Most of us know that things are interconnected, but how quickly we forget. The song "Dry Bones" contains the famous lyrics: "The ankle bone connected to the shin bone / The shin bone connected to the knee bone / The knee bone connected to the thigh bone / The thigh bone connected to the hip bone / The hip bone connected to the back bone / The back bone connected to the shoulder bone / The shoulder bone connected to the neck bone / The neck bone connected to the head bone." Then comes a line I had forgotten: "Dem bones, dem bones gonna walk around."

A real person emerges as ghosts become ancestors and take their place in a pantheon of diverse memories. This person comes back to life, as she inhabits and shapes the present, and aspires to a future.

Collective Level

Turning ghosts into ancestors is the transformative process of a safe, restorative culture and community, not a fetish, an anomaly, or a laboratory concoction. If Roseto sounded bucolic and a bit utopian, let's examine an example from our recent collective history, the tragic shooting in Newtown, Connecticut on December 14, 2012.

I watched the scenes on TV and couldn't help but notice how residents were responding. People were hugging, comforting, and supporting one another. Connecting. We all witnessed and experienced the sudden shock and the utter helplessness. The shearing loss of loved ones and of meaning. And then people came together again, at the interfaith ceremony. Not to meet the President, they said, but to support one another and feel the comfort of one another's presence.

Residents visibly expressed the impacts of traumatic loss: glazing over, shock, numbness, disbelief, utter helplessness, and despair. People were literally blown away. But they made use of every shred that remained of their capacity to respond, to connect—to connect with one another, within themselves, and with something greater than themselves. They created spaces, small and large, where they could come together to regenerate safety, trust, and hope, safe environments where their traumas could be represented. Not forgotten or eliminated but transformed from haunting and disabling traumatic residues into memories we can think about and integrate.

Without conscious effort, residents were "binding" the pervasive fracturing and regenerating compromised capacities for connectivity at every level. Unable to fully process or *understand*, they helped one another *stand* the trauma, stay awake, and stave off the familiar dissociative fog that ensues after such shocking unspeakable loss and horror. The community held in trusteeship, as it were, affects too overwhelming for them to yet explore individually. In the midst of the anguish, it was inspiring to see these healing forces at work, mobilized by the survivors, the first responders, and the surrounding communities, near and far. This was the heart's natural intelligence at work.

Whether an individual, a group, or an institution takes this restorative path in responding to trauma is not assured. The transgressions at VA and DoD described earlier point to a more destructive reaction—a turn toward not only malfeasance but also malevolence. Dysfunctional groups, be they relationships, families, organizations, institutions, or cultures, share many qualities. Here's a description from the field of interpersonal neurobiology of a harmful child-rearing environment that also captures the noxious characteristics in some institutions that care for veterans. For "caregiver," read manager or leader, and for "infant," read provider or employee,

"In contrast to an optimal attachment scenario, in a growth-inhibiting relational environment the primary caregiver induces traumatic states of enduring negative affective arousal in the child. The caregiver is inaccessible and reacts to her infant's expressions of emotions and stress inappropriately and/or rejectingly and . . . instead of modulating, she induces extreme levels of stimulation and arousal, very high in abuse and/or neglect."[3] Punishing whistleblowers, generating derealization and dissociation in well-meaning hard-working employees, and fostering toxic work and service environments induce traumas in their providers similar in form to those the veterans they serve are receiving help for. This is surprising only if we are unaware that war trauma generates traumatic shockwaves that radiate omnidirectionally and continue to detonate in unpredictable ways over generations.

In the process of writing this book, I came upon a book called *Beneath the Crust of Culture* by Howard Stein, professor emeritus in the Department of Family and Preventive Medicine at the University of Oklahoma Health Sciences Center.[4] It was affirming to learn that the model he had developed through his research into events such as the Columbine shootings and the Oklahoma City bombing—"horizontal transmission" of trauma—dovetailed with our Coming Home Project model that emerged from our multidisciplinary therapeutic work with returning post-9/11 veterans, families, service providers, and, to a degree, provider organizations and institutions. Stein focuses in particular on the inability to mourn and invites us into the individual-collective work of "transcending social trauma and repetition."

In response to my letter telling him about our model and how gratified I was to learn about his work, he wrote, "It reassures me that it resonates with your experience. The image/fantasy of omnidirectional trauma came to me first as a visual experience, and only later in words. You are absolutely correct in saying that no one is immune to the shock waves of the traumas of these current wars. Denial, dissociation, and derealization are not signs of immunity! . . . Being a witness is part of what you do. You help people to have a voice—to discover with you that [their voice] deserves to be heard."

The psychoanalyst Vamık Volkan is among the foremost experts on the intergenerational transmission of trauma, a kind of vertical transmission. His writings contain numerous examples drawn from long-term individual psychoanalytic work, informed by an underlying appreciation for the multigenerational dimension. In his book *Bloodlines*,[5] Volkan, also a psychopolitical researcher, presents analyses of a number of ethic conflicts in Europe and the Middle East and develops several concepts, among which "chosen trauma" is perhaps the best known.[6] Chosen trauma refers to the collective memory of a past calamity that remains dormant but may later be reactivated, as it distorts perceptions. It is usually a leader who, for a variety of reasons, reignites the earlier trauma. A close and sometimes overlapping variant is "chosen glory," a historical event that induces feelings of triumph and thus bolsters a group's self-esteem.

Past military losses and victories can serve as either and can be manipulated by leaders to motivate their constituents. Veterans of course are by nature caught up in these often unconscious but nonetheless extensively impactful machinations. One contemporary example of a chosen trauma might be the tragic disasters of 9/11 themselves, how they were used to justify the invasion of Iraq. A chosen glory, say the success of the U.S. surge and the Battle of Fallujah, one of the fiercest and costly in the Iraq War, is of course also a horrific trauma. When the gains made in the battle fall to pieces, as reflected in the fracturing and bloodshed in contemporary Iraq, the traumatic element is revived. It is enough to give the veterans who served in the campaign psychological whiplash.

During a large group check-in a veteran began to get choked up and found it hard to speak; he said we should pass the microphone to the next person. This isn't uncommon and I told her, "It's okay, we've got time." Often the person will relax just a bit, feel better able to modulate their emotions, and continue. This time the veteran continued to struggle with her emotions. It's important to me that grief be welcome in our community. I've become known as the one who says "hold it" when someone rushes in to supply the person speaking with a box of tissues when the speaker's voice is just beginning to waver, before tears have even formed in their eyes. So I waited, then said that grief was natural, we could hear it. She preferred that we move to the next person, and we did. The next person became irate at me, saying that what I had said could cause the first vet to commit suicide. I didn't quite believe what I was hearing and asked what she meant. She said that grief was toxic and made people kill themselves.

It is the inability to grieve that can lead to the hopelessness and despair that often drive suicidal thoughts and behavior. But this participant was not atypical; she spoke for some in the group and for many in our culture.

As a country we are caught up in our collective aversion to profound suffering in general, and the wrenching anguish that is war trauma in particular. We are so blinded that government agencies and corporations, and even well-funded nonprofits, throw hundreds of millions of dollars at programs that do not address the necessary level of experience and so unfortunately come up short when it comes to transforming the anguish of veterans and more effectively preventing them from killing themselves.

As a culture we are allergic to emotional pain. When we sense it we tend to jump in and try to "fix" it. In a *New York Times* blog, Tina Rosenberg describes some current alternative therapies for post-traumatic operational stress injuries. The name of the blog, "Fixes," is unfortunate for an article like this. There is no quick fix for war-related anguish. And no way to create Teflon troops. Further, veterans and service members don't want or need fixing. They want to feel understood and accepted. Some need effective therapeutic assistance in reconnecting, healing, and *coming back to life*. They want the opportunity to use themselves again and make a difference.

In a study conducted by the National Center for Veterans Studies at the University of Utah, the most frequent reason soldiers gave for attempting suicide was . . . intense emotional pain.[7] This is one of those simple truths we all "know" but doggedly refuse to face and let sink in. We need to address our resistance to letting it inform our responses. These commonsense findings have profound implications and, at the same time, they give psychological research a bad name. I can understand somebody responding: "And mountains are tall and fire is hot; tell me something I didn't know." Or: "Did we need to spend millions to find that out?" Psychological researchers are rediscovering that emotional anguish matters, and, along with the desperate sense of futility to alter it, that it contributes mightily to the decision to take one's own life. Better late than never.

Veterans and their families carry a hugely disproportionate load of what veteran war correspondent and filmmaker Sebastian Junger calls "the moral burden" of war. They also carry the lion's share of processing the offloaded and disavowed affect of our war-trauma averse culture. As a nation we're more about cheering up, resetting, new starts, and "resilience," a uniquely American version of our British ancestors' stiff upper lip. Of course, there are positives: military medicine has made enormous strides, as a culture we are no longer spitting on our retuning service members, and there are thousands of examples of veterans and families stepping up for one another in a grassroots way, bucking the healthcare or other systems to really help.

Implied in some "Thank you for your service" comments, one veteran heard, "Now just go away, so we don't have to deal with you." Does some of the pervasive urgency for quick-fix solutions, including even holistic, complementary, and alternative ones, reflect our collective ambivalence about facing the real emotions that suffuse a nation at war?

In March 2013 *60 Minutes* did a piece on the life and death of Clay Hunt, a marine who earned a Purple Heart serving in the Marines in Iraq and Afghanistan.[8] In a blog on *Huffington Post* I wrote that this demonstrated how much we have yet to learn about the epidemic of suicide in our returning troops and veterans.[9] The word "haunted," used by one person to describe what from all appearances seemed like a "poster boy" for how someone should/could return from war, rang a bell. I have heard the word hundreds of times talking with returning veterans. Unprocessed traumatic residues literally haunt and consume the present. The future does not exist. Nowhere in the *60 Minutes* piece do we see Clay finding a way to genuinely process what he had been through and transform the ghosts of his military service, including the losses, the helplessness, and the questions about mission that we hear about. Like thousands of veterans, Clay remained plagued and tortured, despite his stellar *external* adaptation to civilian life. Even his tentative forays at opening up to his parents belied this haunting.

One lesson we can draw is that we each have an *inner* world. Not all anguish can be successfully addressed by "doing something." This includes altruistic public service, and using one's experience to help others. Undeniably noble and often useful to others, we sometimes end up ignoring and bypassing our own inner ghosts and postpone addressing them, sometimes tragically. Some dedicated and well-meaning people and organizations in veteran services today don't fully appreciate this. We underestimate the inner world at our peril. Clearly, many vets are looking for a place to safely articulate this world.

The Ingredients and How to Prepare Them

What are the elements of an optimal healing environment that create a nourishing, safe, restorative culture?

In the safety of a mixed group, fifteen veterans meet during our second retreat. Stephanie tearfully shares how she feels like a failure: as a soldier who served as a captain in the Army; as the wife of Michael, also an Army captain, who committed suicide; as a mother of young Ben; as a person—in every way. She didn't realize the gravity of Michael's distress and couldn't intervene to prevent him from killing himself. Sadness and self-reproach run deep. Several jump in to reassure her: "You have not failed." They provide some consolation: "God had other plans for you," "You now can be of help in ways you couldn't have before," and so on. But Stephanie's expressiveness and emotion dry up as she compliantly agrees. When a third person prefaces his remarks by saying that he will offer something to lift the mood, I say, "That's okay," trying to keep alive the space for acceptance and disclosure that reassuring and uplifting comments often unintentionally foreclose.

Those wishing to offer assurance were genuine. But they did not understand the cultural conditions necessary for transforming the emotional fallout of painful trauma. We've found that even experienced trauma therapists and chaplains need training and practice in working in our small groups and retreats. First they need to learn about military culture. Second they need to become aware of their own assumptions and feelings about these recent wars and about veterans' role in them. Over-identification with the anguish of veterans can be a problem, as can hidden ideological beliefs. It is imperative and challenging to manage their own emotional reactions to veterans' accounts. When a facilitator lurches from listening attentively to the veteran's account into giving advice or "teaching," I will ask what prompted it. Often therapists, even very seasoned ones, can't say, or report being concerned that the veteran was suicidal or potentially homicidal. "What did he say or do that gave you that feeling?" I ask. "Well," they say, and it inevitably turns out there wasn't anything in particular. I've learned that it is usually the sheer emotional force of the affect, be it frustration, despair, outrage, sadness and loss, fear, shame, guilt, or brutal self-loathing. It makes the facilitator anxious and their intervention inevitably stops the sharing in its tracks. In trainings, I now say something counterintuitive: when there's something you absolutely must say or else, do not to say it. Instead, take a few breaths and wait sixty seconds.

I've also learned the hard way not to bring anyone on board in any capacity who uses the phrase "those poor vets." It inevitably reflects an inner wariness covered by a brittle sentimentality and a veneer of pity.

Facilitators learn to track the affect and arousal levels of individual vets and of the group itself. When things are well modulated, when the sense of community has been activated, engaged, and is relatively self-regulating, it's important to let it be. We've seen repeatedly how things take on a power and a pacing all their own; now listening, now sharing, now laughing, now weeping, now silent, now vocal. Providing reminders about the guidelines when things get off track and making sure there's time for those who are less gregarious, we create and maintain a safe and predictable space.

I've talked with some institutionally based therapists who express concern about material surfacing that triggers old traumas. Because of the respect and freedom we provide and the reliable and skilled relational environment we foster, we have never had a situation arise that could not be effectively managed within the group or directly afterward. Participants come to trust that they can regulate the level of disclosure, and they go as deep as feels safe.

Our instructions to participants about small groups are simple: this is not a therapy group; it is a support group. Group members offer support in two ways, by listening and by sharing their own story. Not by judging, giving advice, or trying to fix the others' or their problems. It's counterintuitive for many participants that sharing their own story, a source of anxiety, can be supportive for others who get to recognize themselves in their peers' account. Listening and tolerating short periods of silence can take getting used to; it is not self-evident that simply listening can convey anything but distance or danger. Tolerating certain kinds of silence does not necessarily convey disinterest or distance, to the contrary. Repeated instances of tolerating silence together in small groups, and the freedom to think, feel, and be that accompanies it, provides practical benefit. It helps those considering wading in with a story about their own struggles assess just how deep, safe, and reliable the waters are. When facilitators intervene just as someone's voice is cracking or a fellow participant rushes in with a box of tissues in anticipation of tears, the opposite message is given: emotions are not welcome, it's not safe to bring forth what's buried deep in your heart.

Participants regularly laugh and occasionally gripe about our protocol for leaving the room. We don't want participants to feel confined. So it's fine to get up and leave, for any reason, no explanation needed. But if you're not back within four minutes a co-facilitator or logistics team member will come find you. "Four minutes to go to the can? What's up with that?!" But everyone gets the message: you're free to move, to change the air, to go to the bathroom, or to have a smoke outside. But remember, we've got your back and we're going to check in to make sure you're okay.

Words are cheap; veterans check out our team's actions, follow through, warmth, and sincerity. While a sense of camaraderie and a team-like feeling with fellow veterans is a familiar element from the military setting, some elements are unlike a military setting, and, in their very differentness, help create optimal conditions. One is a change of locale. Programs are better held in simple, beautiful, out-of-the-way places than on base or within an institutional setting. We've also found that a measure of choice and a range of activities, rather than a one-size-fits-all approach, is important. And even though some vets prefer to use virtual means for connecting, sharing information, and relaxing, the vast majority find by the end of the retreat that an environment that promotes social engagement and bonding is deeply gratifying.

Differences from one's usual setting that are initially disorienting can end up being useful. On the first evening of a Coming Home retreat, a former Marine officer reported that someone had stolen the TV in his room. I worried for a moment, but then everyone burst into laughter and I caught on. "Who took my TV?!" Of course his room never had one, and this was his humorous way of registering a complaint. Although not having TV was a stretch for him, he focused on his relationship with his wife and with newfound buddies and found both surprisingly sustaining.

Alcohol and drugs, TV, video games, cellphones and tablets, are ways many veterans regulate their emotions. Retreats invite them to take advantage of other ways: first and foremost, to let being together with their fellow veterans and family members help regulate how they feel; to let in the healing power of nature's beauty; to partake of opportunities for expressive arts and secular ritual; and to participate in time-tested wellness practices like yoga, qigong, and meditation. They present a smorgasbord of pathways within a framework of safety that obviates the need for a weapon or emotional armor for protection.

Of course, staying engaged is not always easy, and can meet with stiff internal resistance, which sometimes manifests in acting out. Two marines discovered that they served in the same location in Iraq at the same time and crossed paths without knowing it. They were tough young men. One was physically imposing and had come by himself, while the other brought his girlfriend. For the first couple of days they stood back with a scornful attitude, taking potshots at the "softness" and "new age-ness" of the goings on. On the third day one let his girlfriend twist his arm into attending a couples communication workshop. His emotional armor was pierced as they and other couples discussed sexual intimacy. He revealed that on returning from the war zone he was "numb" and completely disinterested, despite having a warm, attractive, and understanding girlfriend. "If you open the spigot a little bit," he said, "what makes you think you can control what else comes rushing out?" It was on or off, and he'd chosen off. His shame was evident, but no one, not his girlfriend nor any participant, piled on. Rather, tough as he had appeared, the emotional shift and the exchange with his girlfriend catalyzed other couples.

The other marine attended a group for single vets, and on the last full day, in a discussion about loss, he "lost it." Grief and pain flowed freely as he spoke about this being his "alive day," the anniversary of a firefight in which he was injured, and when, coincidentally, his cousin was killed in another location. Later that evening at the talent show, the shift in these two veterans was palpable to all. No longer were they distant and intimidating. The next morning in the closing circle one described how much closer he felt to his girlfriend, while the other revealed that he had recently learned he was a father and shared both his apprehension and his excitement to meet his young daughter.

They stayed in touch and we heard things were going well. The pair signed up to come to the next retreat. On the way to the site, along with a third veteran from the past retreat, they asked to stop for some medicine at a drugstore. But the medicine, it turned out, was a half-dozen fifths of hard liquor. At dinner they began pouring the liquor in their colas and spiking other participants' sodas. It didn't concern them that some of these veterans had TBIs and were on medications that didn't react well with alcohol.

We informed them that they couldn't return for at least a year and then, only after writing us and speaking to our staff. The third veteran apologized and asked to return to retreats. But the pair reacted as if the authorities had come down unfairly. They stayed in touch from time to time with a longtime Coming Home volunteer, a kind Marine mom, and we learned that relationships with girlfriend and new daughter were going pretty well. The last we heard, one had returned to the war zone working for a military contractor providing security.

Using social engagement and peer supports as a source of safety was new and unsettling; it needed practice to become a consolidated trait. Their opening up in the presence of fellow veterans set off time-release internal alarms and gave way to familiar maladaptive, even malevolent, ways of coping with stress.

Seen and Unseen

Veterans, families, communities, institutions, and leaders have a tough time with emotions, especially those they are unaware and wary of. We read earlier of Jessie, blinded while in Iraq, treated as if invisible by caregiving institutions upon his return, and how important it was for him to be seen. The impacts of war are legend. Some are visible, but many are not. There are injuries we can see and injuries that are invisible to the eye but nonetheless radiate deep and wide into a person's life, health, and web of relationships. TBI patients and their families have a saying: "When the hair grows over." When the visible injuries heal, the unseen wounds to mind, heart, soul, and spirit often go ignored. You're now a "walkie-talkie." You look great, you're up and ready to go. And your inner experiential world simply does not exist.

I call these *unseen* rather than invisible injuries. Their impacts are clearly visible if we care enough to want to look, and we know what to look for. And if we can listen. But it's true that most of us perceive and believe what we can see, hear, taste, and touch, what is materially there and able to be apprehended by the senses. When we see a serious physical injury we're often understandably moved. And as a country we're moved to invest large amounts in treating these injuries. Veterans with PTsxD, PTspD, and mild to moderate TBIs, however, do not receive the same attention. Some suspect they are malingering, making things up, or trying to gain more benefits than they're entitled to. Others think they're making too much of it, and should just grit their teeth and bear it like the stereotypic mythic heroes of old.

This dynamic came to the fore during a controversy in 2009 regarding whether unseen injuries should qualify a veteran for the Purple Heart. John Fortunato, military psychologist at Ft. Bliss and founder of an innovative military-based treatment program for post-traumatic stress, said: "These guys have paid at least as high a price, some of them, as anybody with a traumatic brain injury, as anybody with shrapnel wound, and what it does is it says this is the wound that isn't worthy, and I say it is."[10] Are emotional, psycho-neurobiological, and spiritual injuries real wounds? If you can't see the physical scar, does it exist? How can we know? What about a TBI? If one's head was split open, okay, but what if the contents of your head were seriously jangled around one, two, or ten or twenty times by IED blasts, resulting in closed head "mild and moderate" TBIs? What then? Do the demonstrable cognitive, emotional, and physiological damages count? How about the family, social, employment, and other related impacts?

Defense Secretary Robert Gates, when asked about Fortunato's remarks, responded that the issue was "clearly something that needs to be looked at." And look they did, bureaucratically speaking. Based on a review by the Defense Department's Awards Advisory Group, David Chu, undersecretary of personnel and readiness, decided that post-traumatic operational stress injuries do not meet the criteria for the Purple Heart. "Historically, the Purple Heart has never been awarded for mental disorders or psychological conditions resulting from witnessing or experiencing traumatic combat events (e.g., combat stress reaction, shell-shock, combat stress fatigue, acute stress disorder, or PTSD)," a spokesperson said. The criteria for awarding the Purple Heart required the wound to be caused by "an outside force or agent"; this requirement was found to be "a fair and objective standard." "But, medical science cannot provide such a standard for troops suffering from PTSD." Such is the investment in the visible materiality of suffering that others in the article in *Stars and Stripes* said simply that only those who shed blood should get the award.[11]

If you can't see it, if you didn't shed blood, if it wasn't caused by an "outside agent," if "medical science" can't provide a standard, then it's just a mental *disorder*, a psychological *condition*. The implications are clear: it's not really real. Since others exposed to the same circumstances didn't "get it," it must be something "inside" you, your own personal peculiarity, maybe a "preexisting condition." Some may see this viewpoint as a bureaucratic conundrum relating to standardization and certification. However it would not be a stretch to conclude that maybe it's your own fault. What is implied is the diminishment of the entire range of war-related unseen injuries and those who sustained those injuries.

Tyler Boudreau, former Marine captain and author of *Packing Inferno: The Unmaking of a Marine*, made an excellent suggestion. Why not recognize these unseen injuries with a Black Heart Award? "Certainly the hearts of these soldiers are black, with the terrible things they saw and did on the battlefield," he writes. "Certainly the country should see these Black Hearts pinned on their chests."[12]

What is "invisible" to the eye of many is only unseen for want of the proper ingredients. The emotional, neurobiological, social-family, and spiritual impacts of war, what I'm calling unseen injuries, can only be seen through *an act of empathic responsiveness*. Without this simple and radically human act, what is unseen does not exist. The one suffering feels like she doesn't exist. This can make you feel crazy—can drive you crazy. And this is how many veterans and family members feel, for want of basic recognition.

Healing war trauma is not a religious conversion, suddenly seeing a white light, coming to Jesus, Buddha, or Allah. It is not a state without pain or discomfort, the permanent eradication of all traces of trauma. And it is not simply the elimination of symptoms through "evidence-based" therapies.

We once had a family whose members came together from all around the country at a retreat. There were two young Iraq veterans, with wife and fiancée, and their parents. They were a multigenerational military family and proud of the tradition. In the opening circle the father, himself a veteran and a pious Christian, said he came to help with the healing. I remarked that it's not unusual for those who come in order to help others to end up feeling supported themselves and learning something new. Each time one of the sons' partners or the sons themselves indicated the slightest interest in learning something that could help them, they would shoot a glance at the family patriarch and find a stern look of disapproval that froze them back into the party line: "We're here to help others heal." Finally, in a parents group whose members had lost children and were taking care of injured children, the father said that if the other parents had only had more faith, these horrors would not have happened to them. The facilitator confronted this false verbal assault that blamed the survivors for want of faith. We dialogued with the elder veteran because we could see how much his sons and their partners wanted to stay, but he was intransigent; in the morning he took the entire family and they left.

Most participants describe themselves as "spiritual but not religious," the fastest growing sector of the American population. But this father's view of healing not only excluded those who did not adhere to his beliefs, but also condemned other approaches and blamed those who found value in them for war's inevitable damage, much like Stephanie's church blamed her and her husband, Michael, for Michael's suicide. The entire group of facilitators and participants found such behavior appalling and cruel. Far from encouraging an atmosphere of mutual support, respect, and compassion, it proved to be an object lesson in how to stop it in its tracks.

What drives the remarkable opening to connection reflected in many of the examples presented? It is not religious or psychological ideology. Rather it is the power of a most human compassion that creates a field of unconditional acceptance and love. Acts of loving responsive attentiveness, with each of us supporting and being supported, activate a field that becomes the vehicle, the "bigger container" that holds the grief, the loss, the anger, the powerlessness, the damage. And the precious shards of hope. Everyone can feel its power: the trust, the safety, the deep care. This collective field of compassion also grows capacities for withstanding, regulating, expressing, and representing inner anguish. The healing environment helps transform trauma, turning inner demons, ghosts that haunt the present and foreclose the future, into ancestors. A community of real people along with real inner capacities becomes available. We take in and make our own the comrades, the camaraderie, and their beneficial qualities. We enjoy being and learning together. New possibilities for being alive open up. All this is the activity of healing.

When veterans feel safe, and engage their ghosts by risking and representing their true experience, they are challenging not being seen. They are articulating their voice and re-realizing all they have been through, are, and can become. We have seen over and again how empowering this can be to self and others.

Claudia is a female Iraq veteran who came with her 18-month-old daughter and her sister from Tucson. She had met Tonia and Ken, fellow veterans on the retreat, while on the TBI ward at the Palo Alto VA. She is friendly and sincere but also seems vacant and taciturn. During a breakout group she stands around the perimeter, but toward the end she begins to speak, tentatively. Although she says she doesn't want to read what she had written earlier during a journaling exercise, it seems that part of her longs to do so. With a little encouragement, she begins to read: "My world has narrowed from what it was . . ." Her voice trails off. She describes her TBI and the difficulty she has remembering simple but important elements of her past. She feels that a crucial piece of who she was has been taken from her: she can't even remember her daughter's birth. She needs her sister's help with tasks of daily living, as her short-term memory is also impaired. She is battling to retain custody of her daughter. Claudia's reading has a palpably catalytic effect on everyone. When families gather later, the aliveness of her young daughter, the glimmer in her eyes, juxtaposed with Claudia's memory impairment, her sense of vacancy and helplessness, are striking, poignant, and sad.

Claudia had serious problems to navigate, from cognitive impairment to profound feelings of depression, and family challenges with her husband who was leaving the marriage and filing for custody of their daughter. But she and her sister/caregiver left feeling reinvigorated, connected with many comrades who would be of immense practical help. She continued to write and give shape to her story. Regulating, risking, and representing, parts of the process of transforming ghosts, have their own value and impact.

If collective denial, dissociation, and derealization remove war from our sights then the wars do not exist. If wars don't exist, how can veterans exist? How can we know our veterans when we don't want to know our wars? If we don't hear and see the stories and face the real costs of war, we will not be able to see and hear the stories of veterans and their families and providers. We will miss their humanity, only see the stereotypes, and be unable to provide the social connective fabric in which they can reclaim their humanity.

At a retreat on beautiful Tomales Bay, we contracted with a kayaking company well respected for its long experience working with able-bodied and disabled individuals alike. The founder didn't think they needed to learn about military culture, but I insisted, and she gave us a mere thirty minutes. When we all gathered for orientation on use of the kayaks, the instructor was demonstrating how to paddle. Then, apparently trying to connect using humor and what he thought was a veterans' idiom, he took the kayaking blade and mimed firing a machine gun, with full auditory accompaniment, then saying this was not the way to use it. Several vets recoiled and then bounced back as the instructor laughed, realizing nothing of what had transpired until we debriefed later.

In our culture, veterans themselves are like unseen ghosts, apparitions flashing by in a movie reel of highlights. In their efforts to become whole and real, to participate fully in civilian life, they want to feel alive, make close, reliable interpersonal connections, develop functional regulatory capacities, and discover anew a sense of meaning and purpose. Engaging in safe, facilitated environments of their peers and turning their own inner ghosts into ancestors directly challenges this social perception.

Info

As illustrated by recent and past VA scandals with secret waiting lists, false access reports, and doctored suicide figures, broken and toxic systems exercise control over the flow of information. Another example is our being prevented from seeing the very human costs of war—the coffins returning to Dover Air Force Base. And more: Alex Sinha, author of the Human Rights Watch and American Civil Liberties Union report, *With Liberty to Monitor All: How Large-Scale U.S. Surveillance Is Harming Journalism, Law, and American Democracy*, warns that "large-scale surveillance is seriously hampering U.S.-based journalists and lawyers in their work."[13] Journalists Brian Ross from ABC News and Jonathan Landay from McClatchy News Service said recently that they are made to feel more like criminals than journalists,[14] given the NSA's tracking of their metadata and resultant access to their sources.

In today's society, honest, useful, usable information is at a premium everywhere. Service members and veterans have been showered with countless PowerPoint presentations and URLs to dense user-unfriendly websites. I've come to see that information becomes usable and digestible when it is relationally mediated, that is, shared in a safe, confidential setting with other people whom you trust. Otherwise it leads to a glut of undigested data, a not uncommon problem in our data-rich, usable information-poor culture. Informational and relational registers need one another.

It is difficult to describe the relief of veterans and family members when they get to hear the road that each has taken in navigating the systems back home to receive the benefits, care, and support they earned. First, they learn that they are not alone and are not living in a parallel universe. What they have gone through really does happen, and not just to them, but to many. Second, the content of what they hear, the specific "inside baseball" details of how to navigate broken systems, never conveyed in the PowerPoints and websites, proves extraordinarily useful. Third, in a safe and confidential setting characterized by integrity, ghostly traumatic experiences can surface, and be shared. Witnessed with love and acceptance, they become a source of growth.

We've seen with Rory having the opportunity to be *regulated* relationally by the active duty officer, and with Claudia risking and representing her deepest emotional experiences, that any one element of the process of transforming ghosts can have in itself tremendous value. At our second retreat in 2007 participants seemed to be talking about logistical details of the VA and DoD systems to the exclusion of their emotional and family experience. I was thinking that they might be apprehensive and wondered why, especially since the first retreat had been so open and for some cathartic. During a break I spoke with my co-facilitator, and he suggested we trust the process; participants were likely using the time and setting in the way that was most important for them at the moment. Sure enough, the participants' pragmatic exchanges gradually gave way to the emotional toll their logistical struggles had taken, and before long the frustration, outrage, and sense of injury became front and center. The group, with a little help, was regulating itself and making use of the free flow of information as it needed.

We learned another lesson about empowering veterans and families. Early on we discovered that the sense of stigma and the fear of being "dinged" or demoted, losing one's security clearance, or being humiliated and shunned, evaporated after a few days at a retreat. We utilized this fortuitous development to invite in representatives of governmental and nonprofit organizations to offer information on medical and mental health benefits, housing, education, employment, legal, and financial resources. Participants themselves drove the information-gathering process rather than be force-fed PowerPoint slides during detested transition briefs or have to navigate the impenetrable bureaucracies all by their lonesome. After all, participants were beginning to ask us about resources they had become interested in.

We had our first resource fair at Middleborough VA outside the DC metro area at a family retreat in 2010. We were surprised who actually showed up, driving all the way into the country on a weekend afternoon: representatives from the Departments of Labor, Health and Human Services, Housing, and Education, Substance Abuse and Mental Health Services Administration, VA and Vet Centers, DoD support programs, and other top echelon institutions. Food was available and there was an upbeat atmosphere with participants moving from table to table asking questions, taking flyers, sometimes making appointments or signing up for benefits. They were able to cut through the red tape and access the information, services, and care they had earned, while they were not plagued by stigma but rather were open and receptive.

This was another example of how logistics mattered, being free to make adjustments in the environment that augmented and leveraged the safety, confidentiality, and integrity that were the cornerstones of our optimal environments. "Leave the driving to us," to "we pros," was replaced by an empowering 360-degree information-sharing that was as benevolently omnidirectional as war's shockwaves had been destructively so. Tonia, who had successfully battled the Palo Alto VA professional bureaucracy to be part of Ken's care, would have been happy.

Learning from Experience

I want now to place turning ghosts into ancestors, the organic transformative process we adapted and utilized, into a wider context, and explore how it fosters learning from experience, a capacity we as individuals and as a country tend not to be very good at, especially when it comes to getting into devastating and needless wars. Learning from experience is contingent on the regeneration of memory and a sense of time, both capacities damaged by repeated war trauma.

During the upwelling of antiwar sentiment that followed President Barack Obama and Secretary John Kerry's decision to "punish" Syrian President Bashar al-Assad, media pundits commented endlessly about how we had become "blinded" by Iraq and "war weary." The implication was that we were living in the past, so tired of war that we could not see straight in the here and now, unable to protect our own security interests and act on our native moral outrage. Bill Clinton spoke of the need to learn lessons from the past "without becoming a general who fights the last war. Every new encounter will be shaped by different forces." The message in effect was: don't get caught up in and replay past traumas, unable or unwilling to respond afresh in the here and now to new challenges. Fair enough, and a tip of the hat to those who can do it.

But I heard scant references, save Chris Matthews on *Hardball* and a few others, to the necessity of actually *learning* reliable lessons from the past so that we do not repeat them, over and over again. We know the famous saying, "Those who cannot remember the past are condemned to repeat it." But with our collective attention deficit disorder, our short-term memory is shot. Most of us don't know that the philosopher Santayana also said, "Only the dead have seen the end of war." The "repetition compulsion" was Freud's term for how we tend to repeat unsatisfying and maladaptive emotional and relational patterns. But it can describe equally well our collective penchant for amnesia when it comes to waging war. How quickly we forget the devastating costs. How ignorantly and recklessly we label the crucial act of remembering as "blindness," and judge ourselves and others for our understandable weariness. "Buck up," such shame-inducing implies, "the past is past, get over it." When someone observed about Vietnam that the war was over, a veteran replied: "Yeah, over and over and over."

War weariness is a state: it comes and goes, just like our passing grasp of the costs of war. Life continues, we move on, we forget. War wariness, however, is a trait, a vital quality of attention we can reliably access when we need it, to keep us focused in the here and now, to help us protect our country, our world, and all its creatures from the deluded knee-jerk tendency to believe that the next war will be better than the last one. We are certainly weary of the anguish of needless wars. But we could be more wary.

Learning from experience requires a proper past we can think about, a present we inhabit and treasure, and a sense of the kind of future we want for ourselves, our children, the world's children, and all living creatures. There's no way to engage this process without the willingness to face war-related suffering and our participation in it. As we saw in the example of the two marines who tried to highjack a retreat after deriving real benefits at an earlier one, this shift into living time and memory, and the accountability it makes possible, meets with stiff resistance from diverse quarters. It can be painful, disturbing, distracting, inconvenient, and brings to light how co-responsible we all are, be we leaders, legislators, or voting citizens.

A ghost is not instructive; it provokes harmful reactions mediated by denial, dissociation, distancing, and disavowal. It provides leaders with fodder to reignite chosen traumas in the service of murky, self-absorbed, and often malevolent goals, keeping them alive and repeating over and again the cycle of war. In Buddhism ghosts are represented without bones, clinging to bushes and grasses. They hang around and haunt; left unaddressed, they predispose us to replay the traumas that helped create them in the first place. This collective repetition compulsion comes complete with what psychoanalysts call secondary gain—getting something out of our symptoms. We like it when our ideology is superior to the enemy's, when we enjoy the inflation that comes from feeling purer than the enemy.

In baseball, managers speak about "putting us in a position to win." Reclaiming our humanity by turning ghosts into ancestors "puts us in a position" to learn from our experience, which is after all our ancestry. This key missing capacity requires but is not limited to the ability to track the flux of cause and effect, the impacts of our actions, conscious and unconscious, individual and collective.

If traumatic residues become elements to think about, respond to, struggle with, grieve, dream, express through art—if they become things we can engage with and make real—then we have a chance to access our reflective ability and remember the costs of going down this particular road when the need appears. We are able to stop, look, listen, and assess, based on learned-from experience. The past then becomes instructive, if we are open to learning from it, if we turn our full attention to it.

We can now remember the past because we have a past to remember. We have reclaimed it from the traumatic deep freeze. The past becomes a factor of waking up rather than of haunting, put to the service of a different end.

Reinhold Niebuhr's words, now memorialized as the serenity prayer, capture the same spirit when they invite us to generate the serenity to accept what cannot be changed, the courage to change what can, and the wisdom to know the difference. In Zen Buddhism, the second of the Four Great Vows, "Greed, hatred, and delusion rise endlessly, I vow to put an end to them," too, does not promise to excise suffering forever from human experience. Likewise, in attachment research our sense of security depends less on the traumas we've undergone than on our ability to reflect on and make meaning from those traumas.

Turning ghosts into ancestors mobilizes an ancient alchemy that finds resonance in many change traditions. The lotus grows from the rich earth of discarded recycled garbage. This human process "puts us in position." How we respond to stress and to trauma makes all the difference. Let's investigate the possibilities and limits of our adaptive hearts and minds, bodies and brains, and examine some illuminating neurobiological perspectives.

III. Resilience, Trauma, and the Limits of Plasticity

Trauma—Can't live with it, can't live without it.

War trauma packs a double whammy. Troops are overwhelmed by the horrors encountered in the war zone, while the capacities necessary to process and transform these traumas are disabled at the same time. This catch-22 is the "can't live with it" part. Cumulative trauma also makes an insistent and persistent claim on our awareness. It can become so seared into our visceral circuits that it is like glue; we can't get away even for a moment. Right around the corner, in the next moment, we don't know when, a painful and disorienting barrage can hit, unbidden and outside of our sphere of control. In addition, the cascading rush of stress hormones our bodies generate to help us get through, themselves can become addictive, creating a high that is hard to resist. This is the "can't live without it" part.

Many vets, such as Gable Darbonne, whom we met earlier, want to return to the war zone. Along with the deep ache for lost bonds with battle buddies, we heard in his account the heightened sense of intensity and how it exerts its own draw. Recall Jeremy Williams too: at a Coming Home retreat, the former marine was paddling in a family kayak expedition that turned into an impromptu competition. When he and his wife reached shore first, Jeremy exclaimed, "I'm so high!" He had recaptured in a new postwar setting a taste of the visceral exhilaration that would accompany firefights, woven in as it was with fear.

Reclaiming lost elements of our humanity—exhilaration and aliveness, bonding, a sense of meaning and purpose—and transforming the traumas of war is not identical to promoting readiness in our troops. However, the two efforts overlap. Resilience training began in the military as an effort to promote reintegration into civilian life after deployment. It arose from the awareness that there would likely be future deployments and stressors for service member and family to manage.

Getting More from Less

It's July 2002, nine months after U.S. and British forces began airstrikes in Afghanistan. Thirteen hundred U.S. troops helped drive the Taliban from Kabul. Soon the Taliban-held city of Kandahar would fall. Osama bin Laden and Mullah Mohammed Omar, leader of the Taliban, escaped, and Hamid Karzai was elected to lead a new interim government.

On July 26, 2002, nearly identical headlines flashed across multiple publications. The National Council on Child Abuse and Family Violence lead was "Rash of Wife Killings at Ft. Bragg," while the *New York Times* article was entitled "Rash of Wife Killings at Ft. Bragg Leaves the Base Wondering Why."

In a period of six weeks, there had been four homicides and two suicides on base and one homicide off base in nearby Fayetteville, North Carolina. Henry Berry, manager of family advocacy programs at Fort Bragg, said, "It's mind-boggling. We're going to look at these cases to prevent them from happening in the future."[1]

Fort Bragg is the Army's headquarters for Special Forces and Special Operations units, and hundreds of soldiers had deployed from the base. Sgt. 1st Class Rigoberto Nieves, who served in Afghanistan with the 3rd Special Forces Group, shot his wife Teresa, then shot himself. Master Sgt. William Wright, a Green Beret recently returned from Afghanistan, strangled his wife Jennifer. After being back six months from Afghanistan, Sgt. 1st Class Brandon Floyd shot his wife Andrea in their bedroom and then shot himself. Sgt. Cedric Griffin, a cook with the 20th Engineer Brigade, XVIII Airborne Corps, allegedly stabbed his wife. Army Reserve Maj. David Shannon, who worked in Special Ops Command headquarters, was shot while in bed at home in Fayetteville. Police arrested and charged his wife.[2]

In the wake of this eruption of family violence, the Army developed the Deployment Cycle Support program "to ensure that soldiers and their families are better prepared and sustained throughout the deployment cycle . . . and to identify those who might need assistance."[3]

In October 2003, Gregg Zoroya reported in *USA Today* that at least 11 and as many as 25 service members had committed suicide in Iraq over a seven-week period.[4] Most of these occurred after major combat operations had been declared ended. The Army constituted a Mental Health Advisory Team that surveyed soldiers in Iraq and made a number of recommendations regarding soldier resilience training, war-zone behavioral health care, dwell time (recovery period between deployments), sleep management, stigma reduction training, leadership training in psychological support, suicide prevention, ethics training, and strengthening families. Sadly, implementation has been spotty, up to today.

The Walter Reed Army Institute for Research initiated a program called "Interventions to Enhance Warfighter Psychological Resilience." Battlemind, a resilience approach developed by military psychologist Carl Castro and colleagues, was one of its "products." According to the Army Medical Command, "Battlemind is the Soldier's inner strength to face fear and adversity with courage. Key components include: self confidence: taking calculated risks and handling challenges, and mental toughness: overcoming obstacles or setbacks and maintaining positive thoughts during times of adversity and challenge."[5]

Initial versions focused on utilizing this training in the war zone, while later versions addressed treatment and self-help. The medical command noted, "Battlemind skills helped you survive in combat, but may cause you problems if not adapted when you get home." In the interests of reintegrating soldiers successfully into life back home, the initiative included a postdeployment mental health briefing, and eventually became a training program for soldiers and families across the phases of the deployment cycle.

The Walter Reed Army Institute for Research reported that stress and anxiety levels of deployed soldiers who attended the training were lower than those who had not. After returning home, and 3–6 months later, they also measured a reduction in mental health symptoms for those who took the Battlemind training. Neither study appears to have been professionally peer reviewed.

Other studies at the institute measured the mental health impact of the Iraq and Afghanistan wars on service members. They documented significantly elevated levels of PTSD, depression, anxiety, substance use, overall health problems, and marital issues in soldiers serving in the war zone. They also found that longer deployments, multiple deployments, and insufficient time between deployments were associated with a higher incidence of mental health problems and ethical mistreatment of civilians.

As suicides continued their alarming rise, Battlemind gave way to suicide prevention programming developed under Assistant Army Chief of Staff Gen. Peter Chiarelli, and also to a controversial resilience approach favored by Army Chief of Staff Gen. George Casey, Comprehensive Soldier Fitness (CSF), spearheaded by Col. Rhonda Cornum. The rationale was that increased resilience would translate into a reduction in the need to resort to suicide. Over one million soldiers have been required to participate in CSF, yet evidence for its effectiveness with service members was nonexistent when Martin Seligman from the University of Pennsylvania, whose research on learned helplessness was utilized in developing U.S. torture protocols, was awarded a rare no-bid contract for the materials used to develop it. The evidence for its effectiveness in two large studies since has been inconclusive at best, and Army claims for its success have been examined by a group of researchers and discredited.[6] There have also been complaints about the program being mandatory and about the results of CSF screenings being sent to commanders in advance of soldiers' arrival on base, resulting in negative consequences for those soldiers.

E. Cameron Ritchie, a psychiatrist and the Army's chief behavioral health officer from 2005 to 2010, and now chief clinical officer in the department of mental health for the District of Columbia, said that there were 120–180 separate resilience programs across the military services. She added that resilience prevention and treatment efforts had to draw from the same strapped resources. There was "extreme pressure" to respond to the growing incidence of suicides and other mental health, substance abuse, and family problems. Based on her experience, and the recent Institute of Medicine Report, Ritchie said of the many programs, "it has been difficult to measure their usefulness."

The Defense Centers of Excellence for Psychological Health and TBI, or DCoE, was created to cut through the glut of unsubstantiated program recommendations and bring clarity and efficiency to psychological health and TBI efforts. In November 2007, Deputy Secretary of Defense Gordon England formally announced its establishment. Eight blue ribbon panels and commissions had been established in 2007 to examine PTSD, TBI, and other combat-related health issues that had been increasing exponentially. DCoE was designed in response to several of more than 300 recommendations by policymakers, representatives of federal agencies, war veterans, academics, health-care experts, and scientists convened to address the care of warriors and their families.[7]

In February 2008, Gordon England laid out the DCoE's mission to the Senate Committee on Armed Services: to facilitate coordination and collaboration for psychological health and TBI-related services among the military services and VA; to promote best practice development, research, education and training; to lead clinical efforts toward developing excellence in practice standards, training, outreach, and direct care for the military community regarding psychological health and TBI concerns; and to serve as a nexus for research planning and monitoring.

More than $1.1 billion dollars were appropriated and distributed by DCoE in its first five years, yet there has been a remarkable dearth of original programming or best practices developed, researched, disseminated, effectively incorporated, and documented. DCoE did co-sponsor a special issue of the journal *Military Medicine*.[8] However, this issue appears to contain articles composed almost entirely of literature reviews, with recommendations based upon these same reviews.

The "Theater of War" was an original program funded by DCoE and implemented with some anecdotal success. It presents dramatic readings of

Sophocles' *Ajax* and *Philoctetes* to military and civilian communities. The intent was to reduce stigma, increase awareness of soldiers' mental health issues, and foster greater resilience in troops and their communities.[9]

The DCoE did conduct a comprehensive study of hundreds of functioning reintegration programs across DoD, the VA, and the wider community, using criteria developed by the respected Samueli Institute for the Joint Chiefs of Staff, which gathered dust. My colleagues and I repeatedly contacted DCoE to find out why they were sitting on the data contained in *A Review of Post-Deployment Reintegration: Evidence, Challenges, and Strategies for Program Development*, rather than disseminating it to all DoD and VA departments, to Congress, and to the Executive, which had been clamoring for such data.[10] Among eight reintegration programs discussed, the study featured one, a CBO, the only program in the country to meet all of the DCoE's criteria and to have a solid evidence base: Coming Home Project. Few of the appropriate leaders in the military services, the VA, the corporate sector, and Congress were briefed, read, saw, or even knew about this report—even though the study represented precisely what they had been clamoring for from the DCoE for years. What works? Where shall we responsibly invest our monies? By then most of them had given up on DCoE for what was perceived as not fulfilling its well-funded mission, and didn't bother to read the report.

In March 2013, after twelve years of war, Jackie Garrick, acting director of the Pentagon's Defense Suicide Prevention Office and Lt. Gen. Howard Bromberg, Army deputy chief of staff for personnel, each predicted in testimony to Congress that the alarming rates of suicide would continue to increase, despite 900 prevention programs. Lt. Gen. Bromberg said that a major cultural shift was needed to reduce the stigma of coming forward for mental health care. "Experts are still struggling to understand suicidal behavior," Garrick said. "What makes one person become suicidal and another not is truly an unknown."[11] Not knowing, even nine years and nearly two billion dollars later, is a good place to start. But in their efforts to find the silver bullet to answer "why this service member, and not that one?" they ignored Gregg Zoroya's report in *USA Today* on the results of a study that cited emotional pain as the reason most often given for service members attempting suicide, as well as a study sponsored by the Marine Corps that cited conflicts over values and meaning as important factors.

The Yellow Ribbon Reintegration program was founded to help National Guard members, reservists, and their families connect with community resources before, during, and after a deployment in order to minimize the stress of deployment and family separation. Events provide information about benefits, educational and employment opportunities, financial counseling, legal assistance, suicide prevention, and psychological stress and resources. Tens of thousands have attended these programs and many have derived benefit. From limited experience as a subject matter expert, I've observed that the content and quality of programming varies significantly. To my knowledge, no systematic research has been done on the effectiveness of these programs.

There seem to be two standards, one for nonmilitary programs, where research evidence is required, and the other for the military's own programs, where evidence of effectiveness is not necessary.

Some years ago Rob Gordon, deputy assistant secretary of defense for military community and family policy, introduced me to Dave McGinnis, assistant secretary of defense for reserve affairs. We talked over breakfast in the executive dining room at the Pentagon. During our conversation, Dave said, "Coming Home is the logical follow up to the Yellow Ribbon." He had me contact the appropriate people under him. Nothing happened; it died in the water. Apparently middle managers did not want to share their buckets of money or spheres of control over a number of services.

My colleague David Rabb and I put together an innovative integrative program of services for a National Guard unit and their family members about to deploy to Iraq. It covered predeployment, deployment, and postdeployment. It would cost the National Guard nothing since it was to be funded by private donations. Our proposal was rejected. It was simply not politically correct to be seen as unable to take care of your own, and having to link with a CBO. I since learned that staff at Fort Gordon, Georgia had independently brought to the DCoE their own proposal for a similar wrap-around program. Like ours, their proposal was not a big flash, high-publicity project, but rather a group of experienced medical corps staffers proposing an innovative community-building support program with a serious chance of working. It, too, went nowhere.

From this limited review, and from the continued incidence of suicide, domestic violence, and substance abuse, a strong case can be made that *the vast majority of military resilience, mental health, and suicide prevention programs have failed.*

In their testimony to Congress, Jackie Garrick and Lt. Gen. Bromberg neglected to address a central factor. In addition to chronic compartmentalization, internecine warfare, personal agendas trumping collective benefit, organizational stigma, incompetence, an allergy to collaboration, and the impossible task of keeping up with the burgeoning impacts of a reckless military decision—the 900 programs they referred to were not targeting the *level* of experience necessary to transform the profound anguish that so many service members and veterans experience and that often leads them to take their own lives. The suggestions

Garrick and Bromberg put forward—stigma reduction, availability of screening and mental health care, peer counselors—are good ideas, even if the track record for their implementation has been poor. But they are *not enough*. Not drawing on proven programs that leverage a powerful intrinsic resource hidden in plain sight—community—borders on malpractice.

Making Sense/Nonsense

Let's pull the lens back a moment and take in the wider sweep: two wars engaged without adequate planning, one based on faulty or manipulated intelligence, no planning for healthcare impacts, miscalculations galore, ideological and personal hubris, and recklessness. The Iraq invasion was nothing like the promised "slam dunk." The "shock and awe" backfired, and as it rippled across multiple sectors, we gradually realized just how in-over-our-heads we were. Everyone needed to do more with less. Resources were threadbare, with the heaviest load falling on service members and their families with multiple tours, inadequate dwell time, and the hated stop-loss policy whereby service members about to return stateside from the war zone would have their tour of duty extended. Overload and chaos began to spawn systemically, breeding abuses and abuse. Impossible expectations, pressures, and insufficient resources caused institutional stigma and defensiveness to spike. Nobody wanted to be, or appear to be, the weak link in these misconceived, undersupported, and dysfunctional systems.

In this wider context, building resilience was less a noble healing enterprise than an operational necessity: get more out of each service member, ask more from his family, his stressed providers, and their unprepared healthcare systems. Resilience training was part of a rather desperate effort to play catch-up, control the damage, and appear to be doing something.

With a nod to Shakespeare, "The readiness was all"—no matter the rhetoric about enhancing psychological health, reintegration, and so on. With few exceptions, resilience training conveyed that service members can and should thrive in the midst of the storm, as well as upon returning home. "Staying positive" was the ticket, creating in effect Teflon soldiers and family members. Many broke under the load. Without a sufficient and steady supply of troops, some service members were simply medicated and sent back into the field. Brutal stop-losses devastated families; harassment and abuse thrived in a chaotic and unbound culture. A series of systemic unethical and dishonest dealings ensued in the VA. It should not come as a surprise that toxic environments of deception were the natural result.

A glaring early example of insufficient preparation was the lack of armor on Humvees, which made dangerous IED blasts even more lethal. Resourceful and desperate families went online to buy their own armor and shipped it over to their sons and daughters. Their children would jury-rig the armor to protect themselves and their buddies. The image works as both an on-the-ground reality and a metaphor: no protection, flimsy support, and inadequate resources. One veteran said, "Armor? Heck, I'll just throw on this here resilience blanket, and I'll be fine." Fears of being stigmatized, ostracized, punished, even physically harmed were real. But they weren't the only obstacles. Earned distrust also figured prominently.

The saddest thing is that, based on Coming Home Project results, we are convinced that well-informed and integrated planning, preparation, and practices can make a difference for service members and their families. System-wide, such support was not provided by the military.

Getting Granular

Let's turn our attention now to resilience itself. How shall we understand it? Why is it consequential? While suffering is part of human life, war is a prime example of highly distilled traumatic agony. The encounter with suffering, and how we manage and come back from it, is a central motif of human living.

Patrick Martin-Breen and J. Marty Anderies write that in order to sustain things we need and value, we try "to reduce risk, mitigate [risk] in anticipation, and bolster the speed and efficacy of responding in a crisis." They describe three variants: engineering resilience, systems resilience, and resilience in complex adaptive systems. Engineering (or common sense) resilience implies "bouncing back faster after stress, enduring greater stresses, and being disturbed less by a given amount of stress."[12] According to this framework, if my friend is resilient, he should recover from a big shock, he should recover quickly, and distressing things shouldn't upset him so much. Why the term "engineering" resilience? Because "engineered systems, such as bridges, buildings, and infrastructure, are often designed to handle large stresses, return to normal, and return quickly when the stress is removed." The object with engineering is to prevent or limit disruption. Change isn't a friend. Most of the military's resilience programs fall into the engineering category.

Change, nonetheless, does happen. I recall a conversation with a former therapist of mine when we happened to meet after completing our work together. "So how do you think people change?" I asked him, in the midst of my own training to become a therapist. "How do they not?" he replied. For Martin-Breen and Anderies, authors of the review, "It is not just a matter of inherent properties: the income of households, or hardy personalities of people." Rather, "It is about the system they operate within, and how law and *community*, slowly changing variables, affect the resilience of those who have undergone or will undergo expected crisis, a fast change." Cultivating a regular meditation practice, whether we need it or not, is one example of a slow, barely perceptible change that becomes more available in times of crisis, indicating a well-functioning response system.

Systems are dynamic and their parts, like individuals, families, and communities, influence one another. So system resilience is about maintaining function when change (or disturbance) visits. This capacity depends on parts communicating well with one another, something the institutions we've been examining have done poorly if at all. Parents and some bosses commonly try to get their children and employees respectively to do what they say, not what they do. But this is not how people learn. We learn from, and with, people who walk their talk, who embody what they're conveying verbally. Our purported resilience institutions lack resilience, and this is another reason for the failures of their programs.

Now if a government fails or a disaster occurs, (or both happen concurrently, as in Hurricane Katrina) a system within the overall dysfunctional matrix can respond adaptively by creating a new form. This ability to adapt and "self-organize" (or reorganize, as it were) characterizes resilience in complex adaptive systems. Here, resilience is the "ability to withstand, recover from, and reorganize in response to crisis."

The earlier example of Tonia, struggling to be part of Ken's recovery from a life-threatening TBI, is instructive. She and Ken and their kids, Tasha and Alishya, endured the pain of the injury, along with the subsequent struggles, intimidation, isolation, and more. But her response was adaptive; rather than causing harm, it benefitted not just Ken, but many other families to come. This was also the case with a Marine mother, Mary Ellen, whose efforts during and after her son returned from the war zone led to the creation of a series of statewide collaboratives in California that short-circuit the bureaucracies and isolating silos and connect veterans, families, services, organizations, and communities. And there is Cynthia, Rory's mother, who helped scores of families and their service members struggling with TBI understand and navigate the system effectively. These partners and parents, and thousands like them across the country, stepped in at the grassroots level where DoD and VA had failed. They created robust, responsive, and effective networks where these were absent or where what existed was obstructive, even harmful.

There is novelty and innovation in adaptive self-organization, and it is accompanied, even generated, by the coming together of distinctive and diverse voices, ideas, and backgrounds. This was how we finally developed our research protocols at Coming Home Project, and how our retreats come together afresh each time, creating a reliable structure everyone can engage in and benefit from. This is the obverse of the scattershot, crisis-driven, single variable, quick-fix mentality behind the efforts at responding to the suicide epidemic.

Martin-Breen and Anderies then address ethical obligations and potential value conflicts by posing two questions: "Resilience of what?" and "Resilience to what?" I would add, "Resilience at the service of what?"

The Resilience Trade

Military resilience efforts have been geared around readiness. Readiness is about maintaining and enhancing peak performance. It does not focus on healing, the integration and transformation of traumatic residues. Many in military medicine are skilled, devoted, and well-intentioned, but the bottom line is the driving force. When financial, personnel, and healthcare resources are stretched beyond the limit, the underlying question, even if it's not addressed publicly, is how to maximize the performance of service members so they can better endure the horrors of war, perform well, and "bounce back" reliably from setbacks and traumatic shocks.

Can we "build" a better service member? Is it worth the huge investments going into research to answer this question? Hollywood has given us the Six Million Dollar Man, the Bionic Woman, and other half-man half-machines whose humanity has been trained out of them and whose physical capacities dwarf those of mere people. The compelling story of the black-ops special operator Jason Bourne is in effect the story of returning to the human, the story of a well-trained machine-like being, inured to emotional anguish, reclaiming his humanity. This return is not the province of military resilience programs.

David Sutherland was a decorated commander in the battle of Fallujah and now is a respected advocate and consultant. We discussed strategies for partnering with corporations on a service Coming Home Project codeveloped in order to foster mutual understanding and productive interactions between corporate HR and supervisory staff and prospective veteran employees. "You have to speak to their bottom line," Sutherland advised. How will hiring veteran employees increase their profits?

Resilience programs try to make it easier for service members and families, but there's no guarantee these efforts will prevent disturbance or reduce the costly need for care and services. Try as we might, we cannot escape the fact that service members are human beings. Fighting for your life and your buddies' lives takes a toll, a toll that also exerts pressure on family members and care providers. What disturbs me is that most resilience efforts—driven as they are by the bottom line and "extreme pressure" from above—became incorporated into efforts to wage "war on the cheap." This cheapens the profound and extensive impacts of war and devalues the suffering of veterans and families.

I support and contribute to adapting and employing the best practices to ease the road home for service members and families. It's the context I'm concerned about: "In service of what?" I've come to see that it's often been in service of an attitude and conduct epitomized by our former secretary of defense, Donald Rumsfeld, "You go to war with the Army you have, not the Army you might want or wish to have."[13] Translation: "My, aren't you pushy. You want what? Well-armored Humvees? Robust support programs for your families and children? Enough dwell time between deployments? Responsive, expert, accessible mental health options in theater and back home if you need them? How demanding. How selfish of you, you should know there's no 'I' in 'team.'" This repugnant, twisted appeal is an affront to the immense willingness to sacrifice that characterizes so many service members. This is the D in PTspD—D as in "dissed."

The get-more and do-more-with-less ethic is part of the quick-fix approach to care we've been discussing. During my fundraising travels, I met in Washington, DC, with the executive of a large company that worked with the military. He had done his homework and was interested in Coming Home Project. We got along well personally; I was encouraged. In our last meeting, he asked, "So how much could you reduce the length of your retreats?" I responded that we preferred one to two weeks but had found five days to be the minimum for families and four days for provider and veteran-only retreats. He began, first using humor, then quite intently, to ask, "Could you distill it into a weekend? A day? A half-day? Could it be presented in an hour? Could we package it into an online 'module?'" Here was the businessman, bottom line all the way, understanding nothing about what would be lost in translation, mistaking apparent bottom-line efficiency for substantive durable effectiveness.

I was asked variations of this "How does it scale?" question often, as if our approach could be compressed into a distributable commodity without altering it, a "product" that would appear to be reaching all service members with "top-shelf" content. When I met with Comprehensive Soldier Fitness and Wounded Warrior leadership at the Pentagon, I responded to this question by describing how, with genuine interorganizational collaboration, we could leverage shared staff and infrastructure to manage costs and, in about three years, could become not only the best but the default reintegration program for all returning troops and families. The "natural follow-up to the Yellow Ribbon program," as Dave McGinnis from Reserve Affairs had suggested. Three years? They wanted to "stand up" something right now, to show the brass they were doing something. Hurry up to wait.

They wanted fast change, quick-fix engineering resilience, rather than deliberate and sure complex-systems adaptive change. It brought to mind what I had told a group of long-term therapists quite a while back in a seminar I was teaching on brief therapy. They were anxious about having to find a way to cram months or years of intensive work into four sessions to please the insurance companies. "Slow down," I said. They stared at me with disbelief. To move expeditiously and effectively, take your time, take in the data across multiple channels, let yourself think. Individuals and organizations reeling from traumatic impacts are unable to do this and often react maladaptively by pressing the accelerator pedal to the floor.

Healing and performance-enhancing resilience training overlap but are quite different. Healing is not fundamentally goal-oriented. Its salutary effects derive in large part precisely from not being so. Healing begins with taking a sounding of body and mind, heart and soul, the entire bio-psycho-social/family-spiritual living organism we are. It involves observing, processing, and integrating what emerges, the "full catastrophe" as Zorba the Greek called it, with the unqualified, nonjudgmental, loving support of the community. We come to understand that repeated trauma does not disappear but rather recedes into the background, into deep storage, "archived" rather than "deleted." Relegated to the archives, it no longer haunts but helps create the pantheon of time zones: a proper past, a present, and hopes for the future.

We must not underestimate the anguish inherent in this process. There is struggle, there is fierce moral outrage, there is helpless rage, shame, guilt, and self-loathing. Having a proper past enables genuine mourning, a gateway to emotional growth and restoration.

Shrapnel in the Basement

Kamel Ibrahim Al-Najjar, survivor of the 2014 Israeli invasion of Gaza, spoke about his experience,

> We were safe at home when the bombs rained down on us for no reason. It was just me and my family in the house. There was a lot of shelling. We needed to get shelter under anything, anywhere. We went to our neighbor's house, and we found out that they had a basement. The basement was full, about a hundred

people. The next day at 6:00 a.m., an F-16 strike hit us. Shrapnel fragments entered the basement through the windows, and the basement collapsed. There were 120 people in the basement; ninety percent were women and children. There were only about ten men. I didn't know where I was. Shrapnel went into my eye and my head. I couldn't see anything because of the smoke from the F-16 strike.[14]

A few years ago I was invited to meet a group of social workers, psychologists, and other helping professionals from Gaza at the Human Rights Watch offices in San Francisco. The idea was to informally discuss the traumas that come with serving in the military and living in a war zone, our ways of working with the individual and collective impacts of war, and our personal experiences working therapeutically with service members, civilians, and their families. It was extremely difficult, my Gazan colleagues said, to treat people whom the therapists knew would be traumatized again. Sometimes it felt like an ethical conflict, like a doctor treating a victim of torture, and helping her heal, only for her to be tortured again.

While the experience of service members in a war zone and civilians caught in the destruction of war have their differences, there are many overlaps as well. When Israel bombed and invaded Gaza in August 2014, I was acutely aware of the suffering in all quarters. I was especially sensitized to the added work the Gazan trauma therapists I had met would have at the very time their material and emotional resources were spread the most thin. Then I read that one of the therapists I had met, Hassan al-Zeyada, had lost three of his brothers, his mother, his nephew, and his sister-in-law, when an Israeli bomb hit their house. Like Kamel Ibrahim Al-Najjar, Zeyada articulated what many survivors of massive trauma experience: "I am so afraid in this building. They may hit it at any time. There is no safe place. Psychologically, that is the problem."[15] His family had had "absolute faith" that Israel would warn them if their house was going to be bombed, but there was no warning. Because of their trust, the attack on their home and the sudden losses created a breach that was completely "unexpected." He noted that his young daughters have now experienced three wars. "Can you imagine what that means to the new generation? Scared parents cannot assure or secure scared children."

"Shrapnel in the basement"—sudden destruction we cannot predict, in a place we were convinced was safe. A catastrophe wrapped in a shockingly unanticipated violation. There is first the horrific literal reality of the shrapnel embedded in the bodies of veterans and of civilian victims. Then there are the metaphoric reverberations, the buried "emotional shrapnel" veterans and their families have to deal with for decades.

Echoes from Our Neurobiological Substrate

Neuroscientist Stephen Porges, developer of the polyvagal theory,[16] explores the neurophysiological foundations of emotions, attachment, communication, and self-regulation. When I first discovered his model, it piqued my interest but was difficult to grasp quickly, so I put it on the back burner. I returned to it recently and was stunned to discover a neurobiological framework and rationale for the diverse experiences of trauma survivors, including war veterans. It was also gratifying to learn how his ideas help explain the effectiveness of Coming Home Project's approach. Porges' work illustrates the paramount importance of safety and the grave dangers of helplessness, immobilization, and utter unpredictability.

The root of his theory is that "in the absence of the ability to fight or flee, the body's only effective defense is to immobilize and shut down."[17] This can manifest as nausea, defecation, fainting, even death. It is a feature of an ancient circuit used by our reptilian ancestors to defend themselves, and is mediated by the vagal nerve, which runs from the brain to the stomach. We also have a more recent mammalian (vagal) circuit that exerts calming influences on the heart through social engagement and social bonding, which relationally helps disconfirm danger. But unlike this uniquely mammalian pathway, the older reptilian circuit, which humans are still heir to, is only effective as a defense when the newer pathways, including the fight-flight system, are no longer available for interaction and defense.

"Our reptilian ancestor was similar to a turtle," Porges says, "and the primary defense for a turtle is to immobilize, inhibit breathing, and lower metabolic demands." "Although immobilization may be effective for reptiles, it can be life-threatening for mammals, and for humans it can lead to states of dissociation."

The polyvagal theory helps us see symptoms like dissociation as adaptive reactions to cues in the environment that trigger our physiological responses to perceived dangers. The "thousand-yard stare" memorialized in the photo referred to earlier and the extreme shutdown or freeze response, not uncommon in the war zone and often a source of paralyzing shame, illustrate this mechanism at work. Precipitating circumstances for this response might include a unit being pinned down under enemy fire, with air support unavailable and ammunition running out. In the case of Gaza, civilians escaped from their houses to a neighbor's basement or to United Nations shelters, only to have those bombed too. This left them stranded in a life-threatening state, scared to death, and with no further options for shelter. One could also imagine such circumstances as a breach in unit leadership that results in the loss of a buddy or commiting or witnessing an act that compromises deeply held values. All are events one cannot do anything to alter in the moment, while one's own survival and the survival of one's comrades is at stake.

As Porges explains, "For reptiles and more primitive vertebrates, the primary defense system was *to disappear*—to immobilize, stop breathing, and look like you're dead (a mouse in a cat's mouth). For mammals [however] immobilization is a risky business. Humans have to be selective about whom we can feel still, calm, and comfortable with." This is all the more so for troops during war, and, to some degree, in its aftermath. For troops and civilians alike, the inability to distinguish what is a safe zone, who is to be trusted, and who is a mortal threat, is profoundly disturbing. We've heard from veterans who, following policy, ran over civilians who didn't clear out when a convoy came through. Such split-second decisions can become the source of inconsolable anguish for years to come.

It's not uncommon for returning war veterans to have difficulty "immobilizing without fear," a capacity Porges says is necessary to play and be emotionally and sexually intimate. I became acutely aware of this in our first couples communication workshop when the subject of physical and sexual closeness emerged, brought up by female partners. As described earlier, one veteran found it better (read safer) to turn the emotional faucet off completely rather than risk closeness. Immobilization, even when it involves a man lying down in a bed next to the woman who loves him, triggers fear and shut down. Porges writes, "those who survive [traumatic] experiences [often] don't want to be immobilized. They find it difficult to be held and calmed, even by people who are trying to be helpful. This is often expressed as anxiety and the need to keep moving." Counterintuitively, such people sometimes "adaptively become anxious and go into panic states to avoid this immobilization state." In far milder form, it's not uncommon for veterans to manage vulnerability and anxiety by finding ways to hype up their energy level, putting the foot on the gas, so to speak, rather than a system-wide slamming on of the brakes. I recall my son as a toddler getting ready for bed; he would jazz himself up as he fought off the sandman.

The mammalian pathway for modulating the sense of threat and defensiveness uses social communication. According to Porges, this has less to do with words and syntax than with intonation, gestures, and a cluster of behaviors he calls biological movement. "The face is moving along with the voice and hand gestures. The behavioral features trigger areas of our brain outside the realm of consciousness and change our physiology, enabling us to feel closer and safer with another. *Good therapy and good social relations, good parenting, good teaching, it's all about the same thing—how do you turn off defensiveness?*" When I read this, it was as if he had attended a Coming Home Project retreat and observed firsthand the physiological changes visible in veterans and their family members from the time they arrive until saying goodbye after closing circle. "When you turn defense systems off," Porges says, "you have access to different cortical areas for more profound understanding, learning, and skill development." Optimal environments for healing are also, by their nature, optimal for new learning.

This helped me better understand how unconditional acceptance and compassion, without judgment—the "secret sauce" I was convinced was the active ingredient in the benefit veterans and families experienced—might actually work at the neurobiological level. We react to our environment with physiological shifts outside our conscious awareness. Being safe is really the body's response to the environment.[18] Many wellness practices leverage the value in learning to read these bodily responses by which we adapt to shifting people, places, and things.

On the other hand, we also telegraph defensiveness: "do not approach" and "it's not safe to be around me" (I'm primed to fight or flee). This occurs when some people first arrive at retreats; it's not hard to read their body language. Knowing this helped me appreciate how the "atmospherics"—the overall emotional environment of safety, trust, belonging—work to deactivate threat, fear, and danger, and unleash the potential of the social engagement and bonding systems, which is only available when the individual feels safe and the newest neural circuit is activated. An unqualified "welcome," another key element here, means that social engagement signals are being sent, and, eventually, received. Porges has coined the word "neuroception" to describe how people pick up on one another unconsciously, engage and bond socially, send and receive a range of social cues, reciprocally disconfirm danger and threat, reduce defensiveness, and open to a range of new learning and more joyful, creative, and libidinal experiences.

As if he had sat in on our evaluation team meetings, Porges says, "If we are smart, and science can help here, we will start learning which features in the environment functionally trigger our nervous systems into fight-flight, behavioral shutdown, immobilization with fear, and states of dissociation. And which allow us to move into a state of safety and recruit the social engagement system." This is what my colleagues and I have been learning over the past eight years. The beauty of the model, says Porges, is that we know the features of neuroception that trigger the social engagement system, the uniquely mammalian part of our autonomic nervous system that enables social interactions to calm our physiology and to support health, growth, and restoration.[19] *It is felt safety that gives us access to this mode of social regulation.*

The core of Porges' theory, then, is the quintessential quest for safety and the elements that contribute to feeling safe. If we're not safe—and most vets who return from war feel this way—we are in a chronic state of evaluation and defensiveness. But if we can engage the circuits that support social engagement, we can regulate the neural platform that enables social engagement behaviors to emerge spontaneously. From the polyvagal perspective, this is the objective of all therapeutic activity.[20] The relational ingredients and environmental qualities that characterize Coming Home Project retreats provide these very ingredients.

Let me give you an example of an experience I had some time ago that did just the opposite. I had arrived early for a presentation to a group of several hundred military veterans and their families gathered for a day of postdeployment educational programming provided by the military. The brief that preceded mine was on suicide prevention. The briefer began in a loud and strident voice, "Listen up, this is serious," followed by a series of videos featuring family members from all walks of life whose loved ones had committed suicide. They conveyed the awful impacts suicide had on them. The dramatic music and overall framing gave one message: "Don't do it, you'll be hurting those you love." It used fear and guilt as motivators. I could feel the traumatic currents course through my body and through the room as each story unfolded, replete with emotionally charged projections of family photo albums.

After urgently emphasizing the need to identify those who were contemplating suicide, the briefer put the group on the spot by asking, "So what do you say if you suspect that someone is suicidal?" No one raised their hand. After some prompting an officer who outranked the presenter took a crack, "I'd ask, 'Are you having suicidal thoughts?'" The crowd nervously half giggled and half gasped. "Yes, okay" the briefer said, "but not that fast." What followed was a confusing mishmash of contradictory research on what drives service members to attempt suicide and just as contradictory recommendations for how to prevent it—plus a personal story of how the briefer had missed a sign of suicidal intent in a colleague who did attempt to kill herself but failed. The briefer's anxiety and guilt were palpable but overridden by insistence. There was little to no clear, useful information. The best part of the forty minutes was a video of Terry Bradshaw, the famous quarterback, speaking from the heart about his own emotional struggles.

A much less dramatic and exhortive presentation might have provided clear practical background information delivered in a modulated and heartfelt tone, with a few stories of real service members. It would have made time to talk things over in small groups with comrades, to write about a relevant theme, and to give and receive feedback from each group. Something this simple, informed by the basic principle of creating emotional safety to facilitate learning, would have had a very different impact. As I got ready to receive the microphone, it was all I could do to muster the wherewithal to bite my tongue and not try to repair the damage. I breathed deeply and launched into my talk and instructions on meditation, and we had an opportunity to practice together.

Porges believes that transmuting the fearful immobilization that results from shutdown into "relaxed immobilization," mediated by social engagement and bonding, sponsors physiological processes that promote health, growth, and restoration. Once this ability becomes internalized—a reliable trait rather than a passing state—we are freer to mobilize and activate without being in fight or flight. We can really play, and not just solitary video games. We can enjoy sympathetic arousal and excitement because it is being modulated by the social engagement system whose cues convey "just pretending—not going to harm you." This is illustrated in the jumping for joy, the sheer exhilaration that Jeremy Williams expressed after the kayaking expedition (race) across Tomales Bay. Veterans reclaim this aliveness, formerly associated with the survival-driven war zone. It becomes available to them in a civilian setting, allowing them to experience thrilling, high arousal levels while simultaneously connecting with their wives and their buddies.

There is a "two-fer" that goes like this: safety gives us access to a prosocial system that helps us regulate strong emotions, a neural circuit only available to mammals and only available when we feel safe. It not only facilitates social interaction and enables it to foster growth, health, and restoration, but it also downregulates our reactiveness and the neural circuits that evolved for defense. The sequence, says Porges, operates in this order: when the social engagement system is working and downregulating defenses, we feel calm, we hug people, we look at them, and we feel good.[21] This is precisely what we have observed at Coming Home Project retreats, with upwards of twenty-five hundred people, reliably, over a seven-year period.

However, when risk increases, the two defense systems take priority. In response to danger, our sympathetic nervous system takes over and ratchets up metabolic motor activity for fight-flight. When well-regulated, this is adaptive—for example, for service members as they engage conflicts downrange. But, says Porges, if that doesn't help us become safe, we automatically recruit the ancient vagal circuit and shut down.

Porges sheds light on something else we frequently hear about from veterans and family members. Features in the medical environment often trigger a neuroception of defense, rather than comfort, reassurance, and safety. For example, they often remove access to the moderating social support features that we have in our normal everyday life. As I told the chief of a large VA psychiatry department who asked why so many of our participants returned or recommended our program to friends, "There has to be a 'there' there." Experiences at some VA and DoD hospitals and clinics trigger experiences of heightened defensiveness adaptive for the war zone.

Porges says that "the most profound way of engaging many [traumatized] individuals is to functionally change the physical context. Get rid of low-frequency sounds; enable music or melody to engage people using prosodic voices, voices with great intonation, don't bark at people."[22] At Coming Home Project, we discovered early on that holding programs off base, eschewing large, noisy hotels, and instead locating programs in tranquil, beautiful, natural settings helps participants self-regulate and feel safe. Earlier I mentioned it is not the traumas themselves, but rather our response to their overwhelming impacts that is key. Porges writes that, for some people, specific physical characteristics of an environmental challenge or threat will trigger fight-flight behavior, while others may totally shut down to the same physical features in the environment, "The same event can trigger different neuroceptive reactions in different people, resulting in different physiological states." He emphasizes the need to understand that "it is the response, and not the traumatic event, that is critical."

In terms of war trauma, this helps explain the "testing, testing, testing" dynamic we often noticed during retreats, which varies from person to person. It's critical for veterans to disconfirm through trial and error their apprehensions, which keep war-zone defensive mobilization primed, activating involuntarily in social settings back home. They can learn to put that aside and come to trust: "they" are there for me and "have my back" (peers, other families, Coming Home Project facilitators, instructors, leaders, logistics team, even facility personnel like cooks); I am not really taking my life into my hands, even though it may feel like it; they are not going to hurt me— physically or emotionally—via exclusion, rejection, shame, humiliation, scorn, shunning, and so on. As a veteran or family member, they make a mostly unconscious assessment: I am safe enough to engage transforming my ghosts—to learn to regulate, risk, represent, reexperience, and reencode. Free enough to have a memory again, to reanimate past, present and future—free from the "sentence" of perpetual haunting and terror.

Porges affirms our discoveries when he says, "Safety is functionally our transformative state and neural exercises of this safe state enable the social engagement system to work. The neural exercise would be to enable it to dampen sympathetic [high-arousal and fight-flight] activity. Play literally becomes a functional therapeutic model, the exercising of the neural regulation of the face through song, through listening, through music, and through reciprocal social interactions. So in a sense talk therapy can be a neural exercise."[23] And, I would add, in a support rather than a formal psychotherapy setting, giving voice to one's story and listening to others' stories provides the same "neural exercise" that safety represents. Veterans creatively articulate and narrate experiences that have haunted them for want of having been encoded in a memory system that enables their recall and processing.

Porges presents a neurobiological rationale for the evolution we have seen over seven years with thousands of participants from across the country: a shift from interest tinged with skepticism, and in some cases mistrust and hypervigilance, to feeling safe, more emotionally buoyant, and hopeful. Veterans express these emotions behaviorally through increased playfulness in interpersonally connected ways.

During one interview with Porges, the popular singer Johnny Mathis entered the conversation. Mathis has a particularly smooth and relaxing voice that used to serve as the musical backdrop for many romances. "But what we didn't know at that point in time [when Mathis was at the height of his popularity]," Porges said, "was the prosodic features of Johnny Mathis's voice were triggering the neuroceptive circuit to make us feel safe. And we felt safe and therefore we could be in physical contact. In a sense, the defensiveness was greatly diffused by Johnny Mathis."

Earlier I wrote that, given half a chance, veterans and families want to reconnect with one another, their communities, and within themselves. Porges puts it this way, "The point I am making is that our nervous system is sitting there *waiting* for Johnny Mathis; we are sitting there *waiting* for intonation of voice. We *want* it! And when we start getting it, it changes our physiological state."[24] A sense of safety and community, characterized by an emotionally warm, responsive, and sustained welcome, provides just this. But it does not work when it is faked or where profound unconscious ambivalence prevails. As Gilbert and Sullivan wrote in their 1878 operetta *HMS Pinafore*, "Things are seldom what they seem. Skim milk masquerades as cream." Veterans' BS detection system has evolved, out of necessity, to become acutely sensitive.

Practicing

I wrote earlier how in 2007, a moment of silence at our first Coming Home Project retreat prompted toddler Ben to spontaneously speak about losing his dad, Michael. Later that morning I introduced the adults to a simple focusing on the breath meditation. During the ten-minute guided practice, two people in the circle left the room. One was Rory, who told me later that becoming aware of his breathing and body amplified some unpleasant anomalous physical sensations in his head and neck he thought were related to his TBI. It worked better for him to practice walking meditation. Stephanie was prompted by a feeling of being disloyal to her own religious tradition, even though what we were doing was not framed as a religious practice. Prior to the retreat, she had asked to speak privately and told me that her church back home had ostracized her after Michael's suicide, blaming both him and her. She was in despair and had come searching for an alternate community and perspective for dealing with her pain. Stephanie's experience poignantly illustrates the "can't live with it" aspect of cumulative trauma. During early retreats, I learned that for veterans one size definitely did not fit all, and tailoring the practice to the needs and abilities of individuals brought greater benefit.

Recall the former Marine officer who, on the first evening of a Coming Home retreat, reported that someone had stolen the TV in his room. I worried for a moment, but when everyone burst into laughter, I finally caught on. "Who took my TV?" indeed. He realized he would not have access to TV for five days.

Silence can be challenging. Not speaking unless spoken to, or being seen but not heard, is stultifying. Enforced quiet is painful. Trying not to think or talk about something that's on your mind is stressful and often futile. Atten-huh! does not meditative attentiveness make. But many veterans, family members, and providers tell us what a release it can be to arrive at a retreat, feel the beauty of the surroundings, and experience the whole body begin to ratchet down. Coming home is coming to rest; allowing ourselves to unwind, unburden. And yet it's a struggle. We keep on the go, revved up, the foot stuck on the accelerator pedal. We're plugged in alright, but into what? We're connected, but connected to what?

We live in a culture of distraction. We text while walking, our heads buried in our phones, eyes fixed on a tiny screen; music beating in our ears, we plod along and into others. What's meant to improve efficiency and connect us often does neither. I talk to veterans about the guy I saw who was trimming his beard and checking for missed spots in the rearview mirror while navigating traffic in San Francisco. And a lady who was applying makeup, brushing out the tangles, and conversing while driving around town. I describe my favorite, the bicyclist who, plugged into his earphones, burger in one hand, texting with the other, and leaning on the handlebars, was dashing around town.

I describe how we tend to create more problems for ourselves by how we react to our problems. Take war trauma. Returning stateside from the war zone and driving the Harley around sharp curves at 100 mph after knocking down a fifth of Jack, how's that working as a coping mechanism? Or screaming at your kids? Or pushing your wife around? Or holing up and not coming out for days and weeks at a time? "Stop, look, and listen" is the beginning of meditation, but it's easy to say and often hard to do. But it's worth a try if trauma is haunting you and the strategies you're using are making things worse.

I tell the story Sylvia Boorstein, a fellow meditation teacher, told me. One day her husband, Seymour, a psychoanalyst, came home from seeing patients and said, "You know dear, I really love understanding." She responded, "Me too, but sometimes I like 'standing' even more." When waves of strong emotion rush through us, it's a good thing to be able to "stand" (contain) them and not just react in our usual ways. So the ability and the willingness to experience what's going on in and around us, the good, the bad, the ugly, and everything in between, is an important component of a supple heart and mind. Cultivating acceptance, not resignation—a wide welcoming awareness, short on judgment and long on compassion—takes time. But it is possible, and it can change our relationship to suffering.

When consumed with anguish, we automatically react by closing off or ramping up, foot stuck on the brake or foot stuck on the accelerator. Instead of just reacting, we can come to a full, purposeful stop. When I was living at Plum Village in the early 1980s, then a mostly Vietnamese community that welcomed displaced and traumatized families, the teacher, Thich Nhat Hanh, made a large calligraphy for the meditation hall. It said, "Breathe. You are alive." Stopping. Breathing. Returning to life. The path to rest and refreshment begins simply. When haunted by war-related or other trauma, the buoyancy of a community is often needed for support.

It's remarkable to be with veterans as they learn to safely let down their guard, to slow down long enough to hear themselves think, smell the tree sap, listen to the birds, enjoy their children's laughter, and see loved ones as if for the first time. Service members learn to deploy into war zones and to deploy lethal force. But deploying attention and putting it at the service of reconnecting and healing is something else again. Quiet can't be forced but it can be cultivated: an attentive energized stillness rather than a vegetative quiet that shuts the mind down. When it arrives naturally, when hypervigilance abates, it is a relief and a surprising pleasure. It feels good to just be.

I explain to veterans how meditation utilizes purposeful awareness and can be practiced in a variety of ways: in tumultuous times it can help restore our emotional balance, and when we're about to "lose it," it can keep us from saying or doing things we will regret later. We can also meditate regularly, say a few mornings a week to start, whether or not we think we need to. This is like putting a penny in the piggy bank. The "return on investment" compounds slowly, imperceptibly, and is often first recognized not by us but by those we're close to. Eventually, we have more access to "stopping, looking, and listening" when we need it. The many moments of everyday life can themselves become a field of meditative practice, as we engage with the most mundane or even irritating activities. By directing our awareness—forgetting ourselves as we water the garden, clean the bathtub, or write a report—simple activities can become gateways to quiet pools of composed energy. Finally, practice can help us break through entrenched misunderstandings. Cultivating qualities such as compassion, equanimity, and wisdom, we can more deeply grasp the meaning of our coming and going, living and dying lives, which veterans are only too familiar with.

The purpose of meditation, I explain, is not to stop our thinking but to create conditions for rest, peace, and understanding by cultivating our attention. Say we notice our awareness becoming consumed by small details, by preoccupations with the past, or worries about the future. We can think three Rs: first *recognize* what's happening; then *remember* that we can practice with it; then gently let our awareness *return* to being here, in this body, in this moment, breathing and alive.

I ask veterans to think about a moment of great stress that blindsides them when they least expect it. Our capacity to reflect has been highjacked. But, we can learn to stop, look, and listen. We can recognize, remember, and return. We are not pretending that everything is hunky dory, but rather, we become aware of what's going on, even if we don't fully understand it. We *recognize*. And we deliberately take "the pause that refreshes," remembering that there's a way to practice, even with this. We lean into the discomfort and *return*, to our breath, our life, right here and now. We don't expect the stress to go away forever. But gradually, with diligent practice, space opens up, life looks and feels different. Pain doesn't disappear on command, but neither does it consume and derail us as frequently. Inner peace and composure are gifts beyond price, but they are available to each of us, and they develop when we invest in our own intrinsic powers of attention.

In this way we come to our senses. We sow seeds that help us come to life. We are not passively resigning ourselves or becoming inactive vegetables. We're not rolling over or going belly up. We accrue energy with each attentive moment, a kind of meditative "equity" with which to enjoy life more and to face and transform the traumas that plague us.

An activity such as fishing can be the nonmeditator's meditation. Then the dojo is the great outdoors: the lake, the river, the ocean. For some, fishing is a good excuse to "zone out" with no recriminations, and to "zone in" on the activity at hand. For others it may be cleaning the house or digging in the ground. Fully engaged, giving ourselves over, our burdens surprisingly lift. As the old baseball legend Satchel Paige said, "Sometimes I sits and thinks, and sometimes I just sits."

At Coming Home Project retreats, we've found it important that participants attend meditation practice when they want to and are ready to try it, not because it's required. The relational context—a cohort, a group, or a dyad—is also critical. In the early stages, it's helpful to listen to guided instructions, and the voice itself plays as much a role as the words' content. Participants come to feel open enough to ask questions, which allows us to customize instructions to suit the particular individual. As noted, the majority of families we've welcomed describe themselves as "spiritual but not religious," and they appreciate that the practices—meditation, yoga, or qigong—are framed in a secular humanistic, rather than an organized religious, way.

I gradually came to realize that the three Rs—recognize, remember, and return—were not only Zen instructions I had heard forty years ago in the dojo, or secular meditation guidance I was adapting for at-risk youth and later for veterans, families, and care providers. It dawned on me that these attentional activities were also at the heart of responding adaptively to emotional anguish in general, and traumatic pain and loss in particular. Since trauma is so often dissociated—for fear of becoming overwhelmed, for want of confidence in our ability to process it constructively, and in the interest of staying the course, say on a military mission—the anguish is sequestered away in the recesses of our body and brain.

When a daily life event triggers associated symptoms, say a racing heartbeat, shortness of breath, or constriction in the chest, we tend to react by gunning the motor, foot heavy on the accelerator, or by slamming the brakes, trying somehow to override or avert them. This reactive strategy may work in the short term, but it ignores the opportunity the symptoms present to work with them in the interest of integration and healing. The three Rs help us develop the psycho-physiological habit of stopping, looking, and listening: recalling, and then breathing into the reactive bodily contractions that involuntarily accompany emergence of traumatic symptoms.

Each time we do so we build our capacity to engage the visceral reality of the present moment. With practice, our "meditative muscle" or emotional hardiness grows, along with confidence in our capacity to respond to strong waves of emotion and our composure. This is a benevolent cycle. We can access a sense of peace and well-being more easily and a sense of intimacy with our surroundings and circumstances, especially the natural world, an experience that is available only in the present moment. These elements then serve as ballast when the next storm comes, as it inevitably will, given our common humanity.

Suffering is not enough; we must have access to nonsuffering, however slight, however passing, in order to be willing and able to fruitfully encounter emotional anguish when it arises. When the entire screen goes dark, when we are completely consumed with pain, it is extraordinarily difficult to make our way back. But when even one corner of the screen is letting in light, given the right relational ingredients, we can work with the darkest of experiences. Resilience practices, at their best, help us develop this corner of light, this awareness of the present moment, and ideally the ability to use this skill in daily living and bring it to bear when it is really needed.

At Coming Home Project retreats, participants learn this approach within the framework of a supportive community, characterized by emotional and relational safety—an optimal setting. Qigong and yoga both place a premium on attentive movement, and help connect mind and body in relaxing and energizing ways. Remember that the setting is not just an accompaniment to these practices; it is central. From the beginning the environment is helping participants regulate their emotions, and this provides incentive to explore new practices. In turn, these practices and the attentional possibilities they open up and train encourage participants to participate actively in their small group meetings and give voice to their war experiences. These two pathways, regulatory and expressive both, become mutually enhancing partners in liberation.

When we first began Coming Home Project we wanted to focus on veterans, those who had separated from the military, and their families, who were no longer in limbo regarding a possible new deployment. But it turned out to be impossible, and I felt, unethical. Parents, siblings, partners, and even older children of active duty service members and reservists called to apply, as did some service members themselves. We could not turn them away. They have since become part and parcel of our retreats. Having participants and families at various stages of deployment turned out to be enriching, supportive, and instructive for everyone. Yet service members who know they will be redeployed often have a slightly different experience than those who know they will no longer serve in the war zone. The same is true for their respective families. While active duty service members enjoy the camaraderie with new buddies, some of the wellness practices, expressive arts, and recreation in teams, and the connection with their own and other families, it can be more difficult for them to engage the full range of emotions in small veteran groups, to plow the ground of traumatic experiences, and to engage the process of transforming ghosts into memories. This reflects the words of my Gazan colleagues, who describe the difficulty of working with trauma survivors they know will be retraumatized again. A part of the mind remains prepared, in performance-readiness mode, not giving over into what Porges calls "immobilization without fear."

I recall one service member due to be deployed again, who made a large pastel drawing of a soldier riding his noble-looking horse, part of a "Shadow Brigade" of Afghan and American troops. I was moved when he gave me the drawing and it's been on my wall since. I remember him by it. I also remember how he danced, quite romantically, with his wife after our talent show on the final full day, when many participants get loose without booze and drugs. I remember how they relished their time with another military couple they gravitated to. He listened attentively during small groups, but often in plenary settings he poked fun, distancing himself. I think he knew at some level that there remained, in the shadows, residues he did not feel completely safe letting rise and engaging, elements that might have led him to make the drawing. I went so far as to imagine myself, along with my colleagues, as a different kind of shadow warrior, one that helped create conditions for the safe emergence and expression of ghosts, so they might, with everyone's support, be integrated.

Humans are not infinitely plastic; we all have our breaking point. I was discussing this book with a close friend and colleague who is a psychiatrist. She asked about the word "healing." It sounded to her like I might be implying that our retreats eliminated trauma once and for all. She had endured the tragedy of losing her young child several decades ago and said she still occasionally had pangs of fear regarding her two grown children. Traces still reside, she believes, in her amygdala (part of our brain's limbic system that mediates emotion and motivation, in particular those that are survival-driven) and hippocampus (the "seat" of long-term memory).

In different circumstances, I recall how, after the 1989 earthquake in the San Francisco Bay Area, I would awake from sleep each time a truck went by and the frame of the two-story wood frame duplex I lived in rattled. I had never noticed the rumbling before. I would instantly and automatically connect the dots in my body and brain into "aftershock" and react with a jolt of anxiety. This may have been adaptive: better to experience it as a present danger than be taken by surprise for want of vigilance. After a while, I would awake with apprehension that the rattling might *signal* a tremor rather than experiencing them *as* a tremor. Gradually, I began to dream and integrate elements of the earthquake. Over the course of a few months, when I heard the sounds and felt the vibrations, I would awake, turn over, and go back to sleep. Eventually my regular sleep patterns returned.

Of course, this kind of traumatic stress can be more serious. As will be discussed later, at a men's veterans group retreat in Virginia, one vet opened up about his problems with anger, thus prompting others to talk about how quickly they "went from zero to 60" now that they were back stateside, becoming almost uncontrollably angry at what they could see later was a minor incident. Their ability to modulate strong surges of emotion was compromised. The defensive fight-flight system was turbocharged, continuing to fire when danger was no longer present. We've heard this frightening example more than once: a partner awakes at night screaming as she feels her veteran's hands around her neck, choking her. The veteran is reacting to a threat from a mortal enemy, albeit one that is not present. Eventually he may awaken *as if* he were being attacked, then as if he were being threatened, then with apprehension about not knowing if his partner is friend or foe. And so on. The danger signals fade and the once-adaptive but now outdated survival reaction is gradually extinguished. There is now a space prior to reacting in which to stop, look, and listen. In this space there is a measure of choice in responding to the emotional upsurge.

What I call PTsxD (sx=symptoms) represents the body and brain's understandable reactions to the overwhelming stressors of the war zone. This psychobiological dysregulation is likely to respond to educational interventions that reframe symptoms as adaptive human responses to threat that take time to fade out in the new homefront setting. Some resilience programs provide education explaining the body's defensive stress system and particularly how the reptilian-like vagus supports an ancient defense system to protect us from life threat. This can be helpful in demystifying the responses that traumatized individuals experience. Porges sees reactive behavior as not necessarily morally motivated but rather intended to regulate physiological or behavioral states. He believes that understanding the shutdown response as an adaptive defense reaction can help trauma survivors respect their bodies' automatically deployed responses, designed as they are to save their lives (and in the case of troops, others' lives), rather than blame themselves.

As we have discussed, the experience of trust and belonging that community engenders helps restore damaged connectivity. But the continuing neuroception of life-threatening danger, associated automatically with a survival response that is no longer adaptive, is more a conflation than a healing connection. It illustrates the "can't live without it" or "bondo" effect of trauma. Education is like an instructional manual that can begin to help destigmatize the entire pattern in the mind of the service member or veteran. Safety, however, allows the threads of this psycho-neurobiological association to tease apart and permits the information received to be practiced, tested, learned, and internalized.

Giving up what made you feel safe isn't easy. We've seen this with veterans who bring weapons to retreats, even though they've read and signed the guidelines that prohibit them. When we remind them in our opening orientation, they leave their knives or guns with us for the duration of the retreat, but not without trepidation. Relinquishing what provided protection and relearning safety is a struggle. Porges says we pay a price when we learn to downregulate our ability to hear low-frequency sounds that, in our history as a species, were associated with predators. Although many returning troops return with a compromised social engagement system, they have a functional advantage in detecting threat. While walking with you, some veterans may "hear footsteps behind you rather than listen to you." Many partners of veterans can attest to this experience of not being listened to.

Although we've been focusing on reclaiming attentiveness and cultivating reflectiveness, Porges reminds us that, neurophysiologically, we are actually discussing shifts in physiological state, not simply cognition. Family members grasp this state shift intuitively when they express variations on the theme of, "the partner who returned is not the one who left." Porges says troops and other survivors of repeated trauma have adapted by shifting neural tone to the middle ear, which makes them better able to hear low-frequency sounds associated with predators or threat. But this comes at the cost of difficulties in hearing and understanding the human voice, a problem that impedes rebuilding relationships and intimacy.

PTsxD can also respond to a range of body-based practices that cultivate the ability to access the "three Rs" discussed earlier. These practices help because they support the brain's natural process of reregulating as it adapts to new circumstances. But when, as mentioned earlier, a partner awakes in terror to find herself being choked out by her veteran, we enter another register, the relational aftermath of war. "Intrusive thoughts" are a symptom in the diagnostic cluster called PTSD. But this term doesn't begin to describe the night terrors or night visitations that vividly recreate experiences long dissociated that cannot be remembered or articulated.

Relational aftershocks complicate the post-traumatic picture, along with betrayals, sudden losses, buried conflicts over the ethics of what a veteran has done, witnessed, or been unable to do, crises of meaning and purpose, and experiences of utter helplessness and shutdown of the kind described by Porges. I recall a number of male vets at our Santa Rosa retreat joining in after one of them shared his credo: "Happy wife, happy life." Would that this saying have simply meant being aware of their needs and behaving empathically and considerately. Their deeper concern actually was: if the wives and partners ever knew what we really have gone through, what we really did, they would never want to be with us, and some would even think we were monsters.

Educational and skills-based interventions usually have limited effect with such reactions. The haunting that plagues these vets can however respond to the transformative "turning" we have been discussing, characterized by its safe, unconditionally accepting, respectful, warm, and responsive environment, and the sense of integrity and justice it helps restore. This environment primes the social engagement and bonding systems and nourishes and sustains veterans and families and care providers as they let in, let be, and let out (express) the impacts of military service. It fosters a process that holds them as they change, through what we might call a controlled unraveling of entrenched defensive and protective systems. Reintegration back into civilian life passes through a kind of "unintegration" or letting go that only felt safety and trust make possible. This permits a self-regulated (supported) reexposure to "immobilization with fear," a profound and emotionally moving reintegration of the warded-off traumatic pieces. Gradually, participants become capable of immobilizing without constant fear, letting their humanity flower again—laughing and weeping, struggling and dancing, tasting the elusive experience of enjoyment and peace.

This is not the province of war-on-the-cheap, quick-fix-heavy demonstrations that we're doing something about the mental health of our troops. This is the slow-change system at work (and play), nourishing heart and soul, body, brain and mind. It was not designed to accommodate institutional bottom lines or the fix-it-now mentality that comes along with them. It doesn't fix, it helps transform. That's how healing war trauma works. It works because it's in accord with how we're made, the bio-psycho-social/family-spiritual organisms and complex adaptive systems we actually are. PTgr moves along the trajectory from addressing overloaded fight-flight (or dissociative vagal shutdown) defensive systems, through catalyzing and remobilizing the social engagement and bonding capacities, to reestablishing development that has been derailed as an operational and occupational hazard of military service. It nourishes four capacities that are key for a life well lived: aliveness, bonding, regulation, and meaning/purpose. It has a different intent and content, and follows a different attentional and neurobiological pathway than the pseudo-resilience products commonly traded in the military.

I'm in favor of expanding the palette of what's available to service members and veterans and families. Since 2007, Coming Home Project has incorporated yoga, qigong, equine therapy, journaling, expressive arts, and secular ritual, among other integrative practices. One size does not fit all and service members, veterans, and their families appreciate options.

A few years ago my colleague David Rabb and I adapted Coming Home Project's community-building approach for a Yellow Ribbon program designed specifically for the families and the surviving soldiers in the combat stress unit that was attacked at Fort Hood in November 2009. We reframed the weekend from the typical series of presentations heavy with PowerPoints, to a connective, reflective, experiential opportunity. We introduced meditation practice and encouraged peer-to-peer communication throughout. We provided small facilitated groups for the soldiers injured in the attack and their families, as well as for the families of those who had lost service members. The result was an emotionally moving and healing weekend for all in attendance—from the organizers, old hands who had put together scores of Yellow Ribbons, to the unit's families, to those who had lost or injured service members in the Fort Hood attack. "We talked with each other, we connected," one said, commenting on how unusual it was. Here mindfulness was not only a practice that we taught, but also an overall approach that cultivated a safe environment with a wide, unqualified sense of compassion and acceptance.

Variants of "positivity" that really convey the message, "buck up and look to the bright side," can rob a veteran of the experience of developing and utilizing emotional inner strength. Finding solace in a rose garden, or riding an inner tube down a river with the kids, provides the corner of light in an otherwise dark screen, a glimmer of renewed faith in life's possibilities, and ballast to meet the next storm. Such experiences are encouraging and nurture a fledgling inner strength that helps engage a deeper healing. They have nothing to do with hollow "positivity."

The benefits that participants derived from Coming Home Project retreats remained stable two months after the event. We don't yet know, save from anecdotal accounts, the fate of these gains over the long haul. Could an early intervention, prevention, and treatment program like ours keep service-related post-traumatic stress, both the PTsxD and the PTspD varieties, from developing into debilitating chronic conditions that erode multiple elements of veterans' health and well-being? It would take additional funding for a longitudinal study, funding that has not been forthcoming for reasons we have discussed.

Some years ago, Trish O'Kane, a human rights investigative journalist, lost her father to cancer. "During his last days," she wrote, "he loved to watch the birds come to his feeders." She thought, "If watching birds could help my father die, maybe it could help me live and teach." So she bought two bird feeders, sat on a stoop, and watched sparrows. She came to notice their pluck, and how they focused on their immediate needs. "If they couldn't find food, they went somewhere else. If they lost a nest, they built another. They had no time or energy for grief. They clung to the fence in raggedy lines heckling one another like drunken revelers on Bourbon Street. Their sparring made me laugh." Her "sparrow show" got her through the mornings, while visits to nesting grounds of migrating birds and ducks "got [her] through the afternoons." She realized then that the birds had become her teachers. Now, as a doctoral candidate in environmental studies, she uses birds to show her students "how we are all connected to one another, humans and nonhumans."[25] This is a wonderful illustration of how a profound connection with other living beings in the natural world can enhance genuine resilience.

I was struck by the author observing that the sparrows had "no time for grief." In a more extreme example, recall the retreat participant who fearfully and angrily equated grief with suicide. I suspect Trish O'Kane came around, at her own rhythm and in her own way, to mourning the death of her beloved father.

The sparrows allowed her another way to connect with something bigger than her and her tragedy. This "bigger container" provided a resting place where she could breathe, continue living in the face of tragic loss, and find her way back at her own pace. Maybe it bypassed grief temporarily and provided a sense of agency in the midst of a tragedy that did not consult her. But by making her laugh, the sparrows didn't eliminate grief; they enlarged the narrowed range of her affective life, a range that, I am confident, would later come to include grief. By then, the mourning might even have had a certain tender quality.

Recall the Marine master sergeant who said, "When we meet we're crying, when we break we're laughing." The relational connections veterans make with fellow vets and service dogs, equine therapy horses, as well as birds, support a widening range of emotional experience. My friend and colleague Keith, his feelings also sensitized, supported me in the overwhelming sadness I felt in the ballroom full of personal mementos of lost service members. Real resilience mobilizes and develops the social engagement and bonding systems. It takes other minds and hearts, and sometimes other living creatures, to help us hold our pain in a wider field, to "regulate" and integrate—and not eliminate—it. Seeing war's impacts through unreal rose-colored glasses couldn't be further from this process.

In 1983 Congress authorized a large research study following a protracted debate over the long-term effects of war between those who thought that the nation's 8.3 million Vietnam-era veterans had successfully adjusted to civilian life and those who suspected that many had not. The study resolved the debate and revealed the chronic nature of PTSD.[26] About 30 percent of male veterans had developed the condition and by the late-1980s, half of them were still suffering from it.

A follow-up study examined a huge sample, 283,000 Vietnam veterans—men and a few hundred women now beyond the age of retirement—estimated to still suffer post-traumatic stress disorder from their war experiences in Southeast Asia. The findings are the result of revisiting in recent years Vietnam veterans who took part in the original research. William Schlenger, a lead investigator on the new study, describes the key finding: "For veterans with PTSD, the war is not over. It is chronic and prolonged." About 11 percent of Vietnam combat veterans today still deal with intrusive nightmares and memories, and the tendency toward isolation, numbness, and anxiety that come with PTSD. A third also suffer from major depression. Vietnam veterans with PTSD also had a much higher risk for an array of chronic health problems and the risk of early death is nearly twice as high among men suffering PTSD.

Try as we might to better prepare troops and families for war, we do them an injustice when we pretend that they can skate through the raindrops. My distaste for much of the military's resilience and prevention program stems in large part from it being part of the attempt to sanitize war for troops, families, and civilians. "War is obscene," says decorated retired commander David Sutherland to the hundreds of audiences around the country he speaks to. War is hell, and hell has been happening with striking regularity.

To better prepare our troops, their families, our care providers, and our country for the rare case when war is really essential for our security, it is imperative that we understand and wake up from the dissociative trance that war spawns and realize we have "skin in the game." "You break it, you own it"—would that we would own it, and become accountable for the multidimensional costs of war.

be too upsetting for him. But she felt guilty. I imagine she might have wanted to make faces at him, knowing he can't see her.

Children also have to adjust to a returning parent whose behavior can be unsettling, even scary. Recall Arnold's son Paul and imagine how he experienced his father when, after returning from a gruesome tour in Afghanistan, he would alternately withdraw and explode. After blaming Paul for being "soft," Arnold flew into a rage and shoved him against the wall; he restrained himself from killing him. Then Arnold fled and did not return. The retreat was the first time Paul had seen his father in two months, and Paul was extremely quiet and withdrawn; he didn't want to rock the boat with his father or threaten his own delicate equilibrium. In his family it was not safe to express his emotions. Even at the retreat it took time for him to relax with his fellow teens.

Anna was a sixteen-year-old girl who had come to the retreat with her father, a single military dad who had taken care of her while her mother was deployed. Anna was sullen and surly; no glimmer of brightness crossed her face. Over the course of two days she began spending time with another teenage girl. The two of them, one short and upbeat, the other tall, gangly, and petulant, became inseparable. On day four, at the evening's talent show, they presented a duet about teenagers' war experience, delivered with ironic humor, that brought the house down. Anna's shift was palpable and visible to all. In the closing circle, her father said he never knew what was going on "inside my teenage daughter's head." Tears came to his eyes as he spoke of witnessing her "come back to life like a blossoming flower; the smile returning to her face after five years."

With the support of his male veterans group, Arnold began to face the shame that followed his actions with his son. For a while he was able to consider Paul's experience. During the closing circle, Arnold approached his son and offered a hug, which Paul accepted. This emotional breakthrough moved us all, but it was just the beginning; father and son had much to do to rebuild their relationship.

At the end of our second retreat, Tasha watched her mom and dad renew their wedding vows in a heart-wrenching ceremony, with Ken straining to see Tonia. Tasha began to cry again. Mary Ellen, a family friend and mother of a marine, held her as Tasha sobbed. It was painful for Tasha to see that, while her parents still loved one another, their marriage (and all family relationships) had dramatically changed.

Ben, Stephanie's young son, during a moment of silence at the beginning of our very first retreat, whispered audibly to his playmate Isaiah that his daddy had died in Iraq. Over dinner that evening Ben was restless and looked my way. I suggested we trace one another's hands with crayon, something I learned working with preschoolers. He settled for a while. I gave him my drawing of his hand

and he gave me his drawing of mine. We took them with us as we all parted the following morning—tangible forms of important new memories.

Claudia sustained a severe closed head brain injury that "robbed her of a part of herself," including the memories of giving birth. She was also facing a court motion for sole custody filed by her divorcing husband. As we all gathered for our afternoon circle, Claudia's little girl Juanita was dancing exuberantly, at once letting loose in a safe setting, avoiding the reality of a disconnected mother, and trying to brighten her mother's expressionless face. As she danced playfully, a smile appears on Claudia's face, replacing for a moment the frozen blankness.

Peter, a former marine whose face was disfigured in an IED blast, affecting his speech, has difficulty making himself understood. He brought along his three-year-old son, Sebastian, to the retreat, having recently separated from his wife. On the final day, Sebastian engaged by calling my name a few times. Each time I responded. He liked the give and take; I enjoyed the call and response. Earlier he had steered clear; I was an unknown quantity, not yet safe.

I think of Claudia's little girl, without her father, Ben without his, and Sebastian without his mother. I think of the teenagers, Brittney, Tasha, and Alishiya, both with loving parents present, yet struggling with the enormous rippling impacts of their fathers' injuries. We all step in to fill the gaps. If it takes a village, we become that village. It is gratifying to make use of my own war-related trauma, the experience of my injured WW II veteran father leaving when I was a baby, to help create such an environment.

Parents and Partners

While their partner is deployed, parents have to be there for their children at the very time their own resources, emotional and often financial, are at their lowest. Perhaps the most difficult retreat we ever had was for families with a loved one who was deployed. We received five times the number of applications as we had spaces and simply could not turn away large numbers of motivated families in need. So we had a larger group than usual, 150 partners, parents, children, teens, and other family members from around the country. Understandably, the level of anxiety in the small support groups was higher than we had experienced. Our strategy, to encourage participants to support one another by listening attentively and sharing their own stories when they were moved to do so, didn't last long. For the first few days it was useless to discourage participants from trying to "fix" one another or focus on practical suggestions.

Partners, mostly but not all of them women, were intent on "getting something." They wanted tools they could use now. Sometimes they learned from the self-care strategies we presented, sometimes they dismissed or passed right over them. But the ideas and methods we conveyed were at least a placeholder, helping bind the profound apprehension that gripped them.

Our experience was similar to that of Alicia Lieberman, director of the Child Trauma Research Program at San Francisco General Hospital, and a pioneer in parent-child psychotherapy. Presenting at Coming Home Project's and University of California TV's live nationwide video teleconference on the effects of war on young children, Alicia told the story of a seminar she taught for a group of therapists in the military. She felt their materials were too sunny and optimistic, and did not convey the kind of emotional collapse that can occur with war trauma and the impact it can have on young children. A therapist stood up and said, "I think we have a cultural difference." She said the group emphasized "proactive coping, not dwelling on the emotional nuances." Alicia responded by saying, "Let's try to integrate these two approaches." She saw that sometimes families in their desperation just want to be told what to do. This contrasted with her approach, which was similar to ours—to help families develop the capacity, and take the time, to feel, reflect, and reconnect.

In small groups at our deployed families retreat, parents and partners with a deployed loved one did eventually feel supported and safe enough to share a range of scary and, for them, shameful feelings. They did so at a slower pace than at retreats for families whose veteran had returned home. Some were terrified their loved one would not return or would come home irreparably damaged. Others felt utter helplessness. Some partners were so lonely that they fantasized about a new love interest, and, in one or two cases, had affairs.

Once I visited an organization composed mostly of partners and parents with deployed loved ones in order to provide information about our retreats. They were preparing hundreds of care packages that they would send to the troops. I found them thirsty to talk to someone who'd listen, and they described for me a kind of pony express they had developed. When one of them was concerned about their loved one, they'd put the word out and see what recon the others could come up with regarding the particular unit: where it was and what they were encountering. More news was better than less, until one of their sons or daughters called and was interrupted by the distinctive sound of an incoming mortar and the words, "Gotta go, Mom," followed by a click. It put chills down their spines. I stayed a couple hours longer than I had intended; as I drove home across the Bay Bridge I felt something unusual for a Zen guy like me. In a nonpatronizing way, it felt like this work had become my ministry; these were my people.

My friend and collaborator, Mary Dudum, who volunteered at our first retreat, had her son deploy to Iraq as part of a Marine recon unit. She heard next to nothing about where he was and what he was doing, and I saw the strain it put her through. Being involved with Coming Home Project and helping others was good medicine. Cynthia, Rory's mother, fought for medical services necessary for her son at every step along the way of his recovery. Like the mothers and wives who were preparing care packages, like Tonia fighting the system for Ken and other veterans, Cynthia found meaning and relief in helping other family members understand and access services for TBI, creating robust grassroots networks that filled huge gaps in military and VA services. Eventually, as their situations stabilized, Mary, Tonia, and Cynthia came to face a range of emotions they had avoided in throwing themselves with singular focus into serving the needs of their loved ones and many others. They had put fear, grief, helpless rage, despair, and other feelings on the back burner while helping others, but they came to address them in their own time, in their own way.

> Oh the blood and the treasure and the losing it all
> The time that we wasted and the place where we fall.
> Will we wake in the morning and know what it was for,
> up in our bedrooms after the war?[2]

This is the verse Army wife Angela Ricketts placed on the homepage of her website. You'll recall that while going through a particularly bad time, Angela's friends, whom she calls "the wonderful ladies of Task Force Ghost," suggested she channel her "black soul," meaning go numb for now while staying psychologically alive until she and her deploying husband could reliably face things together. Dissociation can paradoxically protect one's sense of self and aliveness. Throwing oneself into service, often to the edges of burnout, is one way family members manage and leverage their pain for the benefit of others and safeguard their sanity. But eventually, the unseen emotional residues of war trauma must be faced or they eat us alive, as we saw earlier in the suicide of Clay Hunt. It is only in a safe place that this healing alchemy is possible.

Children and Adults in Touch for a Change

Once, as a retreat was winding down, a few parents came up and asked, "How are our kids doing? We want to know more. We've just been thinking about ourselves." It was good they were thinking and talking about themselves; they needed to. They had been so thirsty for support and perspective that, during the small partner support groups, they had forgotten about their children and about the responsibility for others that weighed so heavily. It was a mixed moment: I was glad for the benefit these parents were letting in and for the newfound interest in their children's experience. I also couldn't help but think: the children come last.

It began with a family ritual: group facilitators developed a creative process whereby children and teen groups created mandalas, expressive compositions made of their own drawings, each one a different shape and size. As part of our closing ceremony, members of each group came to the center of the large circle and began to assemble their mandala. It was a bit like doing a puzzle, but using the pieces of their individual art, each of which represented a slice of their experience of deployment. Their parents came up and formed a circle around them, seeing their children's creations and helping them put it all together. They put the pieces together, literally and metaphorically.

The next retreat was the first in a series of four we provided during the summer of 2010, and the first outside the San Francisco Bay Area. It was set amid the rolling hills and streams of horse country in northern Virginia. We invited Larry Long, a composer and singer, to be with us. Larry had the knack of drawing out the creative voices of participants. He used the children's own words to compose lyrics for a song, "What It Means to Be a Family."

The chorus, a simple ditty sung between each verse, went like this, "I wanna tell my mother / I wanna tell my father / I wanna tell the whole wide world what's on my mind." Then children and teens recited the verses, "It was hard for us when you were deployed. We missed you, it made us sad you were gone, always afraid you wouldn't come home or else come back in a casket / We simply want it to go back to normal, to how it was before you left, peaceful, free from the bombs of panic and pain / We have changed, you have changed, and now it's time for us to change together; like a butterfly from a worm to a flower in the sky."

Larry also facilitated the adult cohort as they created a reading for the children based on what it was like to be deployed. Here are excerpts,

> Missing birthdays, holidays, first steps, bedtime stories and butterfly kisses, belly rubs, home cooking, cuddle time.
>
> When I first got over there we had no showers, but we did have mice and rats crawling on our heads!
>
> Through all the hazards, please know we did not forget you.
>
> Now, simply being able to walk on grass is a beautiful thing.

He also spent time with Bob Rodriguez, a Seabee whose unit literally laid the groundwork for the initial U.S. push into Iraq, and his wife Carolyn. From Bob's words describing his war experience, Larry composed a hauntingly beautiful song,

"All Gave Some, Some Gave All," which he sang during the closing ceremony. The song's title provided the lyrics for a simple melodic chorus, which was sung after each verse. Here are the verses, "I feel like a stranger in my own house, fightin' with my kids and spouse, in a moment, in a flash, I'm right back in Iraq / With my kids back at home, with my wife all alone, talking to them on Skype, hoping everything's alright / With mortars all around, my buddy hit the ground, I ran to his side, I watched my buddy die / With shrapnel in my knee, so many casualties, now I have these nightmares, more than I can bear / I don't want to medicate, nor can I wait, to be safe, to be strong, to find peace in this song / When I'm lying next to you, sometimes I don't know what to do, even when I hold you tight, I need your love tonight / I was raised to hold it in, to be faithful, to be a friend, to stand up, to never cry, but I've seen too many die."

And the final verse: "To be safe, to be kind, to feel good to be alive, to know I'm not alone, I need to find my way back home."

These words reflected not only Bob's experience, but the experience of many Iraq and Afghanistan veterans, as well as veterans from other eras. At our plenary closing ceremony, children and teens sang their song, and adults recited the composition they had written. It was moving for everyone to hear and feel our individual and collective hearts open.

The creative experiences Larry helped catalyze inspired us to develop our own adult-child expressive communication ritual. It debuted at the second 2010 retreat, at Mo Ranch in the beautiful hill country between San Antonio and Fort Hood, in Killeen, Texas. Our team developed an interactive social form for children and teens to articulate their experiences, not just to their own parents, but to all the adults gathered, and, in turn, to hear back from them. We wanted to create channels for honest communication but did not want it to become formal family therapy, so we chose to engage the child, teen, and adult cohorts as a whole.

We began by creating art shows featuring children's expressive work. While the children waited inside, the entire adult cohort would walk slowly around the outside display tables in silence, attentively taking in the children's work. A few were mildly uncomfortable at the start, but everyone settled in and really looked at the drawings and read the captions.

Jerri Lee Young, an expressive therapist, had helped the teen group find words to describe their artwork and with these words to construct a collective poem. When adults and children gathered back together inside, the teens took turns reciting the verses of their poem. Most adults had never had such an opportunity to see and listen to the real experiences of their children and other children who had remained stateside during their deployments. This is an excerpt from the teenagers' poem, "Oversea"—"I made that blurry / because that's how it was /

Overwhelmed. Sad. Dizzy. Sleepy / You feel the pain at night / . . . Dad. Gone. Who are you? It makes me feel lost."

I took a live microphone, walked around, and invited the stunned adults to express in no more than three or four words their visceral reactions. Reactions ranged from "amazed," "surprised," "never imagined" to "incredibly real," "courageous," "beautiful," "sad and painful," and "grateful to hear." The children and teens took in every word, every nuance. Adults actually listening and responding to kids? It was strange, but the kids got used to it.

After lunch the following day, during free time, before the afternoon small groups, the adults cohort gathered. We brainstormed, using three questions: For veterans, what did deployment feel like? For family members, what did having their loved one deployed feel like? And for both groups, what were their hopes for their children, the other children present, and this generation of military children as a whole? Later that evening, we condensed their words into a reading, which volunteers read for the children and teens.

Here is a sampling of veteran's voices,

I felt isolated and lonely, even though I had my comrades with me. It was a void, being away from my family.

I felt agonized, as if my heart had been ripped out of my chest. Sad. When I got to see my kids on Skype, I was happy and proud.

I felt this was my last go-around, my last dance on this planet.

I felt like I was betraying my children for my country.

I was afraid when I said goodbye to my kids, I wouldn't see them again.

I felt un-included because I missed my son's first words, first steps, first everything. I was stuck in limbo, and my family went on with their life without me.

I hated that my wife didn't get more support.

At the San Antonio retreat the voices of family members were just as rich and diverse,

I kept asking, "Why am I always the one who has to be strong?"

While he was gone, our daughter almost died. I had to go to the ICU and had to go through all that alone. I was angry he wasn't there.

I found myself looking at the kids and thinking, "Wait, stop!" They were growing up so fast and I didn't want him to miss it.

I had to keep really busy to make it through.

I was proud of him, but scared of having to be mother, father, and everything altogether.

I felt a little guilty, because I did get to witness all those moments; but, since I was there, I also was the one who got blamed. That was hard.

I would sometimes laugh at moments when I wished he was there. Like when I blew up the lawnmower.

Their hopes spanned the gamut,

I hope our kids forgive us for not being there when they needed us.

I hope they never have to go through what we went through.

I hope my daughter can let go of the resentment she feels toward the military for sending home a different father from the one she knew.

I just wish our children can understand that we are peacekeepers, not war makers.

I hope children grow up and learn less violent ways to resolve their problems.

Many children were eager to share their reactions: "Never knew that," "I wish you had said that before," "It makes me sad," were some of the their immediate responses. Even very young children raised their hands to speak. The image of one is imprinted on my mind. She was no more than five, wearing a simple bright dress, with a ponytail. She took the mic and, as we all waited, she stood up and held it in front of her, looking around the room. I tried to comfort and encourage her, until I realized she wasn't inhibited. She was just there, holding the mic proudly. After about thirty seconds, she said, "I liked it." Indeed, she and other children liked hearing adults share their true experiences, and she liked having a voice she could use when and how she wanted.

Our next retreat was in Oceanside, California, adjacent to Camp Pendleton, a Marine base where the barely perceptible sounds of mortars being fired one night during a training exercise stirred up more than a few veterans. It was a beautiful spot. Mission San Luis Rey was full of old trees, flower gardens, walking paths, and cloistered outdoor sanctuaries. Children did yoga on the huge lawns and able-bodied and some injured vets too flew around in relay and potato-sack races.

The children's art show and the teenagers' poems were evocative, "Like a giant mishmoshed clown: / I think someone is mad, sad, nervous / misunderstood— / silent and black. / Depression, heartbreak, sadness and pain— / someone is feeling angry, forgotten. / We missed you. / Daddy, are you still the same? / Something's growing in the heart. / I'm happy we're together: happy OR sad. / The heart is whole. Someone is feeling loved. / Rest in peace."

The immediate emotional feedback from adults visibly moved many children. Later, family members and vets read from their experiences of deployment,

It's hard to take off my uniform; I'm sorry.

I feel responsible for what I put you through.

When you and Mom waved goodbye to me, I put you both away. When I returned home, I didn't know how to come back.

I'm sorry I can't be there with you all for the 4th of July. It's because in my mind the bombs and missiles are still going off.

I didn't write or call as much as I wanted to, but I was trying to protect you.

I did everything I had to, including some crazy stuff, to come back to you.

I so enjoyed putting together that birthday package for you. It pulled me out for that moment.

When your Dad was away I cried every night.

The longer you were away, the longer my agony.

When I read your letter it made me cry: "Dad, what happened to you?" you wrote. "When you left you were so much fun. But when you got back, I didn't know who you were."

Every time the phone rang I was frightened.

While I was deployed I saw a little girl who reminded me of you. She smiled at me.

The faded picture in my vest gave me strength. Sorry I didn't call; I didn't known how to explain the pain.

Vets and family members' hopes for the children were as diverse as they were poignant:

LPU but not W. Love, Peace, Unity—but not War.

I hope you don't have to question my motives but understand my patriotism.

I hope you stand up and fight for what's right.

While I was away, I was scared for you. I hope I never have to go back.

I hope every kid learns how to solve problems peacefully.

I wish you a world without war.

I hope you understand some day this was my job.

I hope you're never hurt again by this kind of separation.

The final retreat that summer, in what we came to fondly call our "dog and pony show," was on the grounds of the beautiful Angela Center, a former convent in Santa Rosa in Sonoma County, California. By now, we were a finely honed team with a traveling core facilitator group supplemented by local assets recruited from DoD, VA, Red Cross, and other groups. They integrated beautifully and we felt like old hands when it came to our expressive family process.

The teens' poem got things rolling, "It's kind of 'off,' like us. / The girl's gray—crying. She's got mixed emotions. / The whole thing is sort of a window / into our inner selves that we don't / let anybody see. / It's all jumbled up—like how you feel / at first / —all these emotions. / After awhile, you're a little numb / you get used to it. / There's a dragon, tears, a broken heart, and art. / I see smiles, agony, the galaxy, outer space. / I see pain, and a poem. / It's nice, a success, creative, beautiful, complete."

Veterans and adult family members then created their reading,

You were the driving force that made me want to return alive.

It hurt being in Iraq; I cried every day being away from you.

When Dad left for the third time, I felt shredded to pieces.

It was okay that you giggled and had fun while I was away. / When I was deployed I was scared—very scared—scared of the unknown.

When Mom was deployed in Iraq she sacrificed so much.

When I'm angry it's not because of you; it's not your fault. (These are the words of a mother, expressing emotions not uncommon for parents: "I was very proud of my son, and also very worried. And I had to hide it.")

Thanks for believing in me when I didn't believe in myself.

We've lost Roland, but we can love and nurture each other. (Written by the wife of a service member who was killed in action)

No matter how much we fight, Mom and Dad love each other. We will see it through.

I'm sorry.

As for their wishes for the children's future, adults expressed diverse sentiments,

I hope you will find some strength in my having been deployed.

I want you to be smart, powerful women and men.

I want you to feel you don't have to do what I did.

I hope you feel confident no matter what path you choose.

I want you to be proud of the vets who come home, for what they did.

I hope you will be more compassionate toward others because of all you had to go through.

I want you to be proud of being military kids, and overcoming so much, especially being apart from Dad.

Couples

When Jeremy and his wife won the kayaking race, Jeremy exclaimed, "I'm so high!" The retreat was a place where they felt alive, hopeful, and connected again. They each talked about the serious problems at home, including Jeremy's frequent anger toward her and their two kids, and her sense of hopelessness that things could change. Just talking about it with peers made a tangible difference for their kids and themselves for quite a while. Eventually, however, like many military couples, the accumulated strains were too much and they divorced.

Earlier we also heard about a veteran couple struggling to reestablish a sexual relationship. The wife wanted more intimacy but was reluctant to speak freely for fear of making things worse for her husband, who was turned off, numb, and easily angered. Their experience was not uncommon. For him, feeling desire for his wife was tantamount to opening the floodgates for all manner of unformulated and uncontrollable feelings. His shutdown strategy was protective, but it had major drawbacks for a sustainable marriage.

Other couples took their lead and began to speak about their struggles with intimacy. I invited each of the eight couples to take turns standing behind their seated partner and, while remaining clothed, massage their shoulders, neck, and head. Amid semi-humorous protest from some of the men, we got started. There was lots of nervous chatter and I encouraged them to try to let in what it felt like. After a few minutes, they switched roles. Something began to shift in the armored presentation of some of the men and a few women. Nearly everyone said they felt closer to their partner. Some couples strolled away, arms around each other, to find a place to talk privately.

At a retreat for couples at Camp Newman, a summer camp and retreat center in Sonoma County, California, it was apparent in the partners group that at least one of the women had experienced domestic violence. It wasn't until the next to the last day that she felt safe enough to speak about her experience, without shying away from the powerful emotions that came along. She had felt terrified, concerned for her kids' safety, and for her own life. The police had gotten involved, and her husband had been taken into custody and gone through a diversion program. It so happened that he was struggling in the men's group with his own denial and becoming more forthcoming. As much as he had his story and was sticking to it—things at home were fine—in a nonjudgmental setting, where fellow male veterans were revealing their struggles with anger, he became less afraid of disclosing his secret.

Although I had witnessed such disclosures before, I was still surprised at what a relief it was for each of them. Several other women began to open up, and one man who had been steadfastly silent and resistant began to let cracks show in his tough, demeaning veneer. On the final day, during the men's group, he spoke with emotion for over an hour about a series of agonizing firefights and losses he had endured. The relief this brought him and his wife was palpable.

One of the most moving experiences from the Mo Ranch retreat was seeing a number of injured and downcast veterans, able to walk only with support and with great difficulty, whose marriages appeared lifeless when they arrived, get up on the last evening after the talent show and dance with their wives. They hadn't shared a dance since before their injuries.

Siblings

LaTisha Bowen is a former specialist with the 350th Psychological Operations Company who served in Iraq in 2004–2005. She first came to a retreat with her sister, LaTonia. They were a vivacious, gregarious walking stand-up routine, their relationship dynamics oozing out of every interaction. But underneath the shtick was the love they had for one another. In a sibling support group, brothers and sisters expressed how ignored they felt within their families. It was apparent how deep their concern ran for their sibling's well-being. Several would be talking matter-of-factly when a strong surge of repressed worry and sadness would surface, often with a flood of tears. Sometimes a sibling was the only one in the family a veteran could speak openly to. Siblings would also provide in-home care to their injured veterans or accompany them to medical visits.

It was LaTisha, in her inimitable fashion, who had deadpanned after the powerful closing ceremony, "Yeah, alright, it was okay. But I keep thinking 'when are you guys gonna break out the Kool-Aid?'"

Later, I had my own sibling experience when my close friend David Rabb deployed for his second tour as commander of a combat stress unit, this time to Afghanistan. I felt like a brother, bearing the apprehension that is always there, only releasing its grip with purposeful effort. My father had deployed before I was born; later I felt the aftershocks. But when David deployed I knew the experience firsthand. A few months after David returned stateside, I drove down from the Bay Area to visit him and his family in Murietta, California. We reconnected like long-lost brothers and talked for hours. I told him I'd written a poem while he was away, "That I Cannot Do" (see appendix), for him and for me, and asked if he wanted to read it. I didn't know how he would react, but I was glad he appreciated it.

Grappling with Suicide

Terri Jones, Coming Home participant, is the mother of three children. She describes her son Jason at the Army Christmas party days before he left for Iraq. "Jason was like any other 21-year-old boy. He loved hanging out with his friends, was funny, and had some of the craziest ideas you couldn't help but get involved with. He loved life and was determined to live his by squeezing as much as he could into each and every single day. Jason was also a talented artist and wanted to study commercial design. He won several awards and there was no end to his creativity. He trained himself to be a skilled martial artist. He wanted to challenge his body to almost do the impossible. He was a compassionate older brother to his sister and brother. He had just begun to teach his little brother all the baseball skills a kid could need. But all that abruptly ended when Jason went to war. A year later he returned home with only shreds of his former self. Little did we know that a silent time bomb was waiting to go off four months later, when Jason took his life due to the trauma of war."

Terri and her family were blown apart. "We were devastated by losing Jason and by not knowing exactly what had happened. We were now suffering from the same kind of trauma Jason had dealt with. There was so much pain in my family, it was almost unbearable. Seeing my daughter and youngest son suffering the loss was enough for me to question whether I could continue to be a parent to them. I sought help and soon learned that not everyone is trained to deal with the realities of war and suicide.

"When I found Coming Home Project I was nervous about meeting more people who 'could help'! But it was a chance I had to take if my family was going to heal. So my daughter, my three-year-old grandson, and my youngest son and myself all boarded a plane and flew to California. We met other families who were also dealing with war trauma and we were able to share our stories in a place where there was understanding and compassion. It felt like we finally had a chance at healing our wounds and keeping our family together. My youngest son Mick was having an especially hard time with all that had happened. I was scared and had no idea how to handle what he was going through. All I could do was ask him to walk with me. We found a Coming Home facilitator who was able to connect with my son on a very personal level. It was late on our second night there that Mick finally felt he had a right to be mad and sad, and was able to 'talk about his feelings.'"

I remember that night. After everyone had turned in, I saw Chad Peterson, a psychiatrist and facilitation team member, sitting on the steps of the main building with Mick. When I returned to the main building about an hour later for something I'd left behind, they were still there, talking late into the night under the big trees of the Angela Center. It is gratifying to our team that Terri felt "Coming Home Project was the most important part of my family's healing from Jason's death," that she has "the tools to survive our war trauma."

"Life does go on," Terri said, "and there is an occasional bump every now and then, but when those bumps occur we are not left alone in the dark. We have so many friends now from Coming Home Project who understand exactly where we have come from, and we can reach out to them. I have been through the valley of death and was able to return with more than I ever expected. Now I am able to pay it forward and help other military families facing the same issues I did so many years before. We could not have healed from this trauma alone."

Women Veterans

In 2009 Coming Home Project organized our first retreat exclusively for women veterans, and one of the first in the United States. It took place on beautiful Tomales Bay, near the Point Reyes National Seashore, in northern California. We had heard many stories and seen for ourselves the need for a program uniquely for women. We reached out to as many organizations as we could, but there were few services at the time in DoD, VA, or the nonprofit sector solely for women vets. We had a robust network and mailing list so we worked up a flyer and program ideas, lined up a core of facilitators, and pressed the send button for the e-mail blast.

Within a week we had received 600 applications for sixty spaces. After we screened people, created a waiting list, and allowed for attrition and changes of plans, we still had to say no to many women. Certainly the numbers demonstrated the thirst for a safe environment. Our team was almost entirely composed of women. During orientation on Thursday evening at the Angela Center in Santa Rosa, one woman took strong issue with my being there: how could a man understand what a woman had experienced? As a harbinger of what was to come, the group discussed it and the women overwhelmingly felt it was fine that I be there. The following morning, after voluntary qigong and meditation, and breakfast, we all gathered in one large circle for introductions. At our retreats, participants speak for a maximum of three minutes, facilitators much less. Every once in a great while, when we have a very large group, introductions extend past the two-and-a-half-hour morning meeting into the beginning of the afternoon gathering. But on this day, the three-minute limit was out the door with the first speaker. In fact, it was gone before introductions began.

After describing the morning's schedule, I asked if people had any questions before we began. Ordinarily there might be a couple of logistical questions. But not this time. The women had all manner of questions. "How long have you been operating?" "Where do you get your funding?" "What kind of legal structure do you have?" "How did the program begin?" "Why did you begin it?" I had never been asked all these questions at once, especially not during a time set aside for introductions. But after a few minutes, I saw that their interest was genuine. They wanted the real scoop, the down and dirty. They were doing their due diligence. If they were going to risk opening their hearts, they needed to be convinced we were legit. It was important that the retreat was off base, strictly confidential, and fully independent from DoD and VA. We soon learned that more than half had experienced sexual harassment or sexual assault while deployed. Being retraumatized was not an option for them; the context needed to be safe.

When introductions began, it was clear that the thirst to tell their stories and have them heard and recognized was likely to extend through the entire afternoon. I knew that it was better to stick to the time limit to lay the groundwork for the more intimate twice-a-day small groups beginning that afternoon. With the first few speakers, after a few minutes I'd clear my throat or explicitly invite them to begin to wind down for the next person. But on this day, each woman wanted to tell her saga, and each was complex and braided with anguish. Telling took time. And despite assurances that there would be more opportunities to share, the time was now. Here we all were, and one story led to another and another. Each was more poignant, more painful, more enraging, and more inspiring than the next.

We were about a third of the way round when a hard-looking Army veteran began to speak. Within thirty seconds, buoyed by the example of her comrades who had already spoken, her posture softened, spaces appeared between sentences, and feeling began to creep into her words. In the next moment a well-meaning vet had located a box of tissues behind a console and was bringing it to the speaker. I cringed and silently screamed "NO…!" Instantly, at the threshold to her story, the speaker stopped in her tracks. The tissues were an unconscious but clear message built of a certain conditioning: feelings, especially tears in this case, were not safe; they could be dangerous. I said, "feelings are okay," but without a word being exchanged about what had happened, the speaker stiffened, her voice became controlled again, and the feeling drained out. Within a minute she was done. The helping hand had struck again, but it turned out to be only a glancing blow. The momentum in the room had a life all its own. The next woman picked things up, and, with time, the original speaker found her full voice. "Introductions" went on through the morning and the entire afternoon.

I knew that women in general tended to be more verbal, open and relationally oriented than men. But I make a point not to cleave to such generalizations because there are, thankfully, so many exceptions. I do think, however, that what transpired was not only a function of participants' wounds and protective strategies; it also expressed their distinctive strengths and mode of connecting.

On the second day, we had a movement experience facilitated by a dance therapist. She suggested that I absent myself so the women could feel more comfortable in their bodies; I agreed. The feedback from all who attended was that this was one of the most exhilarating and connective experiences they had ever participated in. The freedom with which they could express themselves through dance had been contagious. Women felt empowered; they were bold and even bawdy in the safety of their felt sisterhood.

Women's Invisible War

The DoD estimates that more than 26,000 military men and women were sexually assaulted by fellow troops in 2012 while serving in the United States Armed Forces, and that at least 20 percent of servicewomen and 1 percent of men—an estimated 500,000 troops—have experienced sexual trauma while serving.[3]

These alarming statistics motivated documentarian Kirby Dick and producer Amy Ziering to make *The Invisible War*, a film that examines the epidemic of rape within the military, how it affects victims, and why so few cases are prosecuted.[4] Politicians such as Sen. Barbara Boxer of California, Rep. Jackie Speier of California, Lt. Gov. Gavin Newsom of California, and Rep. Mike Turner of Ohio attended the premiere at the 2012 Sundance Film Festival, where it won the Audience Award.

This rare attention came on the heels of a press conference that then Secretary of Defense Leon Panetta held on the subject. Rep. Speier acknowledged Secretary Panetta's confrontation of the problem, "I offer loud applause with a caveat and distinct warning that the Department of Defense's new military sexual trauma policies are not bold enough." From our intensive experience with 120 women over the course of two four-day retreats, I agree. A central issue, more alive today than ever, is the refusal of the military to cede responsibility for investigating and adjudicating cases of military sexual trauma (MST) to an independent review. Most women veterans feel, and my colleagues and I agree, that survivors of MST cannot get a fair hearing in today's military culture.

Coming Home's second women veterans retreat, in 2011, took place at Mission San Luis Rey in Oceanside near Camp Pendleton. It drew 250 applicants for 50 spaces. These retreats were inspiring, powerful, heartwarming, and heartbreaking. More than 50 percent of the participants experienced some form of MST, including rape. Their stories closely resembled the stories of the two women documented in the film. They too conveyed the disabling helplessness and despair that follows being disbelieved. Many women are unable to receive assistance and adjudication since incidents of MST often involve superiors to whom they cannot turn.

Participants listened as we read Chairman of the Joint Chiefs of Staff Admiral Mike Mullen's personal message to them. The retreat on Tomales Bay was covered by the *Veterans of Foreign Wars* magazine. The second, in Oceanside, was covered by the *Los Angeles Times*. Coming Home Project and UCTV went on to produce *Treating Female Veterans of War*, a training video with Darrah Westrup, a leader in research and therapy of women's postwar trauma. Developed for health practitioners, this video, along with thirteen others in the *Treating the Invisible Injuries of War* series, have been downloaded over two million times, indicating more than simply professional interest.

In Oceanside, fifty women vets came together for a truly "purple" gathering: all branches were represented, and status varied from National Guard and reserves to active duty to veterans. There was also a rich diversity in age, rank, type of military experience, marital and parenting status, and sexual preference. Remarkably, one woman had served in Vietnam, the first Gulf War, Iraq, and Afghanistan. Her steadiness and seasoning were a resource for many in attendance. A group of twelve volunteer therapists facilitated small groups where participants shared stories and experiences in an atmosphere of safety, trust, and mutual respect. Like all Coming Home retreats, this was not psychotherapy, but there was much reconnection, healing, and outpouring of joy in the presence of other women vets who "got it." One participant noted that, even in the larger group, she felt a sense of intimacy, as if we were gathering in her living room. We created conditions of safety and belonging that enabled truly open sharing. They were highly receptive to the resources offered: meditation, qigong, and expressive arts like journaling, drawing, movement, and dance. An outing to a nearby ranch for an equine-assisted wellness experience and a nature walk at Batiquitos Lagoon with a *National Geographic* photographer and guide rounded out the four-day program.

When the article in the *Los Angeles Times* appeared, I was shocked and disappointed. The journalist had focused entirely on a couple of stories of women's rage at the system and the men who had assaulted them. This was certainly an element that freely surfaced and was better integrated in the safety of the setting. But the article completely ignored the rest of the story: the permeating atmosphere of closeness, the feeling of family, of sisterhood, and the sheer joy and exhilaration of being together.

KPBS interviewed two retreat participants and me after the retreat. The interviewer asked me, "How are women's reactions to the stresses of war different [than men's]?" Rarely at a loss for words, I became stuck and didn't know why. Later, I retrieved what I knew: brains, bodies, minds, hearts, and souls, male and female, respond more similarly than differently to the impacts of service. The range of post-traumatic stress reactions are the body-mind's normal reaction to extraordinary, overwhelming experiences. What is different are the stressors that women face during their service, including the higher incidence of military sexual trauma and an often hostile and indifferent culture. Many female veterans said they have to work twice as hard for half the recognition in a "man's military." Not only do rates of MST for women exceed those for men, but MST is also associated with a series of serious mental health consequences.

I wanted to be able to return to the question posed on air and say, "Women don't have 'special problems' due to their 'special reactions' to the same circumstances, requiring 'special solutions.' Rather, based on our experience, what women veterans need is fundamental respect, recognition, and understanding of the *unique stressors* of their service experience. They need humane, integrative treatment, and some programming solely with and for their fellow women veterans, where they can feel safe, accepted, and understood. They urgently need serious, comprehensive change in the culture of how women are seen and treated in the military. This would benefit not only them but also the entire military—and all of us."

It was an honor for me to be part of these two memorable retreats. The vast majority of women were glad to have me, a male, involved. In Oceanside, during a large group check-in, one participant asked directly what it was like to be the only man among all these women. I said, "Being around all of you smart, strong, beautiful women, and being the only man? What could be bad?" In the years since, I've reflected on occasion about the fact that nobody took issue with what I said. It could have been heard very differently. Instead the women heard it as it was intended: I was delighted and felt privileged to be in the presence of such brave and beautiful women. My genuine admiration must have come across.

Kelly Von Lunen, a writer with *Veterans of Foreign Wars Magazine*, interviewed a number of participants after our first all-women retreat. Her portraits of them, which follow, place their experiences into the broader context of their lives.[5]

Hlee Yang

Today, Hlee Yang Cruckson readily admits that she "didn't have a very good childhood." She wasn't always willing to divulge her life story, but at 27 years old, she's ready to start sharing and start healing. "I came from a very abusive Hmong family and was married off at 15 in an arranged marriage," she said. She lived through tumultuous teenage years and early 20s. Throughout, Cruckson tried to stay strong for herself and her children. When she finished high school in 2001, her plan was to go to college to study criminal justice. Then one day, Army recruiters were at her mother's house, trying to get her younger siblings to join. "I happened to walk in while they were chatting with my family," she recalled. "I thought to myself, 'Here is my chance.' The very next day, I went into the recruiter's office."

After the September 11, 2001, terrorist attacks, Cruckson went to basic training. But later at Fort Hood, Texas, she was sexually assaulted. According to the VA's National Center for PTSD, 23 percent of female veterans report having been sexually assaulted in the military. Cruckson struggled to cope with the situation, while at the same time undergoing a divorce. "There was an investigation but it didn't go anywhere," she said. "Everyone in my unit looked at me like it was my fault." During that time, her unit readied for action in Afghanistan. She helped prepare for the deployment, but was honorably discharged in March 2003. . . .

In March 2004, Cruckson joined the California National Guard. "Life settled down for me," she said. "I began to pretend that nothing happened and that it was all a very bad dream." Cruckson moved and transferred to the Florida National Guard two months later. In August 2005, she deployed as an automated logistics specialist to Al Asad, Iraq, with HQ Co., HQ Detachment, 553rd Corps Support Bn., 64th Corps Support Grp., 13th Corps Support Command.

During Cruckson's first night in Iraq, her unit was attacked. "I was on the top bunk with other soldiers, and we were getting ready to go to bed," she remembered. "We didn't have any gear on and just when the lights went out for bed, we got hit. The ground shook, and we were thrown off of our bunks. Thankfully, no one was hurt. Some of us wore our helmets to sleep." Cruckson says she also witnessed other soldiers burning to death. "I can hear their screaming for help, and I see them reaching their hands out to me," she said. "I was so scared; I couldn't do anything to help them."

While stationed in Iraq, additional incidents occurred, triggering negative memories that had been buried for a long time. "It then brought back everything that had happened to me in the earlier years." Cruckson served four years in the active Army and National Guard and is a disabled veteran. She now lives in Wisconsin with her new husband and five children.

In the beginning of 2009, she started having trouble again. Cruckson suffers from PTSD, depression, and anxiety. Service-connected back, knee, and internal injuries have put her in a wheelchair, and she is on several medications for chronic pain. "All of my problems that I ignored and pushed away deep down inside of me have come back to haunt me," she said. "Everything in Iraq replays in my head, my dreams, and [real life]. I feel like it's happening all over again."

Today, Cruckson calls the retreat one of the best experiences in her life. "I used to not be able to talk about my past and what I've gone through," she said, "but by watching every brave soul there talk about their experiences, it helped me to break out of my shell."

LaTisha

We've already met LaTisha Bowen; after attending a family retreat with her sister LaTonia, she elected to come to our first women's retreat. A 32-year-old from Cleveland, she said she was overwhelmed by "the beautiful retreat."

She particularly enjoyed meeting women with different backgrounds who served in various units. "I'm not around females that much," she said. "That's one reason I went— I'm not one to get along with females too well. But it was so much fun. I made some good connections." Bowen served in Iraq from August 2004 to June 2005.

"For the things we discussed at the retreat, it was important for there to be just women," Bowen said. "There are certain things that we go through differently. There are double standards in the military. You still have to do your job, but there are certain things you have to do twice as well just because you are a female."

Shauna

Following the retreat, vet Shauna Jones wrote: "The energy that I used to have has come back a little. The energy of all the nice people here has given me a sense of peace, goodness, and warmth within myself that I will never forget." Jones says that through meditation, she discovered that she has a hard time relaxing and just breathing. "At first, I really thought this was not the right time for me to be here," Jones, a single mother, said. "I am a graduate student, and I had a paper to write for the next week. My partner helping me write the paper just bailed out on me the night before I left. However, this retreat has given me the strength that I have needed for some time now."

Tihara

Staff Sgt. Tihara Vargas left the Army Reserves in 2005, but as a result of the women's retreat, is considering rejoining. The 30-year-old Puerto Rico native deployed to Baghdad in 2004-05 with the 4th Bn., 227th Avn. Regt., 1st Air Cav Bde., 1st Cav Div., to start an education center in Al Taji. Later as a civilian, she interned with the VA and researched PTSD for her degree. Working with other veterans who were undergoing group therapy, she found that she had an instant bond with other vets. Vargas says attending the retreat was "life-changing" for her. "I found what I want to do in my life," she said. "I'm exploring the opportunities to go back into the military as a chaplain. I am shocked to find myself even entertaining this." Like the other retreat attendees, Vargas says that women can often feel isolated. However, she was amazed at how well the women at the retreat got along. "There was this instantaneous rapport and openness," she said. "We all just laughed and connected. It was a special time for women to bond as women."

Reviving the Lust for Life

The talent show on the last night in Oceanside was "out of control," as one vet said, "but in a good way." Afterward, Nicolette, our retreat planner, found just the right song. When "We Are Family" by Sister Sledge began playing, everyone got up on the floor dancing. I was reluctant, hesitant to introduce a male-female element into an all-women's gathering. I had absented myself earlier from the movement experience. But the music and fun were just too infectious, and when a female facilitator reached out her hand, I stood up from my chair and joined in.

I grew up in the Bronx and in my teens I would go listen to the best R & B groups: the Four Tops, Wilson Pickett, Martha and the Vandellas, Little Stevie Wonder, James Brown, Aretha. I've been in crowds and on dance floors where it was "cookin." But I have never been a part of an evening such as this. The dancing lasted two hours past the time we had set to finish. The joie de vivre was contagious. Women, whatever their sexual orientations, were letting loose together, in a place where it was safe to fully express their womanhood, their spirit, and their sexuality. It was electric; something remarkable to behold and partake of.

Just when it seemed that things were winding down, two women disagreed about how to do this one dance, and a friendly "dance-off" ensued. Other women joined in, forming a circle, each trying to demonstrate the way to "shake it." The complete absence of self-consciousness or fear was remarkable. At our staff meeting the next day, a female facilitator asked me what the evening was like for me. I commented on how free it was and how free-ing for so many women. Then I added, "It's also good that I have a well-developed capacity for sublimation." We all laughed and continued discussing and marveling at the power of the past evening.

Profound suffering, such as the war trauma experienced by women veterans, needs experiences of nonsuffering, like this, to find its proper place, a place within where it no longer tortures and haunts. For women veterans, this "turning" requires a "family" in which they are held, and hold one another with unqualified compassion and acceptance, without judgment. Then they can create an emotional environment where "the exercise of play," so crucial for healing, flourishes.

Out from the Shadows

In 2008, Anthony "Tony" Loverde was a loadmaster with the 86th Airlift Wing at Ramstein Air Base in Germany. He was a gay service member living, like so many others, in the shadows, under the oppressive influence of DADT (the military's "Don't ask, don't tell" policy). "For years I was lying about who I was," he said. After a deployment to Iraq, he decided to end the lies: "On this deployment, we all became very close. Everyone would talk about their families and their home lives. When it came to me, I either had to lie or just not say anything. I was just tired of not being me. I felt like I was misleading the people I worked with and this started to really bother me." Within months of telling the first sergeant he was gay, and the commander getting the word, Staff Sgt. Loverde was out of the Air Force.

"I love the Air Force, I loved my job as a loadmaster, and I loved all the friends and people I worked with. Not having any of this was hard," he said. He decided to take on the DADT policy and the failure of politicians to change it. "I wasn't trying to engineer a massive change movement or anything. I was just trying to tell my story, to let people know what happened." After reading about his story, the Service Members Legal Defense Network asked Tony to join two other gay service members in a class-action lawsuit they had filed against the U.S. government challenging their dismissals. He wanted to keep the discussion going: "The more time I spent on this case, the more I saw the potential for change."

A photo on the wall of his apartment in Little Rock, Arkansas, memorializes what happened next: in September 2010, President Obama signed the Repeal Act of DADT. "Until that day," he said, "we had to serve in silence and in the shadows, and now we didn't have to be afraid to be who we are." His goal, however, was to return to the Air Force. After being denied several times, finally he was permitted to return to duty in the same career field. Staff Sgt. Loverde was only the second service member discharged under DADT to be reinstated with the same rank, pay, and job he held when he first deployed. There have been 14,000 people discharged under the policy, but since the military no longer asks about sexual orientation, they haven't kept track of how many have reentered the military.

Tony has since qualified again as a loadmaster with the 61st Airlift Squadron at Little Rock Air Force Base and "couldn't be happier." "A lot of people ask me why I would want to rejoin a service that kicked me out," he said. "But I never blamed the Air Force or held a grudge. I blamed policy and knew my commander was only doing what he was legally supposed to at the time. Everything worked out, though, and it's just an amazing feeling to be part of the Air Force again . . . and this time I can be who I really am."

Senior Airman Ashleigh Kohler, an aircrew flight equipment technician with the 19th Operations Support Squadron, said, "Who someone chooses to love doesn't matter to the mission. I don't know anyone that treats Loverde any different from anyone else. He's just a member of the unit that helps us get the job done every day."

Loverde doesn't want his sexual orientation to define him. "At the end of the day, I am more than my sexuality," he said. "I am an airman who loves to fly, and I want to be judged by how well I do my job and not by whom I choose to have a relationship with."

In March 2012, Tony attended a Coming Home Project retreat for student veterans in Yosemite National Forest. He was completing graduate studies at Academy of Art University in San Francisco and saw the posting in a veterans' Facebook group. It was an opportunity to get away, have a break from his thesis, take his mind off the legal suit regarding his reentry into the Air Force, and gain some perspective on his pending reenlistment. He was exhausted from all of this work, beginning to second-guess some life decisions, and he needed a getaway.

Anthony had some apprehension about attending the small male veterans' group since it wasn't solely "gay focused," but he recalled reading somewhere that the Coming Home Project was "inclusive," which he interpreted as gay-friendly. His concerns were somewhat assuaged by descriptions of "spiritual wellness" and "interfaith leaders," which he interpreted as nonreligious, "I wouldn't have gone if I thought one religion or church was behind the organization of such an event," he said, "due to my negative experiences with faith-based ministries regarding homosexuality as sin." But, since he was about to reenlist and be in the company of active duty military, Anthony was eager to experience "coming out" to his fellow straight veterans. "I looked at it as almost a test of what I could possibly face in the future as an out gay man in the midst of military members that would know very little about me." He added, "being gay would most likely be the first thing they learned about me since my personal story happened to be very much about that at the time."

He carpooled to the retreat with another veteran. During the course of the conversation, he told her he was gay and had been kicked out of the military. She asked whether she minded if she shared her opinions. It was okay with Anthony and she began to talk about taking showers and feeling uncomfortable with lesbians. She spoke about her religious views on the sins of homosexuality. Anthony shared his own differing views on how service members were a professional force that would not tolerate inappropriate behavior in the showers, whether or not the "Don't ask, don't tell" policy is the law or not. Sexual harassment and abuse can happen and does happen with or without the law, he added.

They continued talking all the way there. "The great thing about it," he said, "was even though we were at opposite ends with our philosophies, we had a common ground of mutual respect for each other. Not once was either of us offended or upset with what the other person was saying."

They arrived early after a long winding drive and waited for others to arrive. Tony got to meet fellow veterans as they trickled in, which was a nonthreatening way to ease into the weekend, rather than "just showing up in a room all at once." The one-on-one interaction helped him connect with a few people on a personal level, easing the tension of meeting so many new people. He also noticed a car in the parking lot with a Human Rights Campaign sticker on the bumper. Although the driver was already out of the car and he didn't know who belonged to the "pro-equality" vehicle, he did know he wasn't alone.

Although Tony was comfortable being around the other vets, it wasn't until male vets met in small groups and began discussing their lives with each other that he felt a human connection. He had come in order to connect with others and improve his life, so talking wasn't difficult. When he began to speak about being gay and having been discharged under "Don't ask, don't tell," most responded with empathy. A few shared their beliefs about homosexuality but not in a way that felt judgmental to Tony. Most were glad the policy had been repealed and wished him luck on his reentry efforts. At the time, Tony was waiting for approval of a final waiver that would allow him to return to active duty. Every day retreat participants asked if he had gotten the call. He also got some tips about losing the five pounds required for reenlistment. As the weekend went on, Tony discovered a similarity he shared with everyone. "I realized it really didn't matter what our struggle was," he said. "What mattered was that we were stronger than our circumstances and willing to be hopeful for the future."

He appreciated the ground rules about mutual respect and no judgments, but "being a gay guy mostly interested in talking about being gay in the military with a bunch of straight combat veterans was a bit intimidating at first." As he listened to the diverse experiences of his fellow veterans, he began to think about his brother, an Army infantry combat veteran: "It helped me understand my brother more. That was a very unexpected result from the small groups." In the large group, he was surprised that a lesbian also in attendance spoke so freely: "It was rewarding to see her share her story as a gay veteran amongst fellow military members." The retreat confirmed for Tony "the special bond that veterans share, something I always felt was true, but wasn't sure, since most of my veteran advocacy was spent with fellow gay veterans. This was the first group where I went out of my comfort zone."

As part of the closing ceremony, we invited participants to write a letter or make a drawing to themselves that conveyed the best of their experience. It was a kind of message in a bottle that they would receive in the mail one month on. Tony said, "Once in a while I stumble upon the letter to myself with a picture of a road weaving through the mountains at sunset and the phrase 'LET IT GO.'" It reminded him to stay the course without letting the past define his future. "The weekend has provided me the opportunity for wonderful life reflection and the tools to handle my continued service and unexpected life events."

Straight vets learned from their gay and lesbian peers. Mike was a veteran of Afghanistan who attended the same retreat. He was rough and disdainful, and would occasionally comment on anything that smacked of differentness from traditional cultural norms. Mike made a strong connection with Howard Levine, a psychiatrist and Navy veteran who facilitated one of two male veterans groups along with Steve Torgerson. Mike hung out constantly with Howard, much like Rory did with the active duty officer at our first retreats in 2007. The change was gradual but remarkable. He began to open up about the traumas and losses he had experienced and became more relaxed and emotionally expressive. During the closing circle, I was stunned when he directly addressed a lesbian veteran to apologize for some of his comments and told her how much he had learned from her. He felt he was beginning to appreciate people who'd gone through experiences similar to his but who had lifestyles and beliefs different from his own.

Earlier we met James, who attended our San Diego family retreat. After introductions he holed up in his room, refusing to come to any activities, including meals. He wanted only to leave, and felt hopeless about being able to be in the men's veterans group. He and I had a number of talks and finally I told him we were missing him.

He came to lunch and sat next to me. I wasn't prepared for what unfolded next in the men's vet group. He described how worried he had been of not being accepted, of being judged for being different, of being an outcast. He then said he was gay and added that he was certain he would be harshly judged and shamed. The fourteen other men listened with rapt attention. A few spoke, expressing appreciation, respect, and admiration for the courage it took for him to share something so potentially explosive.

This occurred in the "Don't ask, don't tell" days, when "telling" could easily get you kicked out of the service. It's possible that some men in the group were keeping less accepting feelings to themselves, but most saw this gay vet's coming out as remarkable and brave, a leap of faith that entrusted his comrades with a personal and distinctively different part of him. I was moved at how an atmosphere of unconditional compassion without judgment fostered surprising new relational experiences and expanded emotional repertoires.

Healers under Duress

Once I was providing information to a veteran service officer and her staff about the retreat activities Coming Home provided for veterans and families. Her eyes became round as saucers and she said, "What about us?" Of course, I thought. Care providers are not exempt from war-related trauma—to the contrary. If each provider was responsible for one hundred clients, helping sixty or seventy providers learn to care for themselves would yield quite a return. With the support of the Bob

Woodruff Foundation and our program officer, Mary Carstensen, we welcomed 240 therapists, counselors, physicians, chaplains, care and case managers, and nurses to four retreats in the Bay Area over a two-year period. Mary's efforts with the military and the VA made it easier for their employees to attend.

Providers were effusively grateful for being included; they actually found it hard to believe. But one group at our first retreat for providers, from the Burn Unit at Brooke Army Medical Center in San Antonio, Texas, taught everyone an important lesson. The group of three women and one male nurse described long shifts without a break during which they "couldn't even use the restroom." Administrators in attendance from the same facility were stressed, but not like these frontline care providers. The latter felt their fellow participants and facilitators alike weren't grasping just how "burned out" they really were. They tried again to convey the debilitating sense of being immobilized with patients enduring gruesome burn injuries, in medical situations where the slightest lapse on the part of the nurses could prove fatal. Finally, something got through and they felt we "got" them. Tears of relief flowed at finally being understood.

A therapist spoke about how the VA, her organizational "family," came down on her after a patient of hers committed suicide. She had worked tirelessly with a challenging and distraught veteran and was devastated when he took his life. Instead of receiving understanding and support, followed by a helpful exploration of what had happened, she was called on the carpet and blamed; it made the monthly reports look bad. She was devastated, organizational trauma being heaped upon the trauma of losing a patient.

Unfortunately this therapist's ordeal was a common one. The primary source of stress for providers was the organizations themselves, stretched to breaking, and their managers and leaders, who were also under the gun. Workloads were inhumane: over fifty patients per day for one psychiatrist, and impossible caseloads of more than five hundred clients for case managers. And it wasn't only a matter of insufficient resources. Punitive and toxic work environments and managers, described earlier in recent media revelations from whistleblowers, were all too common.

Many providers are also veterans themselves or family members of veterans. Often this helps the veterans they serve feel understood and well-served. But it can also bring challenges of its own. A retired major in the National Guard working at a state university with student veterans was particularly devoted. She would go to the ends of the earth to help a vet in need, and was beloved by her students. But, internally, she was crumbling under the pressure and was utterly unable to let in even a little light into her world to recharge her batteries. "How can I let myself off the hook," she said, "when the vets downrange have no breaks?" She wasn't the only person who was overidentified with the plight of her charges. Many were also trying to compensate through their own sweat and tears for the lack of integrity of the broken systems around them.

John was a big, brash, funny Navy officer and Iraq vet, a psychologist, and he commanded all of our attention at a retreat at Mercy Center in Burlingame, California, a beautiful converted convent. His persona kept him above the fray, until the final day, when, after a number of people in his small group opened up in a personal way, he took his turn. The theme had been how unsafe people felt in their work settings, mostly from a psychological perspective. But when this tall tough active duty Navy officer began to speak, it was in a different, more vulnerable key from anything he'd previously said. He described his work with a patient whom he felt his superiors were underestimating. This experienced therapist found his patient dangerous. For months he had asked for some simple form of security to be installed since his appointment was often at a time when the clinic was beginning to close. He felt he wasn't asking for much: better lighting in the halls, a simple button he could push to alert the secretary to call security. After months of requesting and not receiving help, he had a physical altercation with the patient in which he needed to protect himself and in which both were injured. The psychologist's feelings of betrayal were intense and he spoke angrily for quite some time. No one was laughing at his vulnerability and outrage. Being the brash tough guy he was made his story of feeling unprotected all the more poignant and upsetting to the group. In the remaining days, he shared incidents from his service in Iraq that echoed the betrayal he had experienced as a therapist back stateside.

Humor was as much a social lubricant as in our other retreats. An Air Force chaplain who had earlier attended a family retreat with his wife and children came to the provider retreat at Mercy Center. We liked each other. He was a kind, attentive, and strong man, but he found it difficult to sit still in his men's vets group and listen to his comrades' stories. He would jump in to proffer tissues like a vet had done at the women's retreat. This time, I was reminding the group about how we made tissues available but let people themselves manage their use, and have their own grief. Suddenly, out of the corner of my eye, I saw a box of tissues come flying at me. I raised my hand but was too late, and it hit me in the shoulder. I turned to see the chaplain, a big smile on his face. I broke out laughing, assuring him that he'd get his in due time. The lesson on listening was seeping in.

One of the most meaningful moments occurred at the end of a provider retreat. Participants, who had been feeling ignored and left out in their organizations, described how grateful they were to be included. Some said the absence of judgment was in stark contrast to their work environments. One person began slowly, "I'm not now particularly religious, but what I would say is, this is how church is supposed to feel."

Extending the Circle

From the outset, we had invited scores of community volunteers, many of them civilians with no connection to the military, to help out at retreats. But on Veterans Day 2011, Coming Home Project took another step to help bridge the chasm between veteran families and civilian families, a gulf that benefits neither. That evening, we were preparing to host a benefit concert at the Freight and Salvage Coffee House in Berkeley. Our first community forum and retreat in 2007 were held at the First Congregational Church, also in Berkeley, and our first Veteran Toolkit Workshop, an innovative approach to veteran career development, was held at UC Berkeley's Veteran Transition Services offices. Despite Berkeley's reputation for being a hotbed of antiwar sentiment, veterans from around Northern California who attended these events were, without exception, surprised and heartened by the warm reception. The turnout at one evening community forum was so large and enthusiastic that a vet from Texas said he felt like he had "the wind at my back" as he and his wife went into the retreat the following day.

In the afternoon, before the benefit, we held our first veteran and civilian community art experience, patterned after the interactional ritual we had developed to bring adults and children together in an intergenerational dialogue at our retreats. Civilians, with veterans and their families, crossed the unseen divide, through expressive art discovering surprising similarities, along with the differences in their experience, of ten years of war. Coming Home team members—expressive therapists Jerri Lee Young and Beth Olenberger and art therapist Sandy Kepler—facilitated a remarkable and intimate sharing of visual art, words, and emotion that cut through verbiage and political and ideological identifications. Thirty people were gathered, two-thirds civilians and one-third veterans and family members.

The instructions were simple: feel free to express through drawing what the last ten years of war have been like. People drew on large sheets of butcher-block paper that were affixed to the walls, using pastels, Cray-Pas, colored pencils, crayons, markers, and pencil. Then Jerri asked us to walk around and look at the images. We were then invited to reflect on what words floated up to describe the drawing. With the permission of the artist, we could write those words next to the drawing. Afterward, school-aged children walked around and read aloud the words on the wall while facilitators wrote them down. Other words and phrases emerged, and a discussion developed.

Images included a heart with a jagged fracture running down the middle, and the words "Mend," "Broken Parts," and "Broken Hearts." There was a child's drawing of a gun followed by: "Why?" "When?" "How?" "Where?" A shopping center was depicted in a realistic drawing, complete with familiar store names and the caption, "America, we've gone shopping. What war?" There was a raging fire with a darkly hued phoenix hovering, another broken heart in the midst of a fire, and a simply rendered hand below with the phrase "prayers sent up." There was a large circle with multiple rungs of blended color that radiated warmth and light, with the words: "Wishing vets and their families and all: sense of peace, uninterrupted sleep, and shelter from the darkness." There were chaotic scenes of fighting and planes and bombs falling, alongside a multicolored beating heart and wings accompanied simply by "Love." Phoenixes of all shapes, sizes, and colors were in evidence. A child had drawn a Humvee that looked like a dark grey van with black, jail-like window frames. The room was buzzing with creative foment, save the sound of a hungry infant crying and the gurgles that followed while she nursed.

As we discussed the emotionally charged words that had been collected from the drawings, a transgender woman vet said it was incredible to feel affirmed and recognized by the civilian families gathered. Others added the words "Confused," "Scattered," "It's falling," "Sad," "Renewal," "Flight," "Hot," "Chaos," "Overwhelmed," "Connected," and "Hopeful." Jerri took a crack at improvising a poem from the collection of phrases. With more time, we would have invited participants to try their hand at creating a poem of their own. Over refreshments, people spoke with and learned more about one another. Connections were formed that last to this day.

Mobilizing

As a country, the wars of the past fourteen years have left most of us in a dissociative spell. It is possible, however, to resist the narcotic effects of both war fever and war weariness as the following story illustrates. It was Saturday, January 28, 2012, nine years after the war in Iraq began and four weeks after the last U.S. troops had returned home. Iraq war veterans from across the country converged on St. Louis for the first-ever parade organized to honor their service. Thousands of people came out to cheer them on, braving a cold January wind, with the iconic Gateway Arch glistening in the background. On this day 600 veterans, many dressed in camouflage, walked along downtown streets lined with rows of people clapping and holding signs with messages like "Welcome Home" and "Thanks to Our Service Men and Women." Some of the veterans wiped away tears as they acknowledged the support from the crowd—estimated at 100,000.

The parade was a grassroots effort conceived by two civilians, Tom Schneider, an attorney, and Ted Applebaum, a school district coordinator. Tom was amazed to see that everyone, from city officials to military organizations, to the media, embraced the parade. "It was an idea that nobody said 'no' to . . . America was ready for this." Gayla Gibson, a 38-year-old Air Force master sergeant who served as a medical technician in Iraq said, "I think it's great when people come out to support those who gave their lives and put their lives on the line for this country." "It's just the right thing," said Army Major Rich Radford, a veteran who served for twenty-three years and walked in the parade alongside his 8-year-old daughter, Aimee, and 12-year-old son, Warren. In New York, Mayor Michael Bloomberg had said there would be no city parade for Iraq War veterans in the foreseeable future because of objections voiced by Pentagon officials, who felt that a celebration should wait until all combat troops return from Afghanistan. But St. Louis residents, even those opposed to the war, wanted to thank the troops. "Many of us were not in favor of the war in Iraq, but the soldiers who fought did the right thing and we support them," said 72-year-old Susan Cunningham, who attended the parade with the Missouri Progressive Action Group. "I'm glad the war is over and I'm glad they're home."

The Pentagon thought the idea of a parade for Iraq veterans in New York City was premature. We had "finally" left Iraq but still had troops in Afghanistan. Why not wait until they too returned home so we could honor them all? That time, to honor them all, has not come. We are now engaging in what looks to be a war without end, a war that includes Iraq, Afghanistan, and Syria, not to mention countries such as Pakistan, Somalia, and Yemen, where we are utilizing drones and Special Forces against terrorists.

The organizers of the parade that began under the glistening arch in St. Louis did not wait for approval. Coming Home Project did not wait for government funding that never came. Iraq and Afghanistan Veterans of America and The Mission Continues, two of the most robust nonprofit advocacy and service programs in the country, did not wait for approval. They seized the moment to cultivate a grassroots movement, working shoulder-to-shoulder with civilians in the community on public service projects.

Civilians have had to mobilize, and family members have had to fight, to be recognized as partners in reintegration. Tonia Sargent helped her marine husband Ken "take back his life" after he sustained a devastating head injury. When Ken entered a highly regarded VA polytrauma unit, Tonia was instructed to return home so as not to interfere with his treatment, to "leave it to the experts." But she refused to go away—would not "in a million years" take a back seat in her husband's rehabilitation. She fought doggedly to have the role of family members recognized as integral in the treatment of survivors of traumatic brain injury. Her tenacious efforts, and those of thousands of partners and parents, siblings and grandparents, are gradually changing the face of veteran care—not just for their veterans, but for all. The aspiration to be whole is not just self-directed. With the right ingredients, in the right environment, veterans and families share their quest for inner peace with their comrades and with other families. As their peace becomes consolidated, they share it with their communities, for the benefit of all.

Scott Thompson is a former Army chaplain, psychotherapist, and director of the Veterans Mental Health Coalition, a program of the Mental Health Association of New York City. Some years ago, he was developing programs at Intersections International to encourage social dialogue and peace initiatives. During a planning meeting a young staff member described having had a number of her friends go off to serve in Iraq and not return. On the recommendation of a colleague Scott invited Larry Winters, a Vietnam veteran who had worked for years at Four Winds Hospital in Katonah, New York, to speak with his team.

With fifteen civilians in the room, Larry said, "You all have something I need for my healing." Scott says he nearly fell out of his chair. "What was it," he wondered, "that the civilians in the room could contribute to Larry?" Then Larry said, "And I think I have something you need for your healing, too." Scott said that "laid him out flat," asking, "What is there left unhealed that only a veteran of war can provide?" In part, civilians could take some of the moral burdens from the shoulders of vets and vets could bring fresh perspective to civilians on the realities and costs of war, wars for which we citizens, with our elected leaders, are responsible for.

Thus was born a series of thirty-five public veteran-civilian dialogues. During a conversation Scott had with John Campbell, then deputy assistant secretary of defense for wounded warrior care, Campbell said, "There's too much 'fix-a-vet' going on; you're bringing civilians and the broader community into the mix." Now, Scott is rolling out another community-building project, Stories We Carry, an initiative of the Mental Health Association of New York City that provides veterans, their families, and their communities a safe space, free of politics, to engage in meaningful conversations about the impact of war on all citizens. During a recent event, Jenny Pacanowski, a female veteran who once served as an Army medic in Iraq, read a poem accompanied by cellist Michael Bacon. Animator and documentary filmmaker Dustin Grella showed *Prayers for*

Peace, a short animated film about his brother who was killed in Iraq.[6] MetLife is sponsoring a series of events at University Performing Arts Centers around the country.

I asked Scott to describe a few veteran-civilian exchanges that remain vivid for him. The visit with Larry was uppermost in his memory. Being a vet was less a part of Scott's sense of identity than with many other vets, in part due to his having served during peacetime and not having seen combat. The first meeting with Larry was "a revelation," as if Scott (the veteran) was the civilian in the civilian-veteran dialogue with Larry, reexperiencing in a new way his connection to his own service and the experience of all veterans. It pointed the way for Scott to leverage his experience as a chaplain in the Army and a therapist, and his community and spiritual inclinations, to be of service in a meaningful and energizing way.

At one event, a civilian woman whose deceased father, a Vietnam vet, had drunk himself silly and created a dangerously violent household, sat opposite an actual Vietnam veteran who stood in for her father. He helped make it possible for her to address artifacts of the war that she had kept sequestered for decades. Scott wondered how many others have similar unarticulated stories. At another dialogue, a young woman vet who had just finished college and was interviewing for jobs, described how she found civilian life boring and yearned to return to Afghanistan. A civilian woman came on stage and sat down beside her. She spoke about how she used to be an addict and how often she would return for the high, even when she was on the threshold of putting together a new life for herself. I wondered to Scott how the veteran heard these words; her story could have come off as offensive, as if she was mistaking a love for her buddies and a desire to serve for an addiction. But it turned out the comment was spot-on. When Scott left, the two women were still talking about the excitement and high of trauma and the draw it can exert.

Coming Home Project has welcomed scores of civilian volunteers. The Jerry and Paula Baker Foundation donated their beautiful retreat center in Yosemite National Forest for our student veterans retreat in 2012. Together with their small cooks, their volunteers, and our logistics and facilitator teams, we made a good team. At the closing circle, Jerry and Paula slipped in unnoticed to our closing circle. What they heard was very moving. Before we finished sharing, I introduced them to participants and mentioned their contribution of the site. The genuine warmth and gratitude was palpable. A few vets said as they left, "Some civilians do care."

The night before the retreat ended, we had our first floating-lantern ritual, organized by Mark Pinto, a former Marine helicopter pilot, who had facilitated the teen group at our first retreat. We made small boats from ice cream sticks, with clear sides and a small enclosed candle in the middle. On small pieces of paper we wrote our wishes for those who were no longer here or for ourselves. The family now also included ancestors and future wishes as well. Then we folded the papers and inserted them into the small boats. We walked silently with flashlights down a windy path to a pond and spread out along the shore. There we lit the candles and set our boats upon the water. For a few minutes we watched silently as they bobbed on the surface of the water, candles flickering. Then we wound our way back, chattering, to the warm lodge for hot chocolate.

V. Moral Injuries and Restoring Integrity

The most entrenched emotional pain my colleagues and I have encountered in our work with veterans relates to the unraveling of meaning and purpose. During a small group meeting of fourteen male veterans at our northern Virginia family retreat, Bob Rodriguez, the Iraq war veteran whose experiences formed the basis of Larry Long's "All Gave Some, Some Gave All," spoke about his issues with anger. He'd go "from zero to 60" in a flash, frightening his wife and two sons. This prompted other vets to talk about becoming almost uncontrollably angry at something they later saw was minor. Their ability to modulate strong surges of emotion had been compromised. The defensive fight-flight system was turbocharged, continuing to fire even after danger had passed. This disturbance, what I call PTsxD, was not that difficult to access. Later, with hesitation and anguish, Bob revealed that every night the vision of an Iraqi boy he almost shot wakes him up. He sees the image of the boy's face through the sights of his weapon. It was not exactly a dream, more like a night visitation. Sometimes the face of one of his sons would flicker back and forth in the same sights, switching places with the Iraqi boy. Emotion welled up as he described these disturbing experiences. It was "damned if you do, damned if you don't . . ." he said, "shoot, that is." He was reliving the torturous dilemma he'd faced on guard duty one late afternoon at the forward operating base he and his fellow Seabees had constructed. It was an impossible choice, an agonizing moment as he lined up a suicide bomber in his rifle sights: Take out the young boy leaning against a fence who looked from the drape of his clothing like he might be wearing a suicide belt and risk killing an innocent boy, a boy like his own sons—or wait a few seconds, exercise restraint, give the boy the benefit of the doubt, and risk his own and his buddies' safety. Bob waited the extra seconds; they seemed like an eternity.

A woman nearby called to the boy just as Bob's fingers began to depress the trigger. A split second longer and the boy would have been dead. Bob thought the woman might have been the boy's mother, calling him for dinner. But she also could have been his handler, realizing that something was wrong with their plan and calling him back to strike later. It has pained him since to think he endangered the safety of his buddies. After Bob shared this experience in the company of fellow veterans who listened without judging, you could see the relief on his face and in his overall demeanor throughout the rest of the retreat. Later, he sent us a message for our newsletter:

> This retreat has been the most helpful seminar, vet group, ptsd group meeting, whatever, that I have personally attended. Being a Navy Seabee, many know us . . . some don't. . . . we build anything, anywhere, anytime . . . our combat training is done by Marine instructors, and also Ranger instructors. "Can Do" is our motto . . . we build . . . we fight. That's just what we do. While in Iraq . . . Balad, and Ar'Ramad we were attached to the 1st M.E.F (Marine Expeditionary Force) so we saw some crap . . . did alot of crap, lost seven brothers our first 30 days in country . . . and the list goes on. Your retreat has helped my wife sort of know the "new me." When Military people "come home" from war and are released to the world of life as normal people it just does NOT WORK for us . . . we dance to a different beat than "regular folks" . . . and it seems as though no one understands us. . . . it's like we have formed our own little world, built of distrust, hate, anger, sadness and those @#@@# nightmares that keep on haunting us . . . So our relationship with our spouse has this new added stress, along with money . . . etc. . . . My wife has breast cancer . . . that's our new fight, but we manage . . . day by day . . . oh yeah, no health insurance for her either . . . so you can see and actually feel the stress we have. My wife and I know others have it much worse and just give it to GOD. And we tell the bill collectors to stand in line. I actually tell them to come on over the house and we can chat in my back yard. Anyway learning meditation and qigong has helped me and my wife to relax some. I now talk to my family, my kids, which has helped. And your staff is excellent. Planning was perfect right down to the last minute. I only wish it was longer . . . lol. Thank you so very much and I really hope to see everyone again at another retreat soon.

Using humor to express his ambivalence about the benefits of "sharing," he finished his letter,

> p.s. . . . just an F.Y.I. TO MY FELLOW VETS . . . DON'T. . . RELEASE AND POUR OUT YOUR GUTS TO YOUR SPOUSE AT BEDTIME . . . they just might fall asleep on you . . . . . . mine did . . .

Another vet, a medic who attended the San Antonio retreat at Mo Ranch, spoke without much trouble about how he had been blown up multiple times during his service in Iraq. But as the group coalesced, he revealed that what tormented him most was having shot a child who was about to throw a grenade into a Humvee full of his buddies. As a medic, he saw himself as a healer, not a killer, and had struggled mightily since returning home to make his peace with what he'd done. Many of his comrades had told him his action saved lives, and he "knew" that was true. Amid the rolling hills, his fellow vets and the group facilitators provided a safe space for him to explore the fault lines in his sense of identity—his frozen grief, self-reproach, and sense of being stuck in moral limbo. Slowly and painfully as the ice began to melt, it became possible for him to grieve and the conflicts lost their black-or-white, either-or, disabling effects. His load lightened. At the end of the retreat, balancing himself with a crutch under one shoulder, he got up and danced with his wife for the first time since his injuries.

A veteran from Texas attended the same retreat with his family. He was rangy, restless, and rambunctious. After the medic told his story, this vet began to unpack his. He said he couldn't imagine ever *not* feeling "bad" (responsible) for the injuries to his unit during a firefight. He resisted any discussion that might let him off the hook. Perhaps he was concerned we'd try to make him "think positive" or "let it go." I was reminded of children who blame themselves for awful things that happen to them, often inflicted by parents or others in protective roles. There is a touch of magical thinking involved: if I am to blame forever, at least things are not completely random. The shockingly real trauma can't rear its head unpredictably again. I don't have to face the utter helplessness, the powerlessness to change things. And the grief that often follows. Self-compassion faces this kind of stiff internal resistance. There were additional steps for this vet to take as he considered putting himself in the hands of his comrades and risking experiencing both the terror and the relief this can engender.

These are examples of PTspD or moral injuries. They are not understandable if seen solely as symptoms of nervous system dysregulation (PTsxD). They reflect impossible choices, things done, almost done, not done, or witnessed that compromise one's core values. They generate a profound anguish that lingers for decades.

Sometimes one's whole world comes crumbling down. In 2004, Kenny, the Marine master sergeant in charge of vehicle maintenance, was riding in a convoy near Najaf. During an ambush, a ricocheting bullet struck him under his right eye and exited near his left ear, causing severe damage to the front of his brain. When I visited him at his home in Oceanside a few years ago, after breakfast his wife Tonia got ready to go to church. After all they'd been through, it had been a while before she could go to church again. She had looked around and decided on a congregation that offered more hope. Kenny was staying back. When I asked why, at first he didn't answer. I waited and eventually he said, "Don't get me wrong, I used to be religious, a devout person, went to church all the time." In fits and starts he described how betrayed he felt, how bereft, as if he had not gotten over being forsaken by God, his church, his religion, all of it. "I didn't kill anyone, I was just a mechanic. I tried to help people." Not only his body but his whole "assumptive world" was blown apart—all the unarticulated beliefs, the ways things were supposed to work. No psychiatric acronym can capture the force of this blow, but terms such as spiritual injury or perhaps PTspD might be used.

The helpless inability to accomplish one's mission can also have devastating impacts. Recall the story of Romeo Dallaire, a general in the Canadian Armed Forces and now a Senator, was the commander of NATO peacekeeping forces in Rwanda during the genocide that took place there in 1994. Members of the Hutu ethnic majority murdered 800,000 people, mostly from the Tutsi minority. Lt. Col. Stephane Grenier was his second-in-command. Grenier spoke after me at a conference at the University of Southern California and lit into me dryly for my use of the term "combat veteran," pointing out that a service member need not have been in a firefight to have experienced the impacts of the war zone. I knew that, but I took the hit. He only mentioned tangentially the heart-wrenching story of how he and his boss were commanding the peacekeeping forces in Rwanda at the time of the mass slaughter. It was not what Grenier and Dallaire had done that caused their massive postwar anguish, but what they were not able to do. Upon returning to Canada, having been unable to prevent the genocide or accomplish their peacekeeping mission, they collapsed. Only after long treatment were they able to pull their lives together again. Men and women who suffer similarly say they would have preferred a physical injury to this kind of inner torture.

Survivor guilt is well-known and frequently encountered. "Why me? Why am I here and he, she, or they are gone?" It doesn't make sense. It seems so capricious, so unjust. It can take years for the surviving veteran to reignite his or her joie de vivre. One element of this pain not often discussed is the profound regret that they were unable to live in accord with their beliefs about good conduct. They wanted to do right, to actualize the ethical codes that meant so much to them, but they were prevented from doing so. Many veterans who feel this way were themselves injured and were physically unable to do more to prevent harm or save their comrades, I believe the sheer frustration at having been immobilized, physically unable to move, the factor so prominent in Porges' account, plays more of a role in survivor guilt than we have previously thought.

An experience I had at the conference at USC has stuck with me. After politely excoriating me for using the term "combat trauma" and, to his mind, ignoring war trauma unrelated to being in direct combat situations, Lt. Col.

Grenier sat next to me in the audience as we awaited the next panel. I had not reacted verbally to what he said. As we sat in a mildly uneasy silence, I felt he was sensing around to determine if I was friend or foe. Perhaps I was silently doing the same. Slowly the unspoken emotional atmosphere became more settled and he shifted his posture, narrowing the distance between us. Then he leaned over and whispered a comment about what the presenter was saying. While we didn't discuss our exchanges, I had the sense that the war trauma that had been reignited for him, including not being understood by psychologists like me upon his return to Canada, was becoming contained. I felt emotionally closer to him.

Then, as his cellphone rang, I felt a current of trauma running through him. He apologetically told me he had to take this call and went out for a few minutes. When he returned I was moved and surprised that he confided to me that a colleague had committed suicide and he must now absent himself to make a call. I intuited that he was calling his comrade Gen. Dallaire, about whom he was now concerned, to give him the news personally. Dallaire also knew the colleague, and both Grenier and Dallaire had been suicidal after returning from Rwanda. This intimacy unfolded without a word of acknowledgment. It illustrated the multiple pathways to creating safety and how moral injuries of war begin to be relationally mediated.

Feeling as if it was all for nothing is a devastating blow. When we add the element of betrayal—by a leader, a government, or a healthcare system—it is a potent mix. Then factor in the incomprehensible reverberations of having killed, of having witnessed death and grave injury, of having acted in ways that are diametrically opposed to one's sense of right and wrong, and the mix is explosive.

The fog of war has a long reach and veterans' narratives can become enshrouded. The recounting of war trauma reveals itself over years. Recall Bob Rodriguez, the Seabee who was beset with guilt for hesitating to shoot a young Iraqi boy who appeared threatening, thereby jeopardizing the lives of his fellow Seabees. Recently Bob called to make sure I had his correct email, and we ended up talking at some length about the incident.

Bob said that he found the shell he used. "What shell?" I thought. "Used for what? You didn't pull the trigger." But with his current telling I realized with a start that he did kill the boy. Bob had never explicitly said this at the retreat in the Virginia countryside in 2008. In fact, given the focus on his guilt for hesitating and endangering his fellows, it seemed clear he had not pulled the trigger.

"The five-year-old boy was coming through the wire," he told me. "I was trying to get him out of the wire. I didn't want to hurt him. When I looked at him, I saw the faces of my own sons." He continued, "I saw something in the shape of a book underneath his shirt." The sequence emerges in this retelling,

"Then I got scared, he was coming through the wire, I looked at his face and saw my sons' faces. I hesitated, then I realized I could be dead, my buddies could be dead, and I got pissed off. I blamed myself for hesitating." Then, "I hit him with my M-16 and pulled the trigger. To this day I don't know, was he wearing a vest and it didn't go off, did they not trigger it, or was he not wearing one?" Bob wanted to excise the experience from his mind, "I kept saying it didn't happen. Said this to two buddies. I picked up the shell and put it in my pocket, I didn't want anyone to know, I didn't want to be known as a baby killer. I just found that shell, again.

"There were fifteen guys behind the wire with me. This happened in middle of July, 2004." Then Bob recounted how an earlier event set the stage for his tragic encounter with the boy: "On June 1, 2004, we found a big rocket that had landed nearby but hadn't gone off. The bomb guys came in and detonated it, a huge blast. I thought of what could have happened had it gone off, we'd all have been dead. I tried to put it out of my head—it didn't happen, it didn't happen, it didn't happen." This blast really had *not* happened to them—it had not blown them up. He really *did* kill the boy—that had happened. He *knew* all this, but sorting through the strands and grieving takes time.

As I was completing this chapter, I happened upon a three-part series on moral injury by David Wood, senior military correspondent for *Huffington Post* and winner of the 2012 Pulitzer Prize for national reporting.[1] It is a well-researched, beautifully rendered, heart-wrenching account. Wood confirms the growing consensus among mental health professionals and many veterans that approaches utilized to address PTsxD, the nervous system dysregulation generated by war trauma, are of limited use when trying to address moral injury. I was not surprised to read that "the Pentagon declined to make policymaking officials available to discuss moral injury." Instead, the Defense Department spokeperson said that moral injury is "not clinically defined" and that there is no "formal diagnosis" for it. DoD, she said, "provides a wide range of medical and non-medical resources for service members seeking assistance in addressing moral injuries."

Although the Army produces new training videos that seek to keep soldiers impacted by moral injuries in the fight, the Pentagon does not actually recognize moral injury. The Navy doesn't use the term, referring instead to "inner conflict." The military brass, according to Marine Maj. Gen. Thomas S. Jones, "is loath to use the word 'moral,' concerned that those outside the military 'will think it means somebody did something immoral,' which may not be the case.'"

If it is not in the military or psychiatric manuals, it must not really exist. Perhaps the military services are reluctant to discuss moral injury because it goes to the heart of military operations and the nature of war. This reluctance, however, isn't limited to the military. Michael Castellana, a psychotherapist who provides moral injury therapy at the U.S. Naval Medical Center in San Diego, says, "Maybe people don't want to talk about or know about what can happen to some of our sons and even some of our daughters when they go defend the country. It's not politically correct. It's not attractive, but it's the truth."[2]

Moral injuries don't just arise from illegal activities such as atrocities and other violations of the Geneva Conventions, they are baked into the war experience. Says Castellana, "If you read the suicide notes, the poems and writings of service members and veterans, it's the killing; it's failing to protect those we're supposed to protect, whether that's peers or innocent civilians; it's sending people to their death if you're a leader; failing to save the lives of those injured if you're a medical professional. Nothing to do with the rightness or wrongness of war."

William Nash, a retired Navy psychiatrist who deployed with marines in Iraq, says, "There is an inherent contradiction between the warrior code, how these guys define themselves, what they expect of themselves—to be heroes, the selfless servants who fight for the rest of us—and the impossibility in war of ever living up to those ideals. It cannot be done. Not by anybody there." Nick Rudolph, a former marine, says, "You know it's wrong . . . but you have no choice."[3]

Integrity and morality are motive forces, more impactful in their absence than their presence. When integrity is corrupted or violated, as was revealed during VA scandals where managers knowingly deceived veterans and Congress, the country responded with indignation. When the deception continued, and VA legalistically disclaimed responsibility for veterans who died as a result of employees' misconduct or criminal behavior, Rep. Jeff Miller, chair of the House Veterans Affairs Committee, became irate about the disingenuous word spin and abdication of accountability. But our memories are short, and righteous indignation fades. Integrity belongs to the unseen realm. The potent impacts of corrupted integrity operate much like the unseen injuries of war. They accrue slowly and fester over time if they are not acknowledged and addressed.

Morality is not moralism. Morality arises from realizing that we are all profoundly interdependent. Service members in the war zone and families on deployment back home know this without being told. My life and your life are contingent. My safety and your safety depend on each other. People and creatures are connected beyond words in a dynamic web of reciprocity. When we forget or ignore this truth, trouble ensues. A person (or group or organization) with integrity lives this out. His life embodies it. She is trustworthy, honest, accountable, dependable. He tries to live his values, let his actions speak. Integrity implies ethical alignment, walking one's talk, while having a benevolent impact. We call people like this by various names; a "straight shooter," a "good man," a real "mensch." Integrity is precarious, however; it needs to be renewed each day, like baking fresh bread. We are all a hair's breath away from "there but for the grace of God go I."

"Spirituality" is one of the most overused and saturated of contemporary words, but still I use it. Most retreat participants and a growing majority of Americans describe themselves as "spiritual but not religious." We want to be part of something greater than ourselves and aspire to more than simple self-aggrandizement. We want to be more connected to others and to the lives we lead. We want to live with meaning and purpose, to make a benevolent difference. We want to be of use. To embody our fundamental kinship with one another and with all creatures is to live a spiritual life, though some secular humanists and devoutly religious individuals quibble with the word.

After describing a few of the ways people create and sustain pernicious divisions among themselves, Steve Torgerson, in his talks on spirituality at retreats, says that what unites us is a common desire for peace of mind. Everyone resonates with this. Our team has discovered that in a structured environment of unconditional compassion without judgment, within the most tumultuous inner worlds, a sustainable measure of peace can take root. This was what a military treatment facility provider meant when he said at the conclusion of a retreat, "This is what church should feel like."

Reading Wood's piece I was struck by how spiritual qualities imbue accounts from the few programs in the military that address moral injuries. "'Moral injury is a touchy topic, and for a long time [mental health care] providers have been nervous about addressing it because they felt inexperienced or they felt it was a religious issue,' said Amy Amidon, a staff psychologist at the San Diego Naval Medical Center who oversees its moral injury/moral repair therapy group. 'And service members have been very hesitant to talk about it, nervous about how it would affect their career.'"

Brett Litz, a clinical psychologist and professor at Boston University who is affiliated with the VA in Boston, says, "We have no illusion of a quick-fix cure for serious and sustained moral injury. What's new is that we are trying to study it in a more scientific way and finding ways of treating moral injury—and that's unprecedented. It's a slow process, and I am very proud of the fact that we have brought science to bear." Speaking of the results of new research on experimental therapies, Litz added: 'You can't argue with a clinical trial.'" Actually, we *can and should* scrutinize and if need be challenge results of clinical trials. This is science in action. We should also remember that even good data doesn't always translate from experimental situations into daily living.

Patients using the method Litz helped develop are asked to imagine they are revealing their secret to a compassionate, trusted moral authority—a coach or priest. "The assumption here is if there is someone in your life who has your back, cares for you, is compassionate and you have felt their love for you, then you are safe in disclosing what you did or failed to do," Litz explained. "If there is that compassionate love, that forgiving presence, it will kick-start thinking about, well, how do you fix this, how can you lead a good life now?' And that is the beginning of self-compassion."

Unconditional compassion, without judgment, has been the key transformative element in Coming Home Project's work with veterans from all service branches from around the country for more than seven years. The safe environment at Coming Home Project retreats permits the veteran to go beyond "imagining" a compassionate or trusted "authority." The community of fellow veterans and staff *embodies* compassion, unqualified acceptance, and trustworthiness in their flesh-and-blood presence and responsiveness. That they are brother and sister veterans, not an "authority," plays a crucial role.

I question including "forgiving" among the attributes of an imagined compassionate authority. It sounds presumptuous. I'm not alone. Felipe Tremillo, a Marine staff sergeant, took part in the San Diego program last fall. He was asked to write an imaginary letter of apology. It was addressed to a young Afghan boy whom he had glimpsed during a raid in which his unit broke down doors and threw people from their homes while searching for weapons. The boy had stood trembling as Tremillo and the Marines rifled through the family possessions. The boy's eyes seemed to Tremillo to blaze with rage and shame. He felt that he had violated the boy. "I didn't know his name," Tremillo said. But in his letter, "I told him how sorry I was at how I affected his life, that he didn't have a fair chance to have a happy life, based off of our actions as a unit." Writing the letter, he said, *"wasn't about me forgiving myself, [it was] more about accepting who I am now* [italics added]."

In order for the veteran to accept himself as he is now, the community accepts him or her without qualification. The veteran may have committed acts he or she feels are unconscionable, but the community *nonetheless* holds him or her with unconditional compassion and love that does not judge.

How does the moral weight of war get distributed? Most in the veteran community and many civilians, too, agree that the accrued moral weight or "burden" of the past two U.S. wars has fallen disproportionately on veterans and their family members. Scott Thompson and others want to spread that weight around more equitably, engaging the many willing civilians, some of whom have felt deprived of the opportunity to connect with veterans, in dialogue and community building with veterans and families.

Leaders carry a heavy load when it comes to war. They are not exempt from the impacts of war trauma and the events that follow on the heels of their reactions to such trauma. Wood describes Sendio Martz, a veteran whose moral injury involved the weight of command responsibility and the guilt and shame he felt for having been unable to bring all his guys home safe. Martz sees that incident as a failure because he didn't identify the IED and didn't protect his men. "I'd say one of the things I struggle with the most," Martz said, " is, all my guys got hurt and I let them down. It's a constant movie, replaying that scenario over and over in my head. I constantly question every decision I made out there.'"[4]

Elected and appointed leaders likewise are not exempt. Their responses to the weight of this responsibility vary. Some leaders who led our country into war, such as Robert McNamara in Vietnam, came to question and suffer some of their decisions. Others, like Donald Rumsfeld and Dick Cheney, seemed to have felt and learned nothing. Many laugh at how the commander-in-chief who led us into war in Iraq called himself "the decider," but it is a huge responsibility. I cringe that, looking back, he feels no regret and would do things the same way all over again.

On September 11, 2001, George W. Bush was visiting a classroom and sitting in on story time, when his chief of staff, Andy Card, entered and whispered in his ear, "A second plane has hit the second tower; America is under attack." Bush's six-minute-long reaction was classic traumatic dissociation. Ten years on, the children in the classroom at the time and their teacher shared their impressions. "[His face] was like a blank stare," one said of the president. The teacher recounted, "He had left the room. Mentally he was gone." In an interview for a ten-years-on 9/11 documentary, Bush explained his reaction. He said he knew a lot of people were watching his reaction to the crisis and he wanted to project calm. But in the same interview, he described in one word his immediate reaction to receiving the news, "War." Later he added, "I thought 'War' for seven and a half years."[5] We know all too well the disastrous consequences.

I listened to John Kerry being interviewed by various reporters in September 2013 in the run-up to a new possible war with Syria. Here is Kerry with Chris Hayes of MSNBC:

Hayes: If we strike, if we strike Assad, what happens if he uses chemical weapons again? It seems that we have then committed ourselves to an escalated punitive
. . .

Kerry: Well, I . . . I disagree. And, first of all, let— let— let me make this clear. The president—and this is very important, because I think a lot of Americans, all of your listeners, a lot of people in the country are sitting there and saying,

"Oh, my gosh, this is going to be Iraq, this is going to be Afghanistan. Here we go again." I know this. I— I've heard it. And the answer is no, profoundly no. You know, Senator Chuck Hagel, when he was senator, Senator Chuck Hagel, now secretary of defense, and when I was a senator, we opposed the president's decision to go into Iraq, but we know full well how that evidence was used to persuade all of us that authority ought to be given.

Then Kerry, seemingly out of the blue, volunteered something remarkable, "I can guarantee you, I'm *not* imprisoned by my memories of or experience in Vietnam, I'm informed by it. And I'm not imprisoned by my memory of how that evidence was used, I'm informed by it. And so is Chuck Hagel."[6]

Later in the interview Kerry reiterated the point. He would go on to repeat the same words, "I am *not* imprisoned by my memory of Vietnam," over and over to interviewers. Each time I heard him repeat this statement, I believed it less. The repetition reminds me of the line adapted from *Hamlet*, "Methinks thou doth protest too much." In other interviews, Kerry seemed shaken by the damage caused by bombings and the use of chemical weapons, especially with children, something he surely witnessed in Vietnam. I think his gruesome Vietnam War experiences were triggered beneath the threshold of his conscious awareness, propelling him to feel and remember less and to act more, going into full mobilization mode in the face of threat.

Saying repeatedly with measured rationality that his support of bombing Syria was unrelated to his experience in Vietnam did not make it so. To the contrary, in the mind of this psychoanalyst author, who would have preferred to avoid another war, it was a "show." I was thankful when Kerry later unintentionally cracked open a closed door—with an uncanny throwaway comment about what it would take to reopen negotiations with the Russians—that helped bring about a diplomatic solution for Syria's chemical weapons through a joint agreement on monitoring.

Navy Cmdr. Steve Dundas, a chaplain, went to Iraq in 2007 "bursting with zeal to help fulfill the Bush administration's goal of creating a modern, democratic U.S. ally. 'Seeing the devastation of Iraqi cities and towns, some of it caused by us, some by the insurgents and the civil war that we brought about, hit me to the core,' Dundas said. 'I felt lied to by our senior leadership. And I felt those lies cost too many thousands of American lives and far too much destruction.'" Like Kenny, the Marine master sergeant we met earlier, Dundas returned home "broken, his faith in God and in his country shattered. In addition, he was diagnosed with chronic severe PTSD. Over time, with the help of therapists, friends, and what he calls his 'Christmas miracle,' his faith has returned."[7]

At Coming Home Project, we've heard similar stories about leaders' lack of integrity. But we've heard more grievances about the failures of caregiving institutions. Many veterans, like Jessie, the sergeant major blinded in an IED attack, felt a profound sense of betrayal—a broken compact—the result of systemic breaches of integrity in institutions such as VA and DoD, which resulted in their being denied care and benefits they had earned by their service. Sometimes the aggrieved emotions become so intense as they spiral and amplify that we ask participants if this is how they want to spend their small-group time.

What does integrity look like? What does it look like when someone takes the hit, manages his internal reactions to trauma, and musters a wise response, in accord with circumstances? This story, closer to home and in a peacetime context, illustrates how our response to trauma can make all the difference. On August 9, 2014, in Ferguson, Missouri, a police officer killed an unarmed black teenager, sparking massive street protests. The local police department responded by bringing in military vehicles, using tear gas, and confronting demonstrators, who were primarily peaceful, in a threatening manner, as if they were enemies in a war zone. This inflamed the situation and caused an alarming escalation. When the governor placed the Missouri Highway Patrol in charge of security, things changed. Ron Johnson, a captain in the Highway Patrol, took a different approach, backing away from the ineffective tactics used by the police. He took to the streets by himself to meet and hear from the local people. "We're gonna start from today," said Capt. Johnson. "We're not gonna look back in the past when we talked about boots on the ground . . . *my boots will be on the ground* and actually I plan on tonight myself walking to QuikTrip, that has been called Ground Zero, and meeting with the folks there. And so we are gonna have a different approach, *the approach that we're in this together* [italics added]."[8]

Integrity takes different forms in different situations, and morality can inform decisions differently. But Capt. Johnson's integrity and its impacts were indubitable, in spite of the fact that a very few in the large crowds were provoking a violent confrontation, which brought in the National Guard.

Staying alive and functional with moral injuries requires that service members compromise their own integration by relying on complete emotional detachment, dissociation, and the unraveling of the fluid alignment among values, beliefs, behavior, and emotional experience. In Woods' piece, Marine Sgt. Clint Van Winkle writes about a 2003 combat deployment in Iraq. A car carrying two Iraqi men approached a Marine unit and a marine opened fire, putting two bullet holes in the windshield and leaving the driver mortally wounded and his passenger torn open but alive, blood-drenched and writhing in pain. The two Iraqis may have been innocent civilians. The Marines may have been obeying the strict rules of engagement, but the damage was still done.

"The only way to absorb such experiences," Van Winkle writes, was to 'make it impersonal and tell yourself you didn't give a shit one way or another, even though you really did. It would eventually catch up to you. Sooner or later you'd have to contend with those sights and sounds, the blood and flies, but that wasn't the place for remorse. There was too much war left. We still had a lot of killing to do.'"

Van Winkle's viewpoint has changed slightly. "I tried to make myself and my marines live up to those moral standards," he said. "I mean, we weren't pushing people around. We weren't doing things we shouldn't have been doing, although things happened by accident. *I was doing what I was supposed to be doing, and bad things still happened* [italics added]."⁹

The Turn toward Malfeasance and Evil

Jonathan Shay, the psychiatrist who examined war and homecoming in Homer's *Iliad* and *Odyssey*, writes from the perspective of fundamental interdependence that so many service members in the war zone grasp intuitively.

> The bright line between murder and legitimate killing is something that our most junior enlisted person cares deeply about. When they kill somebody who didn't need to be killed, they are really wounded themselves.¹⁰

Not all service members feel these wounds. Wood recounts the story of Steve Canty, a former marine. During his second deployment to Afghanistan, Canty shot and killed an Afghan who was dragged into the Marines' combat outpost just before he died. "I just lit him up," Canty said. "One of the bullets bounced off his spinal cord and came out his eyeball, and he's laying there in a wheelbarrow clinging to the last seconds of his life, and he's looking up at me with one of his eyes and just pulp in the other. And I was like 20 years old at the time. I just stared down at him . . . and walked away." Then Canty demonstrates Van Winkle's strategy of complete emotional disconnection, "I will . . . never feel anything about that. I literally just don't care whatsoever." He asked himself, "Are you some kind of sociopath that you can just look at a dude you shot three or four times and just kind of walk away? I think I even smiled, not in an evil way but just like, what a fucked-up world we live in—you're a 40-year-old dude and you probably got kids at home and stuff, and you just got smoked by some dumb 20-year-old." Canty continues,

"You learn to kill, and you kill people, and it's like, I don't care. I've seen people get shot, I've seen little kids get shot. You see a kid and his father sitting together and he gets shot and I give a zero fuck.'" He is speaking about going numb, the desensitization and dehumanization inherent in war. He poses critical moral and philosophical questions but without altering his blanket renunciation of emotion, a strategy that holds him together. Canty says, "Once you're able to do that, what is morally right anymore? How good is your value system if you train people to kill another human being, the one thing we are taught not to do? When you create an organization based around the one taboo that all societies have?"

Canty is highly intelligent and seems to never stop analyzing. The constant monitoring serves to fill up all the internal space. There's none available for feeling anything about what happened. "My thought was, you did what you had to. But did I really? I saw him running and I lit him up. It's the right thing to do in war, but in every other circumstance it's the most wrong thing you could do," he said. "'We keep going regardless of knowing the cost, regardless of knowing what it's gonna do,' Canty says. 'The question we have to ask the civilian population is, is it worth it, knowing these mental issues we come home with? *Is it worth it?* [italics added]'"[11]

I agree with Canty. Veterans should pose this vital question to the civilians who direct the DoD, to our commander-in-chief who makes the decision to go to war, to the Congress which is supposed to ratify it, to the departments that carry it out. They should pose the question to all who elect leaders and representatives, and citizens should in turn pose it to their leaders. I didn't speak with Canty, so I may be missing the affect that comes across in the human voice. But when he speaks about civilians and raises important questions for us all, I think he is also externalizing, unable or unwilling to really come face-to-face with the horrors he experienced in war, his actions and reactions, and his inability to feel and care about them.

Although Canty worries he might be a sociopath, with all the moral questions he raises he is missing the sociopath's slick presentation and stone coldness. Recall the service member who asked why he couldn't just will away his inner anguish relating to incidents that were already over. Others echoed his frustration. I paused, uncertain how to respond. "Because you have a beating heart," I finally said, "because you're human." We see Canty working overtime to repudiate his beating heart in the face of the brutality of war, and his own. He keeps one step ahead of his ghosts, fighting off becoming a puddle of tears. He is shocked by the extent to which he goes to disconnect his emotional responses. But unlike a sociopath, there are cracks in his story, cracks he works feverishly to repair. Sociopaths are smooth operators with nary a crack in their presentation. In the last eight years working with thousands of veterans, I've only met one with the symptoms of sociopathy.

The Heart of Darkness

I might have picked it up when he introduced himself in the small men's veterans group by saying that the one thing he missed about military service was being able to do things that are illegal back home. He could simply have been honest, expressing what more than a few veterans feel. I might have suspected it when he surrendered a 9mm automatic pistol for safekeeping after arriving and learning how serious we were about our no weapons policy. But he certainly wasn't the only one who'd brought a weapon to a retreat.

As the group progressed, I saw that he meant it; he had joined the service so he could "do things he'd be put in jail for back home." He enjoyed killing. But this too is a secret kept by some vets and not that unusual given the adrenaline rush and the thrill of combat. I knew we were in different territory when he said he had taken pictures of each of his "kills," including young and old, men and women. He kept them in a special place and would bring them out to view from time to time. It wasn't until, during a discussion about relationships, that it came together. He said he had had a few girlfriends since returning from the war and would show them the photos of his "kills" as they expressed their admiration. A chill went down my spine. There was silence in the group. I glanced around the room; judging from their body language, the other vets took note. But their bond of loyalty with their comrade did not change.

* * *

"Stalking from home to home [Staff Sgt. Robert Bales] . . . methodically killed at least 16 civilians, 9 of them children, in a rural stretch of southern Afghanistan. . . . Residents of three villages in the Panjwai district of Kandahar Province described a terrifying string of attacks in which the soldier, who had walked more than a mile from his base, tried door after door, eventually breaking in to kill within three separate houses. The man gathered 11 bodies, including those of 4 girls younger than 6, and set fire to them . . ."[12]

Staff Sgt. Robert Bales was deployed four times to Iraq and Afghanistan over ten years and was angry about being sent to Afghanistan. The family had hoped to be stationed in Germany, Italy, or Hawai'i.[13]

At trial prosecutors described Bales as "a frustrated soldier prone to drinking and violent outbursts. They said that he had been in deep financial trouble, that he wanted to divorce his wife, and that he was upset about being passed over for a promotion to sergeant first class. They said he was a man frustrated with his career and family, easy to anger, whose rage erupted at the end of his M-4 rifle. 'He liked murder,' a prosecutor, Lt. Col. Jay Morse, said in closing arguments . . . 'he liked the power it gave him.' They described Sergeant Bales as a 'methodical killer,' uncaring and unrepentant, 'Sergeant Bales not only had no remorse, but knew everything he was doing, Colonel Morse said. 'He decided to take out his aggression on the weak and the defenseless.'"[14] The jury agreed, convicted him, and sentenced him to life in prison.

Witnesses recalled him as "a loving son and neighbor, a devoted father, a generous high-school buddy and a brave soldier who endured explosions and bore witnesses to the bloody horrors of Iraq's insurgency." In arguing for parole, the defense team said Sergeant Bales was "a broken man . . . a loving father and a stand-up friend before snapping after four combat deployments to Iraq and Afghanistan." His wife, Karilyn Bales, interviewed on *Today*, said the recent happenings were "unbelievable," and added, "I have no idea what happened, but he would not—he loves children. He would not do that."[15]

At a hearing to determine his eligibility for parole, "Sergeant Bales sat quietly, his hands often clasped in front of him . . . sometimes watching as prosecutors displayed video images of the carnage. He said he understood the terrible cost of what he had done. He offered a tearful apology for gunning down sixteen unarmed Afghan civilians inside their homes. . . . "What I did is an act of cowardice," he said, choking up on the witness stand. "I'm truly, truly sorry for those people whose family members I've taken away. . . . If I could bring their family members back I would in a heartbeat. . . . I can't comprehend their loss. I think about it every time I look at my kids. I know I murdered their family. I took that away from them."

Bales also "spoke tearfully about how he had disgraced his family. And with particular emotion, he apologized for shaming the Army and staining the reputation of the 'really good guys, some heroes' who had served alongside him during three deployments to Iraq and one to Afghanistan."[16] Was his emotional expression of remorse a strategy, staged to buy the possibility of eventual freedom? I wasn't there, but from all accounts, it would have had to be a very good acting job.

Although he did not offer an explanation—"I don't know why," he said— Bales described how "after returning from his tours in Iraq, he slid deeper into a pit of anger, weakness and fear. He said he had attended counseling but quit after about a month and a half after failing to see any improvements. He said he had not been eager to return to combat for a fourth deployment."

It is striking that no medical experts were called at trial on Bales' behalf. My colleague, retired Army psychiatrist Elspeth Cameron Ritchie, has written about the possible involvement of mefloquine, also known as Lariam, an antimalarial drug.[17] "You're ready to take that plunge into hurting someone or hurting and killing yourself, and it comes on unbelievably quickly," said one Special Forces soldier diagnosed with permanent brain damage from Lariam. "It's just a sudden thought, it's the right thing to do. You'll get a mental picture, and it's in full color."[18] Although there is no evidence Bales took the drug while in Afghanistan, Ritchie says the drug can affect behavior years later.

"Sergeant Bales said he had been seeing threats everywhere, spotting phantom bombs and Taliban where other soldiers saw nothing. The day before the shooting, he spent eight hours hacking away at a fallen tree that Taliban fighters had used as a landmark for placing roadside bombs. 'I couldn't let it go,' he said, seeming to refer to the fresh deaths of some comrades in an IED blast he couldn't get out of his mind."

Bales apparently had a history of violent outbursts when drinking and had also been taking steroids. Combined with the effects of the Lariam prescribed in Iraq, this could have predisposed him to violent outbursts. But witnesses describe a very methodical approach, not a blind, impulsive outburst. What triggered his murderous rampage on that particular night? Was it his inability to address the ghosts of the killings of dead buddies?

There are multiple factors at play here. The trial, by its judicial nature, oversimplifies. Prosecutors need to prove guilt beyond a reasonable doubt and rule out insanity. In their narrative, Bales was a murderer who wanted to brutally kill innocent Afghan civilians. There are intimations in the prosecutor's case of the word "psychopath" but the reports I've read don't indicate if the term was used. Again, Bales would have to be quite a good actor to so smoothly pull off the tearful apologies, particularly when he was apologizing to the comrades he served with. He does not sound like a psychopath. The psychotic symptoms a few nights before the killings could have been a result of severe PTspD. If the Lariam primed the fuse, what ignited it? What was the role of moral injury, as well as traumatic brain injury and multiple deployments, on his decision to drink so much or to take steroids?

It's worth listening to someone who knew Bales well, on the job, over a long period of time, "In a letter read to jurors on Friday, a former supervisor of Sergeant Bales said that the heavy toll of combat tours, growing stress and personal problems seemed to reach a critical mass that night in Kandahar. 'I believe he was finally overwhelmed by witnessing the deaths and injuries of the soldiers he loved so much,' the officer wrote. '*The darkness that had been tugging at him for the last ten years swallowed him whole* [italics added].'"[19]

William Nash, the retired Navy psychiatrist who deployed with marines to Iraq as an embedded therapist, says "The ideals taught at Parris Island" [where enlisted marines receive training], are the best of what human beings can do. It's these values that give you some chance of doing something good in a war, and limiting collateral damage, however 'right or wrong' the war itself is. The problem, he said, is that 'war will break these values.' Nash continues, 'there is an inherent contradiction between the warrior code, how these guys define themselves, what they expect of themselves—to be heroes, the selfless servants who fight for the rest of us—and the impossibility in war of ever living up to those ideals. It cannot be done. Not by anybody there.'"[20]

What is the moral responsibility of those who decide to send our boys and girls, men and women—our "treasure"—to war? How do they carry it? Repudiate it? What about the VA managers around the country who lied about waiting times, possibly contributing to the deaths of veterans? How do they rationalize this to themselves? Is it a function of overwork? Dehumanization? Disconnecting the dots of personal responsibility in the face of, or in order not to feel, one's own experience of war trauma? What about feeling justified, entitled, given the strains one is under? What about revenge? What are the steps along the slippery slope that lead to employee malfeasance and the kind of evil Bales acted out?

Civilians are not cut from a different cloth than service members and veterans. We are all capable of inflicting harm and do so daily, in large and small ways. Stanley Milgram's now famous experiment showed just how cruel ordinary people can become with modest impetus and within a very short time. While the impacts of war leave no one untouched, we respond differently. Stephen Canty was forever questioning himself and civilians. Although this kept him from feeling, it revealed that he still has a beating heart.

Canty ponders how, after shooting an Afghan man three or four times, he was able "to just kind of walk away." He thinks he "even smiled, not in an evil way but just like, what a fucked-up world we live in."[21] At least Canty is pondering. In *The Unknown Known*, the documentary about former Secretary of Defense Donald Rumsfeld by Errol Morris, Rumsfeld takes great delight in evading responsibility. The smirk that comes over his face when he parries another honest question is eerie. Canty's smile, and even his disavowal of malevolent intent, is accessible, even as it involuntarily replaces horror, an emotion that seems unbearable to him. But Rumsfeld smiles like a Cheshire cat, leaving me wondering what ever happened to his beating heart.[22]

The internal working models we use to understand things, just under the threshold of awareness, help us see things we otherwise wouldn't. They can also obscure things so they become "hidden in plain sight." I've found the ideas of my psychoanalyst colleague Neville Symington useful in understanding the impacts of trauma, our responses to them, and how some responses perpetuate and amplify the trauma.

Human beings are intimately interconnected. Legend has it that the Buddha said, "This is because that is." In *Emotion and Spirit*, Symington writes of the "unseen emotional action" that occurs within and between people.[23] Although such unconscious activity may not be apparent, it is active and we can become aware of it. It is not secret; it takes shape and operates in our daily interactions. Of course, it also manifests in war. Retired four-star military commander Stanley McChrystal wrote in his memoir "about how breaking down doors in Iraq and scattering the residents made him feel 'sick.' As I watched I could feel in my own limbs and chest the shame and fury of the helpless civilians.'"[24]

Symington describes how—through our unconscious response to trauma—we either repudiate this intrinsic mutuality and encapsulate ourselves, or we embrace it, giving rise to an archetype he calls "the lifegiver." In Hebrew, the word *teshuvah* literally means "repentance," but it also refers to an inward turning toward the truth of the moment. We choose, or not, to attend to what is actually going on, to turn toward the truth of what is happening in and around us. Symington calls this choosing "the lifegiver," an unconscious turning toward inner truth and away from narcissistic self-encapsulation. It requires faith and trust. It also requires (and develops) the capacity to tolerate rather than evade frustration. This unconscious activity begins early and continues throughout life. By choosing the lifegiver, we are generating a source of creative and authentic emotional life. By repudiating it, we are identifying with fragmented by-products of traumatizing situations and people and enclosing ourselves in a narcissistic envelope. We repudiate the lifegiver out of fear of the devastating potential of psychic pain. Recall that in one study of military suicide, the most common element present in attempts was profound emotional anguish.

These ideas don't overlook the role of the surround—the war zone, for example—in the etiology of trauma. Rather, they speak to our responsive, if often unconscious, participation in what evolves. We are not simply a function of what has happened to us, even severe traumas. We are what we make, unconsciously as much as consciously, with the cards we are dealt. When we turn away from pain, death, and war, we may be turning away from life as well. While this is reactive and survival driven, the protective strategies we develop take on a life of their own and can become obstructive, even malevolent, forces to be reckoned with.

I do not subscribe to Freud's theory of a death drive, or Thanatos instinct, although I recognize its power as a by-product of the repudiative unconscious choice Symington describes. Neither do I think humans are innately good. Rather, we are intrinsically capable of good and evil, but neither is written in.

Bales' supervisor believes the former Army sergeant was "swallowed whole by the darkness that had been tugging at him for ten years." He thinks that "witnessing the deaths and injuries of the soldiers he loved so much" triggered Bales' massacre. I suggest the following, mostly unconscious, arc: In the heart of darkness, Bales was consumed by overwhelming emotion, without the inner capacity and social support to bear and transform it. In extremis and unable to undo traumatic losses, he threw in his lot with violence and threw his morality and humanity to the wind. Revenge and helpless rage, buttressed by feelings of righteous entitlement, fueled by a toxic mix of drugs and alcohol, made for a terrifyingly seductive and destructive psychic fuel. Mass killing, whether it follows or breaks military codes of morality, makes one feel alive and purposeful amidst internal deadness and helplessness. Even if it is in service of evil.

Malfeasance and evil behavior are not limited to service members and other individuals. Policymakers, "deciders," and institutions are equally capable, especially when they spout platitudes about "supporting our troops" while not supporting top-flight care for veterans. Hypocrisy is the mother's milk of corrupted integrity. Gilbert and Sullivan nailed it when they wrote lyrics for their operetta, *H.M.S. Pinafore*, "Things are seldom what they seem, skim milk masquerades as cream."

The stated reasons for the U.S. invasion of Iraq were to liberate the Iraqi people from oppression and make the American people and the world more secure from the threat of weapons of mass destruction. That decision, it is now widely agreed, was made on the basis of faulty, and some would say cooked, intelligence. When Rory would seethe with anger at the administration for the death of his buddies, he was expressing a moral injury, a blow to implicit trust. He was reacting to a betrayal of integrity. President Bush's decision to invade, supported by his advisors and our elected representatives, had disastrous consequences, quite different from his stated goals. Many question our country's true motives, citing control of oil reserves and financial gain as among the true, if barely hidden, motives. Others think Bush was simultaneously avenging and showing up his father: avenging (and protecting) him for having had a price put on his head, outdoing him by having the will to finish the job his father had left undone—removing Saddam Hussein from power and bringing democracy to Iraq. It didn't take long for the strategic prediction based on our stated motives—we would be greeted as liberators and the job would be a slam dunk—to be proven wrong. Iraqis came to feel, with good evidence, that the United States had a different set of motives from those we claimed. Most of those we were helping did not feel "helped."

I've learned to refrain mostly from questioning people's intentions. With very few exceptions, people, including leaders and their institutions, have the best of intentions. But motivation is multiple and mostly unconscious, as Freud discovered. Sanctimonious righteousness often covers over more self-serving motives. The road to hell is indeed lined with good intentions. Intention should not be confused with consequences, "A mosquito's intent is to draw blood from you. But the consequence could be that you get malaria."[25]

In Buddhism, it's not our stated goals but our true intentions that matter. In order to know these, we usually have to look back and closely observe the impacts of our behavior. It is possible but arduous to do this in real time. Behavior consists not just in kinetic activity but in conscious and unconscious beliefs, attitudes, and emotions. These all matter. The seeds we plant with our behavior grow in ways we never imagined and they last for a long time.

In 2003, as the drumbeats to war with Iraq grew louder, I became alarmed about the seeds our invasion would plant. I knew they would cause great damage throughout our country and the world, damage that would last a very long time. But I felt helpless to change the direction our leaders were taking us. Something good came out of my struggle, namely the Coming Home Project, a nondenominational and nonpartisan organization that has helped many. But as we've seen, the results of our individual and collective encounters with trauma are never entirely benevolent.

We are now—with the collapse of Iraq, the inability to forge inclusive political solutions, and the rise of ISIS (Islamic State of Iraq and al-Sham)—able to see the fruits of our actions. The seeds planted by that long war did not make Americans, Iraqis, the Middle East, or the world safer or more secure. To the contrary, the region and the economy are in freefall. Yet, we seem to have learned little. As I write, we are beginning another war in a region so complex as to defy realistic predictions and exit strategies.

The ripple effects of these actions and inactions on veterans, families, and providers have been significant. The United States was unprepared to provide high-quality care for our service members and veterans and their families as a result of the wars in Afghanistan and Iraq. In an act of profound ignorance and disrespect, we took our veterans for granted.

I worry we are about to repeat this unconscionable error. We would do well to reflect on the question posed by former marine Steven Canty and other veterans, "Is it worth it?" We would all benefit from a robust national debate. But no one— not Congress, not the administration, and apparently not the general public—has an appetite for the precious and dying Town Hall element of our democratic heritage. The public is war-weary and politicians, concerned almost exclusively about being reelected, are currently avoiding going on record in support of or against war with ISIS. The administration, wary of congressional divisiveness and dysfunction, won't be hamstrung in defending the safety of the United States. The result is the same absence of buy-in, or skin in the game, that has plagued us since 2002.

Since troops come home to communities, if our communities are not strong and *integrated*, the warriors cannot *reintegrate*. What matters most is building the connective tissue of mutual support—otherwise veterans and families may once again fall through the cracks, their care providers may become more overwhelmed, and the integrity of our institutions will remain compromised. At this writing, we are again abdicating that responsibility, thus planting seeds of inattention, disrespect, and grave damage.

The Obama administration claims its authority to go to war with ISIS from the 2001 authorization for the use of military force against al-Qaeda following the terror attacks of September 11, 2001. "I could not disagree more," Tim Kaine, senator from Virginia, said. "You don't ask people to sacrifice their lives until the nation has debated and committed to the mission. *It's immoral.*"[26]

The slippery slope to a wide-scale war has been engaged. Just as President Obama was telling the country we would have "no boots on the ground," we learned there are already boots on the ground, and more to come. Just as we learned these boots belong to advisors and trainers only, we heard that the line between advisors and combatants was fuzzier than originally presented. We heard about surgical strikes and imagined that armed drones might create less trauma among drone pilots and their families than pilots who fly manned craft. But this too couldn't be further from the truth. And we lean heavily on valiant Special Forces without comprehending how profoundly they and their families suffer through ten and more tours of duty.

It is a breach of trust to indulge in sanctimonious self-serving rhetoric while being chronically inattentive to the consequences of going to war on service members, veterans, and families. Our refusal to engage a democratic, inclusive, and integrated process with regard to starting or entering new wars compromises our collective morality. Such betrayals, as we should have learned, do not bode well for veterans or country. They sow the seeds of future moral injuries. Only by acting with integrity, activating a robust, diverse community fully invested with skin in the game, can we hope to attenuate the wounds of war, helping veterans transform their ghosts and become full participants in civic life. We are unfortunately headed in the opposite direction again. And the kicker is that by now, this dissociative spell, this trance of oblivion, feels so normal.

Integrity is intimately tied in to integration—diverse parts functioning in good-enough harmony. This requires—before, during, and after war—that we wake up to what is really going on inside and out, and act in alignment with what we learn to be true. It requires welcoming back, individually and collectively, dissociated pieces of heart and mind, body and soul that were sequestered away in order to survive. We've seen how this happens in Coming Home retreats as we create a durable connective tissue of community and provide a safe, diverse culture of social connection, justice, and dignity. We've looked at ways this happens between veterans and families and the civilian communities they come home to. And we've examined how, as a nation, we can address breaches of integrity in a proactive and preventive way, using our own democratic heritage of vigorous cooperation. Together we can knit a national connective tissue, a net of safety and support for veterans and their families, crafted from respect that stops, reflects, learns from experience, and anticipates consequences. This is what "leaving no one behind" means.

What can policymakers learn from this book? The characteristics that help transform war trauma—at Coming Home Project retreats, in clinics that treat moral injury, or collectively in our communities—are the same characteristics that drive a diverse, robust, functional democracy. War trauma is an equal opportunity tormentor; it does not discriminate. Wise, compassionate, united, multidimensional action cuts across the boundaries of individual and collective, psychological and social, political and spiritual. It ripples far and wide and lasts a long time, even when we don't see its salutary effects immediately, and even if we must pass through discomfort and pain to taste its fruits.

Clinical methods alone will not succeed with war trauma. True healing takes a community to restore the scales of justice. Peace (of mind), freedom (expanded behavioral and relational repertoires), and justice (integrity) are interwoven. Optimal environments for healing, learning, and connecting (including those charged with "doing the people's business") are inclusive, diverse, robust cultures of compassion and service, communities of integrity and responsibility.

Although I had a steep learning curve getting up to speed with military culture, it took me even longer to realize just how marginalized veterans are, individually and as a culture. While discussing with my friend David Rabb his presentation on military cultural competency for Coming Home Project's "Invisible Wounds of War" collaboration with University of California TV, he told me about an experience that both disturbed and inspired him. It illustrates another way to restore integrity:

"My wife Kim worked as a substitute teacher at a Bay Area school. She thought it would be great for me to talk to the kids about Veterans Day. The school principal called the day before to confirm. She had one request, that I not show up in my uniform. She was concerned the parents might get upset with my being in the military and talking to their kids. I was torn by this request, as I was on active duty serving as a military liaison at the VA Medical Center and Polytrauma Unit. After some thought, I decided I could not honor the principal's request. I found it despicable and morally unethical. For God's sake, it was 2008, and the military was at war defending the liberties of this country. Service members were being killed in action or severely injured. I couldn't comprehend the callousness and lack of consideration of some civilians."

The following year "Kim was teaching at a private school. Again, she asked if I would speak to the children about Veterans Day. I agreed, as long as I could wear my uniform. The principal was agreeable. When I went to the local library to research books on veterans and the military appropriate for kids seven to fourteen, I was stunned that there were no books at all on the subject for kids. They had two floors of books and three children's librarians, a pretty well-off community. The only book that even mentioned Veterans Day was a book on American holidays.

"The final straw came when I was contacted by the chief of volunteer service at the VA Medical Center who informed me that an after-school teacher had contacted him wanting someone to talk with her students. I was the first person that came to mind, he said. After some reluctance, I called the teacher. She informed me that she had given her class of thirty students a simple assignment: draw or write about what a veteran is. Half of the them drew American flags and the other half (mostly boys) drew scenes of war with plenty of blood and guts. The teacher was stunned. She knew there was more to the military than American flags and warfighting. After I met with the teacher and saw the students' drawings, I was surprised too. I agreed to come and provide information about the role of the military and why we need to honor and respect veterans. After that presentation, I decided to collaborate with two of the students and their parents to publish a children's book, *From A to Z: What a Veteran Means to Me. A Look into the United States Armed Forces Culture and Veterans Community.*"

The book was beautifully illustrated by one of the students with editorial help from her sister. Some time later, at a nearby elementary school, volunteers from Coming Home Project and Google gathered, one for every class. Some volunteers were veterans or family members. As we read from the new book, the kids showed keen interest. They asked simple and disarming questions that dealt with war, death, and the effects on families and civilians. There was real give and take. Just as toddler Ben, during a moment of silence, had spoken the first words at the first Coming Home Project retreat, "My Daddy died in Iraq," these children were modeling the vigorous and honest discussion our representatives and leaders are unwilling to engage in themselves. Inclusive, grassroots community action, inspired by children—that's a way forward to restore integrity.

VI. All the Way Home

———•◆•———

Ancestors

In many traditional cultures, home is where the bones of the ancestors lie. In Pa'ia, Hawai'i, during the annual Obon festival, families gather at the old Zen temple by the sea in brightly colored traditional dress for ceremonial music and dance to honor their ancestors. Many are buried right alongside the celebrants in the old cemetery on the temple grounds. Three and four generations dance, as past, present, and future flow together. The spectacle illustrates how we "stand on the shoulders" of those who came before us, literally and figuratively.

At the San Francisco National Cemetery, on the northern slope of the Presidio overlooking the San Francisco Bay, 30,000 Americans are laid to rest, including Buffalo Soldiers, Civil War generals, Medal of Honor recipients, and a Union spy. A few years ago, I walked to the cemetery from my Land's End neighborhood to attend the annual Memorial Day commemoration. Maj. Gen. James M. "Mike" Myatt was one of the speakers. I had met him before. Myatt is president and CEO of the Marines Memorial Association, which each year hosts a ceremony honoring Gold Star families from across California. This two-day event also includes a peer support workshop organized by the families. A patriot's patriot, he is invariably upbeat.

But on this chilly, drizzly summer day in San Francisco, Maj. Gen. Myatt struck a different tone. He spoke of how acutely he was feeling the burden, more than twenty years on, of having, during the first Gulf War, sent men and women under his command—"My men and women"—into harm's way. He described with some difficulty how deeply responsible he felt for their injuries and deaths and for the sacrifices sustained by their families. His voice trembled, and he paused so it wouldn't crack and he wouldn't begin weeping. When he had collected himself, he said something that startled me so I wrote down his exact words. With complete and sincere conviction, he said, "The costs of war are so great that we just have to find ways to resolve our differences that do not involve killing one another."

Myatt's sentiments made me think of someone very different, artist-activist Pete Seeger, whose song "Where Have All the Flowers Gone?" has become part of our national heritage. It evokes the resting place of our ancestors' bones.

Each verse contains a call and response. The first begins, "Where have all the flowers gone, long time passing? Where have all the flowers gone, long time ago." The response, "Gone to young girls every one," evokes the simplicity of children picking flowers in a beautiful meadow. Each verse ends with, "When will they ever learn? When will they ever learn?" In circular fashion, the second verse asks, "Where have all the young girls gone?" They've "gone to young men every one." Where have all the young men gone? They've "gone to soldiers every one." In nations with a draft or mandatory military service, this is literally true. From flowers, to young girls, to young men, to soldiers, the inevitability of the subject draws us in. The call in the fourth verse, "Where have all the soldiers gone?" brings into sharp focus the heart of the matter: war claims soldiers and so many others, "Gone to graveyards every one." With the last verse the song comes full circle, "Where have all the graveyards gone? Gone to flowers every one. When will we ever learn? When will we ever learn?"

I recall visiting Gettysburg; I must have been in sixth grade. Even then it hit me: all the blood that was spilled on these flower-covered fields. In high school we studied John McCrae's poem, "In Flanders Fields."[1] As with the Marine master sergeant who humorously described the rhythms of laughing and crying, this poem, juxtaposing death with birdsong and blossoming, landed with no small impact in the mind and heart of a teenager who didn't yet understand just how much a child of war he was.

> In Flanders fields the poppies blow
> Between the crosses, row on row,
> That mark our place; and in the sky
> The larks, still bravely singing, fly
> Scarce heard amid the guns below.

Verse two gives voice to those ancestors,

> We are the Dead. Short days ago
> We lived, felt dawn, saw sunset glow,
> Loved and were loved, and now we lie
> In Flanders fields.

In 2009, I spent three weeks in Vietnam traveling the country from north to south with Tran Dinh Song, my guide who became teacher and friend. Song was a veteran of the South Vietnamese Air Force and a former history teacher. He introduced me to Vietnamese veterans of the American war: South Vietnamese, North Vietnamese regulars, Vietcong, and their families. I visited the root temple of one of my Zen teachers, Thich Nhat Hanh, and met with a Zen master who had been Nhat Hanh's fellow novice monk more than sixty years earlier.

In 1983, after participating in a workshop with Nhat Hanh on engaged Buddhism at Tassajara Mountain Monastery in California, I traveled to Plum Village, his community in the Dordogne region of southern France, where I spent the next two summers. When I first arrived after a long trip, the only American at the time in a community of Vietnamese refugees, Sister Phuong (now Chan Không) greeted me and showed me around. Moved by the families and children, the simple, heartfelt sense of peace that permeated the place, and all the work that needed to be done on the buildings and in the fields of plum trees and sunflowers, I said, "If there's anything I can do to help, let me know." She replied, "Just to be is enough." Her response stopped me in my tracks and liberated me from the guilt I realized, with her comment, that I felt over our role in the Vietnam War. I had not had to serve because I received a high lottery number, and I spent parts of that period traveling, on "pilgrimage," and studying Zen.

I took Chan Không up on just being that summer and the next, enjoying the simple company of residents, weeding, walking, playing with children, cooking, meditating, laughing, translating, socializing. The polarities of being versus doing and personal benefit versus communal good fell away. The community held the residents, all survivors of war trauma, with a light yet profound touch. The children were at the center, and their parents felt the supportive power of the village. This was clearly not psychological treatment, and there was relatively little formal Zen practice compared to what I was used to in our Japanese-inspired tradition, but the compassionate embrace was palpable. The seeds planted at Plum Village were among the inspirations twenty-five years later to begin the Coming Home Project and our retreats for veterans, their families, and their caregivers.

In 2009, Song and I traveled up the Perfume River in a small boat to the city of Hue and its beautiful shrine. In 1968, Hue was the site of one of the longest and bloodiest battles of the war. On the way back, I wrote a short poem and texted it as soon as I could to a friend back in the states. "Perfume and Blood" helped me with the feelings of traumatic grief while riding on the river's tranquil waters— waters that just "yesterday" had run red with the blood of so many American and Vietnamese young men.

Home

"Home is where the heart is," but both are hard to find at the "heart of darkness." Home is where the bones of the ancestors lie, but we often don't hear their voices, powerfully conveyed in poems such as "In Flanders Fields" or in the voices of living veterans. "Only the dead have seen the end of war," wrote Santayana.[2] Veterans and their families and children have, however, found a home for their humanity in the environments we created at our retreats. Coming home—to the present moment, body and breath, the beauty of redwoods and rivers, the company of fellow veterans, just being—coarises with the transformation of ghosts into ancestors. The results are therapeutic, and beyond simply eliminating symptoms.

Right in the midst of disabling emotional, ethical, and family turmoil, veterans become able to rest. The "beloved community" (Martin Luther King's felicitous phrase) meets the traumatic shockwaves, takes in and contains them, and enables participants to experience a measure of peace. This rest, this peace, this being "at home" provide a great and unanticipated relief.

While completing this book, my computer began acting up. I brought it to a fellow who lives in Hali'imaile, a small town that is home to some of the most majestic banyan trees in Hawai'i. While waiting for the repairs to be done, I sat at a picnic table under one such great tree, in a row of four massive banyans. As I waited, I began to relax, enjoying the serenity and beauty, letting go of my timetables, and soon I became quiet and peaceful. School had let out and two Hawai'ian women were sitting on the grass "talking story" while their children played nearby, checking in every so often to get a snack. An old man, short and thin, with gaunt cheeks, unevenly dyed hair, and a limp, was slowly circling the area. He sat down at the table, kitty-corner from me. He didn't respond to my quiet "hello" and made no eye contact. We sat together quietly under the great tree for about twenty minutes. My hands were folded simply on the table.

No sooner did I take out my pad and pen than the man got up and walked away. He made his way to a spot in the sun where he sat down and folded his hands as mine had been. It struck me that he might have thought I was praying. A Zen phrase came to mind, "the formless field of benefaction." I wondered if, under the sheltering banyan with the families, me, the singing birds, and other living creatures, the man had been drawn to partake in a benevolent atmosphere. I thought how unadorned and uncontrived the goings-on were. I saw families at our retreats just hanging out together during free time and understood how the same peace that permeated these simple events felt healing to veterans and their loved ones, not unlike the way I'd felt at Plum Village. This relief, this rest, are part of coming home. We realize we're *already* home.

There's nothing we have to do, nowhere to get, no one to become. There's no technique to apply and no worry about succeeding or failing. In this atmosphere, deep intertwined strands of anguish loosen, obstructions fade into the background and lose their grip. There is ease and freedom. Here, under the great Hali'imaile banyans, Hawaiian women sit on freshly cut grass, rooted like the trees beside them. A husband returns from work, sits down next to his wife, stretches out and lays his head on her lap as his kids play with their neighborhood friends. They have all the time in the world.

I realize with a start: "Here it is," the "X factor"— this is the activity a safe environment liberates. Veterans, families, and all of us realize it only when we're *already* in the midst of it. Some participants say, "We're not sure how we got there but here we are, feeling close, feeling good for a change." The elusive "there, there," so conspicuous in its absence in many caregiving institutions, is palpable. It's not a gimmick, it's just our beating hearts at rest, "immobilized without fear," as Porges puts it.

This is how we realize and share the healing potential of our humanity. It is not an add-on, it comes built in; would that we remember and seize the opportunity to connect with it. We can't manufacture or replicate it. It's unique each time, but the same, too. It can't be earned and it can't be forfeited. This bountiful source is always there. This feeling of connection, peace, and freedom is available in the particulars of our daily living. It is our true security. We are home.

The shared experience of safety, harmony, and ease helps us immeasurably. Our research shows it to be extremely reliable. The beauty is that it has no purpose. Purposeless ease—the absence of apprehension and the palpable presence of peace—*is* its activity. People feel it. Veterans, family members, and care providers resolve to pass it on rather than talk about it. For a limited time, anxieties recede and our true home, our birthright of peace, is palpably present.

After the Newtown massacre, many asked, "Where is God?" God comes forth as the "beloved community" of people responding selflessly for the benefit of all (Judeo-Christian); as the sangha, the fellowship of an interconnected and boundless web (Buddhism); as "all our relations," the great family of beings, infused with and conveying the Great Spirit (Native American).

We don't have to belong to an organized religion or even believe in God. We do "God's work" when we bring forth our finest qualities, when we unleash the "reparative instinct" in ourselves and others, when we help mend the connections of body and mind, heart and soul that war fractures, when we rebuild trust and integrity. Our response provides the ingredients. Unconditional compassion is not just the province of the Heavenly Father or the Sacred Feminine. With our tuned-in response to suffering, that heavenly sphere is right here now, amid all the madness, damage, and evil.

My friend and collaborator, Steve Torgerson, calls this grace—right in the midst of brokenness. Such grace is possible when war trauma is engaged without reservation, without qualification, and with the compassion and acceptance of a safe, diverse, and harmonious community. This is unconditional love in action, as human as a warm loaf of good bread. It is not blind infatuation, a cultish trick, or the dissociated or inflated state of a leader or a country. We see *more* clearly, our pain and our ghosts become *more* accessible, not less. We do not pull the wool over our eyes or cover emotional pain with "resilience." Healing happens when we're at home.

Turning: Two

"To everything, turn, turn, turn, there is a season turn, turn, turn, and a time for every purpose unto heaven." The lyrics, written by Pete Seeger, adapted from Ecclesiastes, reprise the cyclical imagery from Seeger's, "Where Have all the Flowers Gone?" Today war has become normalized, part and parcel of our everyday lives. In an interview by Stephen Colbert, former Chairman of the Joint Chiefs of Staff Mike Mullen said we are looking at 30–40 years of turmoil in the flammable, unpredictable Middle East. He thinks the United States must remain engaged militarily, though not unilaterally. And he reminded us that the United States has now bombed seven Muslim countries, agreeing with Colbert that this has not helped our world standing.

We are now in a season of continuous war, and more veterans will be wounded or killed even if the troop levels on the ground do not reach those in Iraq and Afghanistan. The toll on Special Forces, pilots, and drone operators will be especially heavy. Thousands of families will feel the strain. And the American people and their elected representatives seem as disconnected from these wars and from those fighting and sacrificing for them as they have been for the past fourteen years.

Shedding his comic persona, Colbert asked Mullen, "We're asked to be afraid of [the terrorists], we're reminded to be afraid, but we don't have a voice, our representatives won't vote, we're not asked to sacrifice, and we're not told much about what's going on over there. We only have the fear, without any action. We want to stop caring, we don't want [troops] to sacrifice for something that's not right, but we don't have a voice anymore."[3]

There is a parallel between this collective desire not to care, and former marine

Steven Canty's desire not to care about those he's killed or about the war. We can see the struggle to stay emotionally disconnected.

Mullen's response to Colbert, complete with matching body language, conveyed how strongly he feels, "I'm concerned that there's a growing disconnect between our all-volunteer force and the U.S. public. The American people don't have to buy into these wars, we don't have to fight in them, and we don't know who our military is. I worry that our military becomes a version of the French Foreign Legion: '*Go out and fight our dirty little wars for us and let us get on with our lives.*' I think that's a disaster for America. We need to be connected to the American people. We need to do that through the system that's here, those that are elected. Those that are elected ought to vote on what we do, and we ought to have *a fulsome and raging debate* [italics added] about that in this country."[4]

I'm struck by the parallel between Mullen's worry and the title of a drawing an Afghan war veteran gave me, "Shadow Warrior." Our military forces and our veterans are indeed ghosts. Out of sight and out of mind, they enable us to "get on with our lives." We don't want to face the costs and realities of war, but we want them to be fought. By our collective dissociation and inaction, we enable troops to step forward, become invisible phantoms, and turn into literal ancestors, buried in our national cemeteries with full pomp and circumstance but without our knowing them or the wars they fought. "Johnny we hardly knew ye."

The antidote for this, as Mullen and a few in the media, in constitutional law, and on the political stage tell us, is what child psychiatrist Rene Spitz was referring to when he wrote, "Life begins in dialogue and all psychopathology can be seen as derailments of dialogue." Substitute governmental breakdown for psychopathology. Vigorous dialogue, genuine exchange is at the heart of healing war trauma as well as getting the people's business done in Congress and developing working relations with allies and enemies.

I have been struck by a phrase that keeps coming up: "There is, ultimately, no military solution here; this has to be resolved politically." I hear it over and over while pundits and politicos decide whether to go to war, while at war, and while debating whether to end wars. It emerges often when discussing allied governments and how they need to be more inclusive. By not being inclusive, they sow seeds of ethnic and religious humiliation, disenfranchisement, and certain violence. "We'll bring them to the negotiating table by our military action" is frequently the rationale. But when we track the impacts of our policies over the past fourteen years, this has not been the case. Our strategies have helped create chaos and unintentionally spawned the enemies we are now combating. Our responses have engendered more terrorist recruits and spawned new and more deadly groups intent on our destruction.

I'm not a pacifist. I believe we have a right to defend ourselves if our collective safety is threatened directly. I also think it is our responsibility to stop genocide. But before resorting to military force we should exhaust all nonmilitary means for self-defense. "Smart power"—diplomatic and other nonviolent means of "resolving our differences"— is frowned upon and seen as weak. It brings a stigma similar to troops who return home, don't grasp why they are so out of control, and fear they will be weak—and, in turn, lose the respect of their peers, their security clearances, and their place on promotion lists if they seek support.

As a country we must break the stigma that engaging in vigorous debate and dialogue and negotiations within our own democratic system and with our allies and enemies is "weak." With regard to veterans, bypassing constitutional processes for authorizing war means deepening the gulf between military and civilians and betraying a central military (and humanitarian) ethic: "Leave no man or woman behind." Such "forgetting" disrespects service members, veterans, and their families, compromises integrity, and sows seeds of moral injury.

Strange Bedfellows

Who would have thought it, a decorated commanding general and a singer-songwriter-peace activist sharing an urgency for peace? At Coming Home Project's two community gatherings in Berkeley, a total of 350 people came, as diverse a crowd as one could imagine. There was plenty of media coverage, too. Perhaps they were curious about what would happen in ultraliberal Berkeley when war veterans, commanders, their families, researchers, politicians, psychotherapists, and interfaith leaders got together. I was delighted that we disappointed those who may have been anticipating a confrontation. Military officers, religious teachers, therapists, wives who'd lost husbands, mothers who advocated and cared for their children, and veterans from as far back as World War II all came together to learn more about the costs of war and to promote understanding between civilians and veterans. We are all in it together. And we embodied this solidarity through dialogue.

The phrase "strange bedfellows" comes from Shakespeare's *The Tempest*. Trinculo, a jester, is shipwrecked in a storm with his aristocratic keepers on an uncharted island. He comes upon Caliban, a native whom he first takes to be a fish. When he realizes that Caliban has arms and legs and is warm-blooded, he sees that what seemed a fish is an islander. The storm resumes and Trinculo retreats to the nearest shelter, under Caliban's loose-fitting cloak. As Trinculo puts it, "Misery acquaints a man with strange bedfellows." To avoid the storm, he must lie down with Caliban, who thinks he is a tormenting spirit.[5]

I admired former Israeli premier Yitzhak Rabin and his tenacious efforts for Middle East peace. When he shook hands with Yasser Arafat after signing the Palestinian-Israeli peace treaty, I noticed his body language: He could barely look Arafat in the face and he was biting his lip. Peacemaking is far from easy, and for Rabin it was profoundly conflictual, but he knew it was the right thing to do for Israel in the long haul. During the 2014 Israeli invasion of Gaza, I was struck by the comments of two Israeli journalists, veterans of many wars, about strategies for dealing with the existential threat their country lives with daily.

"Look, we tend to beat our enemies and never to listen to them. And many times, listening to the enemy, even to the most bitter enemy, can serve a much better cause than beating and beating and beating," wrote Gideon Levy, journalist for the newspaper *Ha'aretz*.[6] "It is really at our door now to decide. Do we want to go from one cycle to the other, from one circle of bloodshed to the other, not solving anything? Look, I don't want to underestimate," he wrote, "there is certainly fear, for sure, more in the south, close to the Gaza Strip. . . . I just say let's try and solve it once and for all and not go again to the old games, which have proven already that they lead to nowhere."

Uri Avnery is a German-born Israeli who, as a youth, was part of Irgun, a Zionist paramilitary group. He says he was a young terrorist and has some understanding of the new generation of terrorists. Avnery was the first Israeli to meet with Yasser Arafat. "During the battle of Beirut, I crossed the lines into the Palestinian territory," he said. "I met with Yasser Arafat, who was the leader of the PLO, and we had a long conversation about how to make peace. And then I went back to Israel. And we remained friends for the rest of his life." Avnery said they met often, abroad and later in Palestine. "I think the result of this meeting was that it helped to de-demonize the PLO. When pictures of him and me appeared on Israeli television talking to each other, sitting on the same sofa, I think it—to some extent, it helped to change the picture of Arafat the monster into Arafat the enemy with whom we can make peace." Those seeds bore fruit: "Twelve years later Israel made peace with the PLO. It was a peace between the Israeli prime minister, Yitzhak Rabin, and the chief of the PLO, Yasser Arafat." Unfortunately, Rabin was assassinated by a Jewish extremist and "we sank back into a war."[7]

"In order to put an end to a war, you must talk with your enemy, look him in the eye, try to understand him, and come up with a solution," Avnery says. "One of the basic problems at this moment is that Israelis and Hamas [the militant ruling party in the Gaza Strip] do not talk to each other . . . So we don't have somebody who can mediate and who's trusted by both sides. . . . I, myself, would say that there's a very simple solution to this. I think Israel and Hamas must talk to each other. When people are firing on each other and trying to kill each other—indeed, killing each other—the best solution is that they start to talk with each other. I think if the Israelis and the Palestinians would sit together opposite each other at one table and thresh out their real problems, trying to understand, be able to understand each other, the whole thing would look very differently."

Along with friends, Avnery met with Hamas leaders. He found them to be "people with whom I don't necessarily agree, but people with whom I can talk." He feels Israel cannot "wish Hamas away. You can do to Hamas whatever you want. You can kill all the 10,000 fighters of Hamas. But Hamas will remain, because Hamas is an ideology, and Hamas is a political party accepted by the Palestinian people. So, in the end, whatever we do, in the end, after all the killing and after all this terrible destruction, in the end, we'll have to talk with Hamas."

Avnery is not naive. He is pragmatic and understands talking requires a modicum of trust, respect, and common aims, "Do we agree to live side by side with an independent, sovereign state of Palestine? Yes or no? If not, then every further discussion is superfluous. We shall have war, and again and again and again and again, until the end of time."

I hear in his words the prospect of despair at the helpless inevitably of war and the carnage it brings. Hope in the face of such despair must animate this 91-year-old's efforts to build dialogue and peace. Perhaps the internal conversation between anguish and hope also helped prompt Maj. Gen. Myatt's surprising words at the Memorial Day commemoration in San Francisco.

Coming Home Project has demonstrated the effectiveness of bringing together an interdisciplinary staff and a diverse group of veterans, service members, and families— from all phases of deployment, all military branches, and a range of ages, races, religions, political persuasions, and sexual orientations—within a structured environment of mutual respect and compassion without judgment. Helping individual veterans and families heal war trauma coarises with addressing the collective impacts of war trauma on our institutions, leaders, policymaking, and civilians, so as to become able to prevent needless wars. We cannot artificially detach one from the other. Otherwise we are using Band-Aids to patch life-threatening wounds. It might seem to work, but it's only window dressing, and the problem is exacerbated for want of a systemic solution. When examining post-traumatic stress and related trauma, needless war, perpetuated by people with sterling intentions, is an unexamined kernel of the illness.

By its nature, war engenders moral injury. Ed Tick in *War and the Soul* suggests there is a reduced incidence of post-traumatic stress in troops who are fighting for their country against invaders and occupiers. That is not what I found in meetings in Vietnam with veterans of the American war. The injuries I heard about from Vietcong, North Vietnamese regulars, and South Vietnamese Air Force veterans closely paralleled the themes, stories, and experiences of their American counterparts.

As with inner peace, which Steve Torgerson speaks movingly about, bringing tears to many eyes at our retreats, so with the peace (and dialogue) that could turn our dysfunctional government functional again, and so with peace among nations—all require robust associations of strange bedfellows. Our personal and collective ghosts are also like strange bedfellows to us. We need the courage and the requisite conditions to invite them back to be "reintegrated," to reanimate our dissociated connection with veterans and their families and the wars they fight, to restore our buried desire for "ways of resolving our differences that don't involve killing one another," and to muster the integrity to employ such means tenaciously.

Long Haul–Long View

The road ahead will not be short—traumatic war impacts are time bombs. In an article on Army.mil, "The Desire to Be Resilient Can Sometimes Mask Underlying Depression," Col. Geoffrey Grammar, chief of research at the National Intrepid Center of Excellence, says that in an Army culture of "toughness and resilience," soldiers and family members can have a hard time coming forward for help with underlying problems like depression.[8] "It may," says Grammar, "be easier to focus on stomach discomfort" (and other symptoms of depression such as trouble sleeping, concentrating, and fatigue) "rather than on an existential crisis." Severe depression can feel like an existential crisis and, if left untreated, can precipitate suicide. Many people think of depression as a "preexisting" psychiatric condition. But depression does not exist in a vacuum, unrelated to the brutal realities of life and death in a war zone where existential threats abound. War trauma not only can precipitate PTsxD with its painful symptoms of dysregulation. It can also precipitate a range of psychological disturbances, including clinical depression, manic depression, psychosis, and dissociative shutdown. These conditions take time to heal. And Pollyanish "resilience" programs can mask or overlook deeper layers of moral injury and anguish.

While PTsxD is being addressed with increasing effectiveness, there are no shortcuts when addressing PTspD. William Nash, the retired Navy psychiatrist who deployed with marines in Iraq, says that "definitely a majority" of service members return from the war zone with moral injury. "People avoid talking about or thinking about it and every time they do, it's a flashback or nightmare that just damages them even more. It's going to take a long time to sort that out."

It's January 2012 and Nick Rudolph is back home at Camp Lejeune, North Carolina, after three deployments, sixteen months in the war zone, six IED blasts, and one gunshot wound, Wood writes. Drinking heavily, Nick got a DUI and was demoted a rank, losing his prized position as a squad leader. He went to see a civilian therapist, was prescribed sleeping pills, and slept through morning formation, an unauthorized absence. The Marine Corps considered this a "pattern of misconduct."[9]

A year later, his physical wounds have healed, but his war experience keeps insinuating itself into the serene civilian reality he's trying to create. "Coming back, I didn't know what could help, like . . . how do I get those feelings to stop?" Nick said. Much like the night visitations of Bob Rodriguez, who was revisited each night by the face of the boy he shot, Nick feels the rush of combat and watches again as the boy comes around the wall, "The feeling hits you and like . . . I don't want to be like that."

Not only can the symptoms of dysregulation that Nick describes and that characterize PTsxD continue long after the original traumas, so too can the inner anguish of PTspD. Often they are intertwined. Sendio Martz was in "a constant movie . . . replaying over and over in his head" a scenario in which, as commanding officer, he was unable to bring all his men home safe. Three years later, Martz is "kind of stuck." He says, 'I have a hard time feeling comfortable around kids, because it was that kid that we got close to, and to have that same kid turn around and blow you up, it shatters your reality of what's OK and what's not OK. Your trust has been ruined and broken. The only ones you trust are the guys you went with."

Blocking out or willing away the pain may work for a while, but Iraq Marine veteran Stephen Canty says of fighting in war, "*Once you know it, you can't un-know it* [italics added]."

Marine Staff Sgt. Felipe Tremillo is still "haunted by images of the women and children he saw suffer from the violence and destruction of war in Afghanistan. . . . The . . . willful casting aside of his own values broke something inside him, changing him into someone he hardly recognizes, or admires. The wound gets worse with time: 'There is no fairy-tale ending.'"[10]

Can anyone be "inoculated" against the trauma of moral injury? I do not think so. There are ways to reduce the iatrogenic factors in war trauma, the unintended negative effects of policy, protocols, and their implementation, and the cultural factors I've discussed. But "inoculation" is a misguided, expensive, and dangerous delusion that ignores everything we've learned from firsthand accounts that span millennia about the unpredictably predictable cascading horrors of war and their long-lasting impacts. It lulls us into a false sense of security that the troops will be okay, and we can count on them remaining okay (and take them for granted), as we leap, without authorization, into wars without end.

Billie Grimes-Watson, who served in Iraq in 2003 and 2004, drives home just how long lasting the impacts of PTspD can be. A medic, she was devastated that she couldn't help a dying comrade. A decade later, she remains haunted by the war and her part in it. "I avoid talking about it, try to keep it down," she told Wood in a recent phone conversation. "But inside I'm trying to do the happy face so no one knows how much I'm hurting."

In 2013, she began therapy in the San Diego moral injury program. "I have more than one moral injury and I used the easier one and not the bad ones that are really affecting me," she said, eight months after completing the program. Trust comes hard, especially in military or psychiatric settings. I believe that the weight of such war trauma is sometimes too much for the clinical setting.

She told the group about her "small one"—throwing rocks back at Iraqi kids who had begun pelting the troops. "It's something I normally wouldn't do, bullying kids—I have kids of my own, and I can't even think of anyone hurting them like I did with those kids," she says. In therapy, "I explained how peer pressure kind of gets to you and you do things you shouldn't have done and you try to forgive yourself for it. People gave me hugs, a lot of crying and discussion. But I still feel guilty and *I haven't forgiven myself for a lot of the things I did over there* [italics added]."

Trusting oneself and others as one allows in and risks sharing a range of shameful and frightening emotions is more likely, we've found, in a bigger container—a safe, nonpsychiatric, nature-based, residential environment in the company of fellow veterans and caring and skilled civilian facilitators. The "total" setting is more conducive to engaging buried ghosts. Self-compassion always comes hard, but it is more likely to grow in a larger, independent, trustworthy, unconditionally loving culture.

We usually think one-to-one is optimal for psychotherapy, and in many cases it is. But Malcolm Gladwell suggests that, given the critical importance of peer friendships in education, bigger classes sometimes give students a better chance to find someone they can connect with.[11] This also helps explain why, although most retreat participants find small affiliative groups congenial, large-group settings (recall the introductions block during our first women's retreat) occasionally provide just the right holding environment for the massive emotional and moral loads veterans and their families are carrying. Finally, it helps explain why "peer counseling" is, to my mind, not as effective as the organic peer support that develops at retreats, where participants' daily interactions are the basis for their informed choice of who they develop a bond with, and one is not required to self-identify as having a problem.

Billie Grimes-Watson, the former medic, says, "I have all this guilt inside me and I want to let it out but I can't. I want to tell my husband and family what's going on, but I don't. I just put on a happy face until I'm alone."

Involving families is critical. It's all too easy—as illustrated by my chance meeting with the head chaplain at a military treatment facility whose trauma had been "seared into his brain" and who poured his heart out to me, a stranger he'd just met—for veterans to shy away from sharing their true experience with their partners, other family members, and colleagues. I recall telephoning an Army captain during the early stages of Coming Home Project, and within ten minutes, he was telling me about his war experience. "Hold it a second," he said, "I have to go to a quieter place," his wife's voice in the background asking who was on the phone. Then, within minutes, I heard his wife say, "Why don't you ever talk to me like that?"

Fast-forward and Grimes-Watson is seeing a therapist but, she says, "I've started going backwards again. All the emotions and nightmares are coming back. I had stopped drinking and now I'm drinking again, trying to hide it. I can't sleep at night. . . . It's hard to find yourself again, because you're never going to be the same person. I am trying to figure out how to forgive myself for everything I did over there, and it's hard to figure out. . . . I'm messed up. I'm tired of just taking the pills."

"I don't think it ever happens in the therapy," retired psychiatrist Bill Nash said. "Because I don't think the therapy is ever long enough for that to happen. All we can do is plant seeds." But, he added, "as far as I know that's the only route to salvation, and it ain't easy and it ain't quick." For many veterans, maybe most veterans suffering from PTspD, it takes a village, and a moveable, durable one at that.

Post-traumatic Growth (PTgr)

Although the road home from PTspD is long and protracted, the absence of symptoms is not a criterion for post-traumatic growth. The concern is when symptoms continue to haunt, disable, and erode ordinary life. Emotional seasons change even for those fully invested in healing and emotional growth. The process of growing through massive trauma lasts a lifetime. While not eradicating war-related pain forever, transforming haunting war trauma helps it find its rightful place while no longer torturing. The safety and trust of community permits veterans to represent and reexperience the shards of war trauma within a new environment and have them reencoded in their hearts and minds in a different key.

Returning veterans are not the same and will never be the same. They know things they didn't know before, things at once dangerous and potentially liberating. They know what human beings are capable of. They've seen the worst; they know the impacts. While rest, ease, and peace can be transformative, symptoms, as long as they don't prevent us from living fully, help us remember. For veterans, war becomes both their ancestor and their mentor.

Turning ghosts into ancestors, the integrative process we learned and applied with such success at Coming Home Project, requires the right ingredients and takes personal engagement and time. But it's not realistic to expect the suffering to vanish forever. Dysregulation symptoms are more accessible than moral injuries but, unaddressed, they too can be tenacious. With PTspD, there will be occasional storms: ripples of remorse, sadness, memories of traumatic events and the people involved, infrequent traumatic dreams. Practices that build regulation capacity such as forms of qigong, yoga, and meditation help manage them when they come up. Ongoing peer support provides a bigger container, as it helps us remember to practice—whether we need to or not— investing in our meditative-emotional muscle so it is available when we need it. Some Vietnam veterans have found it healing to return to the sites of battles, meet with their counterparts, and be of service, constructing schools and public health facilities. One day, if the region truly stabilizes, Iraq and Afghanistan veterans may do likewise.

I hope veterans are not inoculated against war trauma. They carry our collective memory. The wounds of PTsxD and especially PTspD lie latent, awaiting a safe environment to be transformed, to be redeemed. Adm. Mullen was right to worry about the public thinking of our military as the French Foreign Legion: "Go fight our 'dirty little wars' and leave us be." After fourteen years of war, after real and manipulated terror, we are understandably frightened and on a hair trigger when we witness gruesome terrorist acts. We want it "taken care of" even if, as recent polls indicate, we think it will endanger us more down the road. We are like the crooked politician in a TV drama who whispers to some dangerous-looking man to "handle it." But, we don't want to be bothered by the details, implications, the cascading threats that incur from our reactions, or the costs. It is impossible to take the long view when trauma has us in its grip without our knowledge. Veterans and families in their healing, and nations in their foreign relations, can likewise learn to recognize, contain, and transform unconscious traumatic impacts.

There is a remarkable and encouraging convergence among several factors: the conditions that contribute to healing war trauma, the characteristics of a working democracy, and the qualities of a genuinely peaceful world in which "resolving differences without killing each other," as Maj. Gen. Myatt put it, is a priority. This convergence involves sitting with one another in safety, listening deeply and respectfully to differences as well as similarities, without judging or trying to reform or fix the other, while speaking truthfully from the heart. This kind of dialogue can play a key role both in healing war trauma and in preventing future destruction. Turning ghosts into memories that help us heal and wake up runs parallel to turning collective monsters into enemies we can actually talk to. Collective amnesia and dissociation are set aside. The anxiety, as Porges suggests, is that in "immobilizing without fear," we run the risk of being ambushed, being left with our guard down, and failing to protect ourselves and those we love, even our entire country.

As with veterans, so with nations, we work through our respective war trauma residues, our ghosts, together. We can't erase all symptoms; if we could, we'd wipe away our working memory. Transformed residues of war trauma help us learn from experience, accept ourselves and what we've done or haven't done, right down to the bottom, as Staff Sgt. Tremillo said. Acceptance promotes healthy mourning and leads in the direction of self-compassion. "Thank you for your service," "It wasn't your fault," or "We forgive you" are not particularly helpful here. Growing through war trauma requires forging a bigger container to hold it all and then redeeming it with others. A wider view enables us to grieve, to let in the tender mercies that life still offers, and to live more fully.

I was at a conference with the Dalai Lama, and someone asked him if the continuing occupation and ethnic cleansing in his native Tibet was upsetting. He replied that it was indeed disturbing and very sad. The next questioner asked if he ever got angry. Of course, he replied. Well, another teacher asked, what helped him during his most trying moments? After pausing for quite some time to consider the question, the Dalai Lama replied that, in addition to his regular Tibetan Buddhist practices, he would think, "What would things be like in a hundred years?" To see the long view in action was bracing. His practices were not intended or utilized to magically leap frog and transcend suffering. But they allowed him to retain hope, live through it, stay awake and useful, and envision a future where shifting causes and conditions and moral balance might transform the oppressive status quo.

We've explored how integrity is a motive force and how painful the moral reverberations of wartime actions or inactions can be. Can morality itself be a force for "resolving our differences without killing each other"? In today's terror-filled world we are so driven by pressing fears and the clamor to "do something" that we may be missing a powerful and practical force for transforming the rush to war. Richard Falk, author of *Palestine: The Legitimacy of Hope* and professor emeritus of international law at Princeton University, was recently asked what he meant by "the legitimacy of hope."

"What I mean is that if you look at the way in which conflicts have been resolved since the end of World War II, particularly involving foreign domination or foreign rule in a Third World country, the decisive factor in their resolution has been gaining the high ground of international morality and international law. Military superiority has not produced political outcomes favorable to the intervening or the more powerful side. And so, the hope comes from this pattern of gaining legitimacy, in what I call 'legitimacy war,' being more significant politically than being able to control the results on a battlefield. And that's a profound change in the whole structure of power in the world."[12]

Gandhi's term *satyagraha*, truth force, is akin to what Falk is referring to. It does not imply passivity, to the contrary. Our country as a whole faces a challenge similar to one veterans struggle with. Returning service members know how to fight; their nervous systems and their hearts and minds have compensated to accomplish just this task. In part their struggle is to adapt to new circumstances. As a country, we know how to employ the blunt-force tool of war. But can we adapt to changing situations? Doing so requires understanding the multidimensional impacts of war trauma and how we are all implicated. It requires the capacity to "take the hit" of traumatic provocation while remaining able to accurately assess the real level of danger and the complex, intertwining forces at play. It requires the courage and ability to track the impacts of our actions over time, learn from experience, and make course corrections. It requires challenging the stigma that equates robust, collaborative, nonviolent means of resisting malfeasance and evil with weakness and cowardice. It requires adopting the long view and developing an appreciation for the profound interdependence at play in our world.

Waking Up

What will it take for us to roust ourselves from our dissociative spell and wake up to the costs of war? What did it take for Gen. Myatt to challenge his previous views, go "off-message," and speak as spontaneously and honestly as he did? In the *I-Ching* (Book of Changes), the ancient Taoist wisdom text, the fifty-ninth hexagram (archetypal situation) is called Dispersion. It depicts a time where divisiveness is dissolving. An accompanying image shows the wind blowing over a body of water. For divisive forces to dissipate, the commentary says, "the heart must be seized by a devout emotion." The *I-Ching* is not referring to religious fanaticism but to a profound change of heart, an ethical turning whereby we make connections that had not occurred to us.

I spoke with Steve Torgerson about this in early 2014, during the run-up to the United States' possible military involvement to topple the regime of Bashar al-Assad in Syria. I said our fellow citizens, our legislators, and especially our leaders need to have more skin in the game. What would that take? Drafting firstborns? A high school teacher of Steve's once suggested that if money was not a factor, we might have fewer wars. I thought of outlawing war profiteering. Greed is a common and corrosive motivation that often flies under the radar, benefitting from the cover provided by nationalistic rhetoric. The teacher added that the leader responsible for taking the country to war should also serve on the frontlines. I think all "deciders"—deciders-in-chief and their many co-deciders—should be required to have at least one family member on the frontlines. I'm not naive enough to think this will happen, but it would assure skin in the game. The point is, what would happen if elected leaders and the people's representatives understood *and felt* the intimate connectedness at the heart of our earthly coexistence?

With money off the table and real skin in the game, I would be intrigued to see policymakers go back to the drawing board. Would their decision-making process be different? More thorough, more creative, more patient, more intelligent, more honest, stronger in nonviolent strategies and tactics? Would they resort less quickly to war? Be more resourceful and tenacious in finding ways "to resolve differences that don't involve killing each other"? I wonder.

Taking the long view, the best way to cut through the hypocrisy and lack of integrity and really look out for veterans and their families is to prevent war whenever possible. The vast majority of officers and enlisted men and women I've met over the past eight years, up and down the chain of command, are not hankering to go to war. Their families don't want them to go to war. They aren't cavalier about it. They are devoted, reliable, skilled, and accountable, and will make whatever sacrifices are required if and when the men or women in suits and skirts call on them.

Learning from Experience: Two

Why won't most resilience programs work? Because we can't fix the problems of war. Needless wars *are* the problem. We need serenity to accept what we think we can control but cannot, courage, tenacity, and resourcefulness to change what we can, and wisdom to know the difference. Would that there were a twelve-step program for national addiction to war.

When we forget the costs of war we forget veterans and their families. We leave them behind. There will always be those who want to hurt our country, individuals and groups we need to confront. The question is how. Some may directly threaten our lives and we may, as a last resort, need to employ military force to protect ourselves. But the wisdom in the serenity prayer is contingent on becoming able to learn from experience, internalizing those lessons, and having access to usable memories rather than being driven by unconscious ghosts. We need to remember and factor in the costs of war, recognize the long-lasting impacts of individual and collective war trauma, and enjoin the process of turning our ghosts into ancestors. As we do, we become better able to track the impacts of trauma on our behavior, and the impacts of our responses. This can make us less prone to repeating past errors.

A friend was telling me about her father, a veteran of the Pacific theater during World War II. He saw the atom bomb explode, but never talked about it. She thinks if he were to comment on today's situation, he'd say, "It's hard to fight people who want to die." Groups who provoke you with atrocities, dare you, wanting to draw you into an assured conflagration leading to a quagmire. Malicious groups whose every casualty improves recruitment and creates martyrs. How do we respond intelligently, think outside the box, consider fresh perspectives, and come up with new solutions? Can we track the impacts of past actions, take in new information, and respond in accord? Or are we disabled by unrecognized war trauma and highjacked by our maladaptive reactions to it?

The challenges we face as a nation are not unlike the struggles veterans face daily. Returning service members tend to react to the old (traumatic) situation and they experience certain current events as if they were still in the war zone. It is a long, arduous process to liberate perception and respond to new situations afresh.

When we discussed war trauma and resilience earlier, we explored a conundrum veterans face with regard to war trauma: "can't live with it, can't live without it." This also sums up our current collective relationship with war: we can't live with it, and we can't seem to live without it. We know the colloquial definition of insanity: doing the same thing over and over again and expecting a different result. Chuck Todd, moderator of *Meet the Press*, is not alone when he commented on *The Rachel Maddow Show* that as a country we seem to have learned nothing from our war experience in Iraq. News analyst Scott Shane writes in the *New York Times*, "Despite a decade of war, most Americans seem to endorse 'the politicians' martial spirit.'" In a Pew Research Center poll, 58 percent of those surveyed said the United States should use military force, if necessary, to prevent Iran from developing nuclear weapons. Only 30 percent said no. Yet, 75 percent of respondents said Mr. Obama was withdrawing troops from Afghanistan at the right pace or not quickly enough, a finding in keeping with many indications of war weariness."

One expert who has studied security threats since the Cold War found this puzzling: "You'd think there would be an instinctive reason to hold back after two bloody noses in Iraq and Afghanistan." Another expert on conflict prevention said, "Faced with an intractable security challenge, both politicians and ordinary people want to 'do something,' and nothing 'does something' like military force." He sees an old pattern, *"It's true throughout history: there's always the belief that the next war will go much better than the last war* [italics added]."[13]

In one view, leaders patently manipulate our basic human need for safety and prey on our fears of insecurity and damage. Lawrence Wilkerson, Vietnam veteran, retired U.S. Army colonel, and former chief of staff to Secretary of Defense Colin Powell, thinks war has nothing to do with truth, justice, and the "American Way." Rather, war resists change by aggrandizing the coffers and power of a select few who exert partial control of the governance of our country. From this perspective, leaders manipulate the people by summoning old or new threats and deploying grand ideological themes to provide cover and fuel the fires of war fever for their own benefit and with complete disregard for their people, the enemy, and, of course, military forces and their families.

Gen. Dan Bolger commanded and trained U.S. military forces in Iraq and Afghanistan. In his book, *Why We Lost*, Bolger says our efforts to militarily change the hearts and minds of people whose regimes we toppled, to nation-build, and to "remake them in our image" was responsible for the failure. There are grave dangers, as we saw in the educator John Holt's words, when "the helping hand strikes again."

When asked if he believed that our counterinsurgency military efforts to win "hearts and minds" and nation-build were wrong, Gen. Bolger replied, "I *came* to believe [it]." He went on, "I now have sympathy for the British generals on the western front in WWI. I used to say 'How stupid can they be?' Now I see they were well-meaning men, doing what they were trained to do, and it took time for them to figure out 'this isn't working.'" Bolger now takes responsibility, "The same thing happened for me and many of my colleagues in the military. We realized, as the months built up, 'it wasn't working.'" Bolger says we got it wrong from the outset. If we were going to counter an insurgency, we couldn't, as an outside force, go in there and do that; it had to be local forces that led the way. Here's where it becomes interesting: "We *did* learn that in Vietnam. I *studied* Vietnam, and, as I think about it, I'm appalled that I repeated [the same error] twice, once in Iraq and once in Afghanistan." Bolger says he owes it to the troops he fought alongside to say, "What can we learn from this?"[14]

As we saw earlier, here is the ineluctable tendency to obscure history, get caught up in the spell of trauma, and react by leaping to the conclusion that war is the answer and the next one will be better than the last. We dissociate what we know. We deceive ourselves and others. Would that we would *all* be appalled and wake up to how insidiously this perennial dynamic operates. Whether this tendency is purposeful or delusionally out of consciousness, the impacts are devastating.

As a country, we come to the worksite and encounter a chronically unpredictable, complex, and flammable situation. Without fully considering whether or not the problem is a nail, we use our hammer and think things will work out differently this time. In principle we could respond differently. We could be a seasoned old dog, ripened by experience and able to learn new tricks—an old hand who responds in accord with new information rather than using the same tools on the job that didn't work well the last time.

I worry that the military's dependence on resilience techniques lulls us into a false sense of security: service members and veterans? Covered. We don't have to address the problems underlying their anguish: the isolation that accompanies the growing military-civilian divide, the dysfunction and lack of coordination among monolithic institutions such as VA and DoD, the absence of debate and skin in the game, the pervasive moral injuries that come with compromised integrity, and many others. As news reports about our current war footing convey, few have "the appetite" (read intestinal fortitude and integrity) to step up to the plate, debate, and take a stand: not Congress, not our leaders, not we who elect them.

How do we come home as a nation? By waking up *to* war, coming to our senses, engaging the vigorous dialogue that characterizes the democratic process, respecting one another's views, having skin in the game, and seeing the big picture, the collective impacts, conscious and unconscious. With an understanding of interdependence, we can create approaches characterized both by the resolve to protect ourselves and the ability to put ourselves in others' shoes. We can act with integrity, remaining committed to forging peaceful solutions while anticipating and calibrating actual danger.

We will always have this one deadly tool in our toolbox. There should be a warning label on war reading, "Use only as last resort, highly unpredictable and destructive over many generations in ways you cannot now imagine."

Let's look at it another way: when something goes wrong with your health and your doctor says you need surgery, you try everything else first. You research, consult, talk to people, get second and third opinions, read up, maybe try a few less intrusive treatments, and see how that goes, calibrating risk and reward.

You prefer not having them cut into your body. There can be unanticipated outcomes. Anesthesia is a risk. And there are high rates of infection in hospitals. Finally you meet with the surgeon. You've done your homework and have a few questions: How many of these surgeries have you done? What is your success rate? The rate of complications? How many deaths? How long has your team been working together? What's the hospital's infection rate? The number of deaths from iatrogenic factors?

Imagine that as a nation we are having an international dispute, not a difficult thing to imagine. Our doctor recommends war. What if we asked her the same questions? How safe and efficient is it? How effective? How many of these have you conducted? What's the success rate? Complication rate? Death Rate? Complaints? Lawsuits? Iatrogenic damage? How many times have you had to go back in and redo something you thought was done? What if we had to have surgeries without end for the rest of our lives? What if our children were also burdened with endless surgeries, and they passed this legacy on to their children and their children's children? What if the initial surgery didn't resolve the problem and it kept occurring, even getting worse? Would we keep trying the same technique?

What would it take us as a nation to realize that we have a malaise and that, rather than confront that malaise constructively, we've come to depend on a strategy that might provide temporary relief, but that in the long run often makes things worse? Can we recognize the symptoms of addiction? The substance in question is war. It provides immediate gratification, an adrenaline high, feeling like we're doing something to keep our country safe, striking those who harmed our citizens. But long term, things crash and it's back to square one. Or worse. Can we take a searching and fearless inventory?

The Road Ahead

Bob Bradley, the retired National Guard officer with the booming voice and presence who helped us learn about logistics, also introduced our team to after-action reports. What have I learned from our work at Coming Home Project about the health, well-being, and care of returning service members, veterans, and their families? This book is the response to that question. The following list of twenty-seven recommendations is not exhaustive. Some recommendations are specific, and some may seem general and unrelated to our work. In our interconnected world, all are significant in their own way.

1. Redistribute the massive burdens of war. These loads have fallen disproportionately on service members, veterans, and families.

2. Be clear about motivation and intention, particularly the unconscious kind. They have enormous impacts. Bring actions into alignment. Righteous ideology and proclamations of helpfulness are not sufficient. "Do as I say not as I do" puts us at peril. Lead by example.

3. Acknowledge that real security is built on the quality of our relationships with allies and enemies alike.

4. Unhitch from classical stereotypes of power and strength, and transform the stigma that equates needing help at the individual level and nonviolent means of resolving conflicts at the collective level with weakness and not taking responsibility.

5. Recognize that integrity is the alpha and omega in caring for veterans and families. The absence of integrity corrupts, spoils, and damages. Cultivating integrity is the best hope for attenuating moral injuries.

6. Take the long view. Grasp the interconnection of things, actions, people, and events. Let actions emerge accordingly.

7. Transition from the short view and what comes with it: quick-fix, window-dressing programs, Band-Aid approaches, and deceptive word spin that insults our intelligence, such as "surgical strikes," "no 'combat' troops," "minimal civilian casualties," and "no boots on the ground."

8. Understand that there is no war on the cheap or on the down low. Be straight. Insist on "a fulsome and raging debate" out in the open. It's good for us and it will be better for service members, veterans, and families.

9. Go beyond symptom reduction and address underlying factors. Use resources hidden in plain sight like the awesome power of community and peer support. Let in new information and let it inform new responses. Address the appropriate depth of the problem. Use the right tool for the job.

10. Understand that social and foreign policy cannot be unhitched from veteran policy, especially in such an interconnected world as ours.

11. Recognize that a docile public and a dysfunctional Congress may enable a rapid decision to go to war, but that, in the long run, we will lose out from a lack of robust input and exchange.

12. See ordinary civilians as civic assets, a resource for reintegration and healing. Welcome their volunteer help. When people ask the general question, "What

can I do?" suggest they meet, talk with, and listen to a vet or a sister, brother, mother, father, grandma, grandpa, child, or teenager of a vet. Learn about military culture. Feature stories of veterans and families, focus on military kids. Veterans are a marginalized population; live your multicultural ideals. Learn about the costs of war through human-to-human exchange. Put aside ideology and make contact with real folks. Create civilian-veteran dialogues where you live. Make common cause. Help build social support networks based on forged affinity. Know that this is at once a way to build peace and a proven alternative to some of the existing compartmentalized, medical-model approaches to reintegration. Link up with interfaith groups working to raise consciousness about the moral and spiritual injuries of war. Remember, "Community heals and isolation kills."

13. Become aware in real time of what we—institutions, legislature, leaders, and citizenry—are cultivating with our actions. With each action, we are planting seeds.

14. Approach war's impacts as a public health issue, because they are one. In the national debate recommended by Adm. Mullen and others, include not just policy and immediate decision making but also:

    • Education and dialogue about the impacts of war trauma on vets and families, communities, and on all of us.

    • Opportunities nationwide for real connection among civilians, military personnel, and vets and families. Family-to-family, intimate, not huge big-top spectacles.

15. Understand war as a national enterprise. We are all implicated. Healing from war's impacts cannot be accomplished solely through specialized, professional responses. Just as we need a durable grassroots response to reckless war making, we need a durable grassroots response to postwar healing. War trauma should not remain medicalized, like a microbe we are striving to eliminate. It cannot be eliminated until war is no longer a unilateral, unconscious decision and act.

16. Recognize that community-based, safe, welcoming environments not related to the military or to psychiatry (and not associated with "fixing") are our best bet to facilitate redemption, restoration, and renewal. Promoting mental health includes but is not identical to services rendered in a therapist's office.

17. Replenish our cultural commons, build community as we counter the veteran/military-civilian divide. Create real connection among people in a world that, although linked through technology, leaves many feeling isolated.

18. Develop opportunities for collaboration and partnership, not just window dressing. To make collaborations real and functional, fund them, share infrastructure and resources.

19. Understand that big-top programs, expensive summits on aircraft carriers full of celebrities, and other mega-spectacles have limited value. Better to invest resources into bringing civilians and veterans together in more intimate and ongoing settings. Invest in the development of a nationwide grassroots veteran-civilian consortium. This builds connective tissue, durable healing "infrastructure," and social capital.

20. Continue to hold VA, DoD, Congress, and the administration's feet to the fire, but focus on decentralizing, thinking systemically, and acting locally. Support grassroots advocacy efforts, and service-oriented, community-building programs.

21. Reexamine how we think about veteran benefits. Why do they depend so heavily on a psychiatric diagnosis? Why is the burden placed on veterans to prove how much combat they saw and the degree to which their functioning is compromised? Consider providing care for life: what you need, when you need it, for as long as you need it. If you served in war and find you need more help, you get what you need—an HMO for veterans. Imagine the resources that could be redirected into programming and care. Imagine the additional time and energy veterans could devote to healing, renewing their lives, and contributing to their communities.

22. Start adopting proven best practices and stop complaining about not being able to find "top-shelf" programs while indulging in crony favoritism, profiteering, and pork barreling.

23. Recognize our collective amnesia regarding war is like pulling the covers over our head and pretending things go away. Improve our collective memory. Meet and turn ghosts into usable memories. Learn from experience. This will help veterans with their own reintegrative work. Like veterans, learn to take in new information and respond in accord with new conditions.

24. Remedy overdependence on virtual content and programs. Informational glut is a concern. Porges asks, "Do our institutions want to educate people with more information or to help people become able to reciprocally interact and regulate each other to feel good?" In-person learning complements virtual platforms. "Relational" and "informational" support each other. Cultivate social engagement and social bonding systems and grow relational capacities.

25. Consider rethinking our all-volunteer force. Explore required national service with opt-in for military service. Having skin in the game is crucial.

26. Expand the VA's current tripartite structure of health, benefits, and national cemeteries to include a dedicated reintegration branch. We'll be needing it for a long time.

27. Adopt a well-funded, three-pronged approach for the unseen injuries, including TBI, PTsxD, and PTspD, in which each component enhances the others:

    • First, fund a national network of off-site, confidential, free, peer-support-driven, community-building environments facilitated by trained psychotherapists, chaplains, and seasoned veteran and family members—on the model of Coming Home Project retreats, with participant and facilitator cohorts. Make such a gateway program available to all returning service members, veterans, and their families. It coordinates with Yellow Ribbon programs nationwide. It serves multiple purposes at once: outreach, (naturalistic) assessment and referral, prevention, early intervention, stigma reduction, suicide prevention, mental health, strengthening families, and wellness education and training. Many veterans and families will get most of what they need from these programs combined with regular, local follow-up programs. This creates a robust connective tissue of peer support amplified by access to known health professionals.

    • Second, make widely available a range of evidence-based wellness practices that help veterans and family members with PTsxD. These also help those with PTspD manage the strong waves of emotion that are part of the ongoing process of turning ghosts into ancestors. Remember that these two kinds of post-traumatic stress often co-occur.

    • Third, make widely and affordably available high-quality, long-term intensive psychotherapy. Large volunteer therapist organizations must provide quality control; Coming Home Project has learned that regular peer consultation meetings with senior therapists in attendance work well. Also make available on-demand access to quality residential programs inside and outside VA and DoD.

Coda

———•◆•———

When Pope Francis or the Dalai Lama come to town, crowds commonly swoon. They are almost universally admired. Why don't we listen more attentively to their views on war? Each thinks war is a scourge. Each considers it immoral.

I've met many warriors whom I respect who see themselves as peacemakers and many veterans who feel proud that they have contributed to peace and the freedoms it permits. Many, but not all. Inner peace and outer peace—how critical and how elusive they are. I've learned empirically over the past eight years, as if for the first time, just how intimately connected they are.

From these two beloved religious teachers let's turn to a scientist who is simultaneously a deeply spiritual person. Greg Friccione is associate chief of psychiatry; director of the Division of Psychiatry and Medicine at Massachusetts General Hospital; director of the Benson-Henry Institute for Mind Body Medicine; and professor of psychiatry at Harvard Medical School. Now, just as we leave titles and rank at the door at Coming Home retreats, forget all that. Greg wrote a book, *Compassion and Healing in Medicine and Society: On the Nature and Use of Attachment Solutions to Separation Challenges.*[1] It's a mouthful and it took a long time to plow through it. But it was more worthwhile than I ever imagined.

I met Greg in his small, book-filled office at Mass General. He greeted me warmly and we talked prior to our meeting with Herb Benson, director emeritus of the Benson Henry Institute and a pioneer in mind-body medicine and integration of Western and Eastern medical practices. Herb joined us via conference call. I must have been straining to hear Herb when Greg invited me to move my chair closer to the phone, and to him. There were the three of us, huddled up, Herb on speakerphone, having a stimulating and close conversation about healing trauma. After I read Greg's book, I saw that by inviting me in closer, Greg was un-self-consciously creating an "attachment solution to a separation challenge," instinctively responding to Herb being at a distance, and my not knowing either of them. It made me feel comfortable.

I recognized my own motivations and personal and professional life path in his theory. It helped me understand more about why so many spiritual teachers have navigated early traumatic loss. The anguish provides the experiential ground for exploration and connection with deeper meaning, and with altruistic love, a perennial source for Greg. Liberating the expression of compassionate love in all its particularity in real situations—reaching our full evolutionary potential—is no small part of Greg's motivation. He demonstrates in his book that this love drives the evolutionary bus and will keep us growing as individuals and as a species—if we make use of the separation challenge-attachment solution imperative.

Greg demonstrates the explanatory power of his theory across multiple disciplines, including genetics, evolutionary biology, psychiatry, human development, neuroscience, philosophy, spirituality, physics, and cosmology. A consummate clinician and researcher, he mobilizes the work of hundreds of expert resources, refracted through his own analytic, compassionate mind and heart.

Although he and Herb do research on war trauma, the ideas in his book developed in another crucible of life and death—the bedside of patients facing serious illness and the potential of losing everything. In the face of such separation threats, we are primed to seek healing connections with others and create a deeper sense of meaning—an attachment solution. Our brain has in fact evolved to do just this.

When we look at stereotypical norms of what constitutes strength and what strategies effectively generate safety, security, and well-being, we face the reality that our world is a dangerous place. It's not desirable or possible to eliminate our threat sensors or our capacity to use force to protect self and other. But I believe there is an implicit theory at play, no matter how protective the intent: to stay safe, it's a battle—the survival of the fittest.

Greg finds that evolution does utilize natural selection and there is a bias, a selection preference. The law is indeed the survival of the fittest. But wait, there's more. Who are the fittest? This integrative scientist demonstrates across multiple disciplines, beginning before the earliest history of our planet to this very day, that the fittest—cue the theme from Rocky IV, "Eye of the Tiger"—are those entities, individuals, and groups that forge inclusive, connection-enhancing solutions to the dangers of isolation, death, and extinction.

In a subsequent e-mail exchange, Greg commented on our collective struggles with this imperative: "It seems clear to me from the evolutionary saga that the answer to our challenges, which can all be understood as separation-fear induced, can be found in our creative implementation of attachment solutions. This emerges from our biological pores as our spiritual imperative to be connected. However it is still an open question whether we have actually evolved far enough to actually institute more encompassing attachment solutions that mutualize the interests of out-groups as well as in-groups. I think this is the lesson the Hebrew writer of the Noah story was trying to tell. We can blow it as a species and then the evolutionary process would continue along with another 'chosen' species enjoying a selection bias by accruing traits that provide attachment solutions and their attendant survival advantages. We sure are on an evolutionary adventure."

The world is burning. How we respond to our returning warriors and the traumas of war makes all the difference. Let us together transform the fragmentation and dissociation war creates and truly welcome home our service members, veterans, and families. Let's invest in the resources that make healing possible. Let's use our voices for real dialogue, build peaceful communities, and prevent war.

Three Poems of Love and War

The First Casualties

The first casualties
are thinking, feeling and being
dreaming, imagining, laughing, and crying.

September 11 was an endless loop
a visual blur of pain,
then the announcer stopped,
recited the names of the dead.
one by one
they came to life.

Benumbed or caught up in ill-will
How can we understand when we can't stand?
How can we respond, when response ability is in such short supply?

Monomaniacal thinking hijacks religion
turns it into ideology
the person vanishes
Have I got an idea for you:
    It's to die for
A romance with death.
The precious other
thou
so necessary to think, feel and be,
is sacrificed at the altar of absolute purity

You infect me and mine—I expel you
rid the world of impurity
pernicious sameness reigns supreme
you strike at me, I eradicate you, "evil-doer"
and the beat goes on
tragic misrecognition breeds action that is
sticky
it pulls irresistibly for like-minded reaction
You know how easy it is
we get sucked in.

A teenager once whispered:
"I wish I had the balls of those kids at Columbine."
His father deserted him, he can't grieve and glorifies rage
"Ya feel me?" he asks.
I say:
Maybe it takes real balls not to go off in blind rage - to stop, look and listen.
Maybe the person next to you can help.
Where is the fertile, durable other?

Respond with love, not might, I hear,
  Ugh
What a force love is when founded in standing and understanding and
bearing the impossible.
It takes all our power to stop, look and listen,

to protect and nourish and share
the gift of response ability

That I Cannot Do

"That I cannot do," the Godfather said to Bonasera, when the undertaker asked
for justice on the day Sicilian fathers
entertain such requests.
"Your daughter is still alive"
said Don Corleone.

The undertaker's whispers asked for murder,
Measure is needed even
when dispensing
vengeance

I would if I could
if I had the power of life and death
like the suits

I would prevent harm from coming to David:
Colonel, social worker, father, comrade-in-arms
of peace and healing.
I would protect him and the soldier-therapists,
chaplains, and mental health
techs under his command
Women, men, seasoned hands and newbies
All headed into the hornets nest
we sat, spoke and listened
in stillness
felt the energy of sanctuary
looked each other in the eye
they spoke their fears hopes and struggles,
in two and a half hours we touched

I would if I could
protect and watch over them
like a good father
a godfather
heavenly father
I am not
though my impact is not
inconsequential

I would keep them safe keep them alive,
feel your weight on the chair, sink in, soft belly
rises and falls,
we practice meditation together
after ten minutes I suggest
they shift their attention back

but no one moves
nary a whisper
jumping jacks leaping up for refills of coffee
  are all still
out of the quiet depth they speak
one by one
they speak of their families
the ache of separation: "My mom is sick; who will care
for her?" "I'll miss my first baby's birth. Will she know me
when I return?"
  If I return (unspoken)

jacks in the box
we all sit together
counting our breaths
stopping looking, listening,
recognizing, remembering and returning
to body and breath, flesh and blood, here and now
we wish safety equanimity
strength and peace of mind to loved ones, to all of us,
to ourselves
and no one wants to stop

they say pre-deployment everyone's so
toughened up
but rest, energy, silent closeness,
peace and life are flowing here still
and sure

L'chaim
To life

maybe they don't want it to end
because they know
and they don't know
what is
to come

David calls a break, has to leave early

to prepare for an IED detection field exercise
I know he is leaving
for nine months
enough time for a baby
we hug unabashedly
I cradle his head against my chest
he points to the little Buddha I gave him, tucked inside the chest pocket
of his cammies
I still don't get it until he says "love ya,"
that's what I whispered in his ear at my place
when his friends sent him off,
I get it
he is saying goodbye

L'chaim
To life

I would if I could
heal and protect,
it happens, you know
mysterious energy
like a shaman
I could do it, maybe
but do I want to take it all on? make it mine?
their fate?

I see each one of them in my mind's eye
their beauty, noble and fragile
I let them flow in me
and then, like them,
I get on with it

Passing over the Cascades then Shasta
on the return
the tears come

I would if I could,
if I had the power of the suits, the
power of life and death over

young lives

That I cannot do

"But, if some unlucky accident should befall him, if he should get shot in the head by a police officer, or hang himself in his jail cell, or if he's struck by a bolt of lightning—then I'm going to blame some of the people in this room, and that I do not forgive"—said Don Corleone.

Should something befall David
grief washes over me now
I know
of course
the awful possibility

I can only imagine my helpless rage

this senseless war

Day of Atonement

In a moment of forgetting, gazing at a photo of a soldier,
it comes to me:

I'm born of brokenness
and damage

He was my father but I didn't know him.
driven by the blind struggle to forget, maybe to heal
he took a shortcut to redemption

"I did some things during the war."

I glean a few details here and there, across the decades,
like scattered dispatches from the front,
thirty years after his death

his daughter says
he never spoke about it
my mother too, he never spoke to her

may have killed people
feet froze, almost amputated
surgery in England
Lost his father suddenly, age four
one brother during, one right after
the war

Where did the men go?

 "I did some things during the war."
"I wasn't proud of"
 "I couldn't go back."

threw himself into "The Cause"
empower the disenfranchised workers

swept up in the fight for justice
he threw himself into my mother

I wanted to know
my creation story
"How old was I? Six months? A year?"

her accounts change;
memory and inclination are subject
to conditions on the ground

"He left, that's it," she says.
"I wanted to take you with me," he says much later,
the year he died

* * *

A young man, I'm reweaving the threads
How do the pieces fit?

The holocaust as mini-series with Meryl Streep

I wept all night.
Years pass, the show is on again

"Come watch Dad, it's powerful."
"I've seen too much," he says.

I know him now, met him at 24,
he was 56,
when we hugged the first time in Venice California he
almost squeezed the air out of me.

We repaired fences, pounded nails, smell of cedar planks,
sweating alongside him, whew
  the joy

I laid large pieces of red tile in the ground outside the sliding doors
in the valley of Saint Fernando, on Noble Avenue
when there were still 2 acre plots

collected black walnuts on the ground, from big trees, mixed in
with piles of leaves
some were rotten
apricot, orange, cherry, tangerine, apple trees
some fragrant with blossoms, some heavy with fruit.

* * *

He develops this hacking cough
it's the smoking he says, but he doesn't stop
he's puffing away as we drive to his medical appointment
I'm pissed
I want as much of him as I can get
he ignores his health as he ignored his son
as he ignored the wounds of war
rippling silently through his heart and soul.

The cough gets worse, pneumonia he says, but when I finally get up
the gumption to confront him
—no more of this honeymoon business—

he owns up: it's leukemia.
Thought I had all the time in the world
to repair and reconnect, but no

his condition worsens, four years after we met, his doctor calls
"Come now, if you want to see him again."
I leave Boston, spend three months with him daily in his hospital room.

One day as I arrive at the hospital he's marching madly
down the hall, flailing about
dragging the IV bag on the ground behind him
gown all undone, needle still in his arm,
he's screaming
"They want to kill me!"
    yes

Nurses desperate rush when they see me, "he's asking for you"
like a Commander calling "Medic! Soldier down!"

I get him back to his room, wash off the blood and
change his clothes. He lays down and tells me

"I want to go home." Back to the cherry and apricot trees.

But his wife and his new doctor say no, and I don't have the say
so I'm just his son

* * *

Twenty five years later I ask
why am I throwing myself
into working with warriors and families?
why have I caught this passion?
Helping them knit themselves back together,
build new heart tissue
reweave broken narrative materiel,
Am I repairing my dad? Healing myself?
maybe, not quite, not completely

Born of damage, the brokenness of war,
a man's search to hold together,
to keep from unraveling

"He was the life of the party, he played the piano, he sang show tunes, he was
handsome, he was 'Everything I Wanted,'"
says my mother, now 95

Once over coffee at Mel's Diner on Geary, at 85, she said
"You look like Bob now, the look you have."

my father enters my mother her
mind, from left field,
this time it's a blessing
    their love is palpable
and her eyes grow watery as she describes the look she saw
on my face, his look, on my face

We are what we make of the cards we're dealt
they made   me

Did the passion bind his wounds, knit him together?
was there tenderness? love?
"The Cause" was the gasoline
was lust the spark?
so strong, it made an anxious woman "Risk Everything."
    they risked it all: marriages, kids
their son-to-be

I see myself at five: I'm throwing my pink ball against the wall,
catch a la solitaire,
    a dark cloud trailing
envelops me in loneliness

other kids have dads

Don't get me wrong
I'm glad to be here
grateful for this life

it's just that
coming into this world
this way
filled me with shame
I helped so many with theirs
shame was foreign to me

  a boy feels like a foreigner without his father

* * *

I see him now, as I gaze into the face of the grizzled soldier,
a man's face, features ruddy and rugged,
I remember, on this Day of Atonement:
the image from *Life* magazine, now on the cover of *War and the Soul*
is one he liked

a photo journalist
he knew good pictures when he saw them,
liked them black and white, gritty and earthy

but being drawn to this image
is not a matter of aesthetics.
Something resonates, something missing
in the eyes of the soldier. His eyes say "Vacancy."

I'm up at night, heartbeats out of whack,
What is this? Moan? Muffled sob? Strangled cry? Suffocated scream?
Cri de coeur
Ocean of tears
I can barely form the word: daddy

* * *

Steve, first one I told
he's ex-Army, former Ranger, injured face and hands in explosion
different fathers, different wars, same story
American troops make babies with Vietnamese
women, hell, that's just the tip of the iceberg.

I see now; we're comrades-in-brokenness
we go way back
children born of war's damage
my shame ebbs,
I have plenty of company

They did some things in the war
They saw too much
horrors that hurtled them
toward passion
and a hidden wish: turn death into life

oh the collateral damage, we
kids try to layer back unraveled threads of connective tissue
repair unseen wounds

light enters now, through the breakage
illuminating all of war's casualties
it's not just US—but birds and fishes, air and water and earth, generations

unborn

* * *

I come to the hospital, but he's not in his room.
how far can he get? he's in a renal coma
I search everywhere
finally find him in Med-Surg: emergency peritoneal dialysis.

I push pass the nursing staff, shouts get louder and louder, "You can't go in
there!" I open the door to the operating room

There he is, his body racked by spasms, coughing fits lift him off the table, blood
all over

so much for the blessings of renal failure, a peaceful death
so much for Do No Harm
heroes united in combating
the arch enemy: death.
I vow not to return

Next day I spend with Lizzie
my seven year old niece
Returning from the zoo, she crashes.

I lay down in another room
afternoon sun hot, bright
I doze off and begin falling, tumbling down a long tunnel
at the bottom of the tunnel
clear as day

there he is
sitting up cross-legged in his hospital bed,
distended Buddha belly,
gown up around his thighs.

I begin to speak,
walk him through the last moments,
"You can let go, it's okay," I say

He laughs and says "Buddhism schmuddhism,
I just want you to know
how much it means that you came,
that you're here with me"

And we hug.

Basking, I slowly begin the return back up the tunnel,
When I arrive I try to open my eyes, but I can't.
I'm alert but don't feel any sensation.
When I try to move, I can't.
Must be half hour later, I'm able to move a finger, then a hand
I get up,
shaky, awestruck, full

It's Father's Day, 1979

That night I see a cockroach crawling slowly along the linoleum
near the garbage cabinet
under the sink in the kitchen.

I watch as it moves, slower and slower,
then it stops.

the visible and invisible worlds
are speaking goodbye

The next morning I get a call
when I arrive he's gone

Vacated the premises

* * *

I have become his son, and he, my father.

my passionate flawed warrior dad
   we found each other
   by the bedside,
   in the walnut groves,
   in my mother's eyes,
   in the language
   between worlds

now I wish you

   "the wideness, the foolish loving spaces

   full of heart."

Notes

—•●•—

Introduction

1. Nicholas Kristoff, "A Veteran's Death, the Nation's Shame," *New York Times*, April 15, 2012, www.nytimes.com/2012/04/15/opinion/sunday/kristof-a-veterans-death-the-nations-shame.html?pagewanted=all.

2. Dexter Filkins, "Operators of Drones Are Faulted in Afghan Deaths," *New York Times*, May 30, 2010, www.nytimes.com/2010/05/30/world/asia/30drone.html?module=Search&mabReward=relbias%3As%2C%7B%222%22%3A%22RI%3A12%22%7D&_r=0.

3. "Thousand-yard Stare," Wikipedia, http://en.wikipedia.org/wiki/Thousand-yard_stare (last accessed July 5, 2015).

4. T. Shanker and M. Richtel, "In New Military, Data Overload Can Be Deadly," *New York Times,* January 16, 2011, www.nytimes.com/2011/01/17/technology/17brain.html?pagewanted=all&_r=0.

5. Rene Spitz, *Dialogues From Infancy* (New York: International Universities Press, 1963).

6. "A Review of Post-Deployment Reintegration," Coming Home Project, http://cominghomeproject.net/sites/all/files/images/Complete%20DCoE%20Report.pdf.

7. Richard Engel, in an interview with Rachel Maddow, *The Rachel Maddow Show*, MSNBC, June 12, 2014, available on YouTube at www.youtube.com/watch?v=wbR6jwEfQzQ.

8. "Get Together," written by Chet Powers, Irving Music Inc., 1964.

9. Marine Corps—USMC Community, "Great Quote" [Archive], www.leatherneck.com/forums/archive/index.php/t-15431.html (last accessed on July 5, 2015).

10. Joseph Bobrow "Military Suicides Rise, Despite 900 Programs," *Huffington Post*, March 22, 2013, www.huffingtonpost.com/joseph-bobrow/veteran-suicide-rate_b_2936244.html.

11.   Joseph Bobrow, "Learning from Marines about Military Suicides," *Huffington Post*, March 28, 2013, at www.huffingtonpost.com/joseph-bobrow/learning-from-marines-abo_b_2972854.html.

12.   Dan Lamothe, "New Obama Plan Calls for Implanted Computer Chips to Help U.S. Troops Heal," *Washington Post*, August 27, 2014, www.washingtonpost.com/news/checkpoint/wp/2014/08/27/new-obama-plan-calls-for-implanted-computer-chips-to-help-u-s-troops-heal/.

13.   Sebastian Junger, "U.S. Veterans Need to Share the Moral Burden of War," *Washington Post*, May 24, 2013, www.washingtonpost.com/opinions/sebastian-junger-us-veterans-need-to-share-the-moral-burden-of-war/2013/05/24/726d7576-c3b9-11e2-914f-a7aba60512a7_story.html.

14.   "Remembering Maya Angelou: Bill Clinton," Eslkevin's Blog, June 12, 2014, http://eslkevin.wordpress.com/2014/06/12/remembering-maya-angelou-bill-clinton/.

Chapter I

1.   Romans 8:22–25

2.   Dick Dorworth, www.dickdorworth.com/ (last accessed on July 5, 2015).

3.   Jonathan Topaz, "Mcdonough: Obama 'Madder than Hell' on VA Scandal," Politico, May 18, 2014, www.politico.com/blogs/politico-live/2014/05/mcdonough-obama-madder-than-hell-on-va-scandal-188734.html.

4.   Les Blumenthal, "Senator: VA Lying about Number of Veteran suicides," McClatchy, April 23, 2008, Last accessed on July 5, 2015 at www.mcclatchydc.com/2008/04/23/34718/senator-va-lying-about-number.html.

5.   Eric Lichtblau, "V.A. Punished Critics on Staff, Doctors Assert," *New York Times*, June 15, 2014, www.nytimes.com/2014/06/16/us/va-punished-critics-on-staff-doctors-assert.html?_r=0.

6.   Jennifer Janisch, "Email Reveals Deliberate Effort by VA hospital to Hide Long Patient Waiting lists," CBS News, May 9, 2014, Last accessed on July 5, 2015 at www.cbsnews.com/news/email-reveals-effort-by-va-hospital-to-hide-long-patient-waits/.

7.   "Veterans' Advocate Steve Robinson Dies," Veterans Today, June 16, 2014, www.veteranstoday.com/2014/06/16/veterans-advocate-steve-robinson-dies/.

8.   "DOD and VA Can't Prove Their PTSD Care is Working, Study Claims." Last accessed on July 5, 2015, www.nbcnews.com/health/health-news/dod-va-cant-prove-their-ptsd-care-working-study-claims-n136371.

9.   Joseph Bobrow, "Realizing the Love That Is Our Evolutionary Heritage," customer review posted on Amazon, www.amazon.com/review/RH7QR68N9Y5B4/ref=cm_cr_dp_title?ie=UTF8&ASIN=1421402203&channel=detail-glance&nodeID=283155&store=books (last accessed on July 5, 2015).

10.   "Bush Accepted 4 Cabinet Resignations," *New York Times*, November 15, 2004.

11.   Malcolm Gladwell, *Outliers: The Story of Success* (Boston: Back Bay Books, 2011), 3–11.

12.   Anne Harding, "Sense of Belonging a Key to Suicide Prevention," Reuters, April 2, 2008, www.reuters.com/article/2008/04/02/us-suicide-prevention-idUSCOL2691212 0080402.

13.   Communitas—Cyborg Anthropology, http://cyborganthropology.com/ Communitas (last accessed on July 5, 2015).

14.   "The War Within: Treating PTSD," *60 Minutes*, November 24, 2013, www. cbsnews.com/news/the-war-within-treating-ptsd/ (last accessed on July 5, 2015).

15.   Abraham Lincoln, "Second Inaugural Address," March 4, 1865, available at www.bartleby.com/124/pres32.html.

16.   "The Origin of the VA Motto," U.S. Department of Veterans Affairs, www. va.gov/opa/publications/celebrate/vamotto.pdf.

17.   Donovan Slack, "Embattled VA Watchdog Stepping Down," *USA Today*, June 30, 2015.

Chapter II

1.   Hans W. Loewald, "On the Therapeutic Action of Psychoanalysis," in *Papers on Psychoanalysis* (New Haven: Yale University Press, 1960), 221–256.

2.   *On Being*, http://www.onbeing.org/program/brother-thay-radio-pilgrimage-thich-nhat-hanh/feature/warmth/644 (last accessed on July 5, 2015).

3.   Alan Schore, "Relational Trauma and the Developing Right Brain: An Interface of Psychoanalytic Self Psychology and Neuroscience," Yellowbrick, 6, www. yellowbrickprogram.com/Papers_By_Yellowbrick/PsychologyOfTheSelf_p6.html.

4.   Howard Stein, *Beneath the Crust of Culture* (New York: Rodopi, 2004).

5.   Vamık Volkan, *Bloodlines: From Ethnic Pride to Ethnic Terrrorism* (Boulder, CO: Westview Press, 1997).

6.   Vamık Volkan, "On 'Chosen' Trauma," *Mind and Human Interaction* 3, no. 1 (July, 1991): 13.

7.   Gregg Zoroya, "Study Reveals Top Reason behind Soldiers' Suicides," *USA Today*, July 11, 2012, http://usatoday30.usatoday.com/news/military/story/2012-07-10/ army-study-soldiers-suicides/56136192/1.

8.   "The Life and Death of Clay Hunt," *60 Minutes*, March 3, 2012, www.cbsnews. com/news/the-life-and-death-of-clay-hunt/.

9.   Joseph Bobrow, "A Veteran's Suicide on 60 Minutes: Lessons Learned?" *Huffington Post*, March 12, 2013, www.huffingtonpost.com/joseph-bobrow/veteran-

suicide-60-minutes_b_2849668.html.

10. Donna Miles, "Gates: Purple Heart for PTSD 'Needs to Be Looked At,'" American Forces Press Service, May 5, 2008, www.defense.gov/news/newsarticle. aspx?id=49781.

11. "Pentagon: No Purple Heart for PTSD." C PTSD—A Way Out, March 29, 2011, http://ptsdawayout.com/2011/03/29/pentagon-no-purple-heart-for-ptsd/.

12. Tyler Boudreau, "Troubled Minds and Purple Hearts," *New York Times*, January 25, 2009, www.nytimes.com/2009/01/26/opinion/26boudreau.html.

13. "With Liberty to Monitor All," Human Rights Watch, July 2014, available at www.aclu.org/liberty-monitor-all-how-large-scale-us-surveillance-harming-journalism-law-and-american-democracy.

14. "Mass U.S. Surveillance Targeting Journalists and Lawyers Seen as Threat to American Democracy," Democracy Now!, July 29, 2014, www.democracynow. org/2014/7/29/mass_us_surveillance_targeting_journalists_and.

Chapter III

1. "Rash of Wife Killings Stuns Ft. Bragg," Associated Press, July 27, 2002, www. nytimes.com/2002/07/27/national/27BRAG.html.

2. "Murder at Fort Bragg," www.militarycorruption.com/braggmurders.htm.

3. Last accessed on website of US Army on July 5, 2015 at www.armyg1.army.mil/ dcs/.

4. Gregg Zoroya, "War-years Military Suicide Rate Higher than Believed," *USA Today*, April 25, 2014, www.usatoday.com/story/nation/2014/04/25/suicide-rates-army-military-pentagon/8060059/.

5. "Battlemind," Wikipedia, http://en.wikipedia.org/wiki/Battlemind (last accessed on July 5, 2015).

6. Roy Eidelson, Marc Pilisuk, and Stephen Soldz, "The Dark Side of Comprehensive Soldier Fitness," CounterPunch, March 24, 2011, www.counterpunch.org/2011/03/24/the-dark-side-of-comprehensive-soldier-fitness/.

7. "Defense Centers of Excellence for Psychological Health and Traumatic Brain Injury," Wikipedia, http://en.wikipedia.org/wiki/Defense_Centers_of_Excellence_for_Psychological_Health_and_Traumatic_Brain_Injury (last accessed on July 5, 2015).

8. *Military Medicine* 177, no. 8 (August 2012): 883–998.

9. "The Theater of War," www.outsidethewirellc.com/projects/theater-of-war/ overview.

10. "A Review of Post-Deployment Reintegration," Defense Centers of Excellence for Psychological Health and Traumatic Brain Injury, available at http://

cominghomeproject.net/sites/all/files/images/Complete%20DCoE%20Report.pdf.

11. "Military Suicides Up to Almost One Per Day," CBN News, June 8, 2012, www.cbn.com/cbnnews/us/2012/June/Military-Suicides-Up-to-Almost-One-Per-Day/.

12. Quotes on resilience are from Patrick Martin-Breen and J. Marty Anderies, "Resilience: A Literature Review," Bellagio Initiative, November 2011, http://opendocs.ids.ac.uk/opendocs/bitstream/handle/123456789/3692/Resilience%20A%20Literature%20Review_summary.pdf?sequence=2.

13. John Amato, "Remembering Rumsfeld: 'You Go To War With The Army You Have,'" Crooks and Liars, December 14, 2006, http://crooksandliars.com/2006/12/15/remebering-rumsfeld-you-go-to-war-with-the-army-you-have-not-the-army-you-might-want-or-wish-to-have-at-a-later-time.

14. "As Palestinians Go to ICC, Human Rights Watch Alleges Israeli War Crimes for Shooting Fleeing Gazans," Democracy Now!, August 6, 2014, www.democracynow.org/2014/8/6/as_palestinians_visit_icc_human_rights.

15. Anne Barnard, "In Fatal Flash, Gaza Psychologist Switches Roles, Turning Into a Trauma Victim," New York Times, August 4, 2014, www.nytimes.com/2014/08/05/world/middleeast/gaza-strip-israel-psychologist-trauma.html.

16. Stephen Porges Infosite, www.stephenporges.com.

17. Ryan Howes, "Wearing Your Heart on Your Face," Pyschotherapy Networker, www.psychotherapynetworker.org/home/2013/09/point-of-view-7/.

18. Stephen W. Porges, "Somatic Perspectives on Psychotherapy," November 2011, available at http://lifespanlearn.org/documents/somatic%20perspectives%20porges.pdf.

19. "The Polyvagal Theory for Treating Trauma," teleseminar session transcript featuring Stephen W. Borges and Ruth Buczynski, National Institute for the Clinical Application of Behavioral Medicine, www.naturalworldhealing.com/images/stephen_porges_interview_nicabm.pdf.

20. Porges, "Somatic Perspectives on Psychotherapy."

21. Mary Jo Barrett, "Don't Try This at Home," Attachment Disorder Healing, August 22, 2014, http://attachmentdisorderhealing.com/tag/mary-jo-barrett/.

22. "The Polyvagal Theory for Treating Trauma."

23. Ibid.

24. Ibid.

25. Trish O'Kane, "What the Sparrows Told Me," New York Times, August 16, 2014, http://opinionator.blogs.nytimes.com/2014/08/16/what-the-sparrows-told-me/.

26. Gregg Zoroya, "Vietnam Veterans Still Dogged by PTSD," USA Today, August 8, 2014, http://www.usatoday.com/story/news/nation/2014/08/08/ptsd-vietnam-war-research-veterans/13721131/.

Chapter IV

1. Anita Chandra, "Children on the Home Front: The Experiences of Children from Military Families," video, RAND Congressional Briefing Series, March 1, 2010, www.rand.org/multimedia/video/2010/03/01/children_on_the_home_front.html.

2. "The Beginning after the End," Christopher Seligman Evan Cranley, BMC Rights Management US, LLC, http://songmeanings.com/songs/view/3530822107858674852/.

3. Hayes Brown, "Pentagon: Estimated 26,000 Sexual Assaults In Military Last Year," Think Progress, May 7, 2013, http://thinkprogress.org/security/2013/05/07/1972241/pentagon-sexual-assault-report/.

4. "Sundance Documentary Examines Rape In US Military," *NewsOne*, January 26, 2012, http://newsone.com/1825575/sundance-documentary-examines-rape-in-us-military.

5. Kelly Von Lunen, "Vets Connect, Heal at All-Female Retreat," *Veterans of Foreign Wars Magazine*, March 1, 2010, available at www.readperiodicals.com/201003/2012681071.html.

6. "Prayers for Peace," video, https://vimeo.com/7520674.

Chapter V

1. David Wood, "Moral Injury: The Grunts," *Huffington Post*, March 18, 2014, http://projects.huffingtonpost.com/moral-injury/the-grunts.

2. Ibid.

3. Ibid.

4. Ibid.

5. "Moment Bush Learned of 9/11 Terror Attacks," ABC News, September 11, 2012, http://abcnews.go.com/US/September_11/photos/moment-bush-learned-911-terror-attacks-14476011/image-14476160.

6. "'This Is Not Iraq': Video," transcript of Kerry's MSNBC Interview," *All in with Chris Hayes*, MSNBC, September 5, 2013, www.msnbc.com/all/not-iraq-video-transcript.

7. Wood, "Moral Injury: The Grunts."

8. Betsey Bruce, "MHP Captain Ron Johnson Takes Charge in Ferguson," Fox 2 Now, August 14, 2014, http://fox2now.com/2014/08/14/missouri-highway-patrol-to-take-over-policing-in-ferguson/.

9. Wood, "Moral Injury: The Grunts."

10. Ibid.

11. Ibid.

12. Taimoor Shah and Graham Bowley, "U.S. Sergeant Is Said to Kill 16 Civilians in Afghanistan," *New York Times*, March 11, 2012, www.nytimes.com/2012/03/12/world/asia/afghanistan-civilians-killed-american-soldier-held.html?pagewanted=all.

13. Elisabeth Bumiller and John H. Cushman Jr., "Suspect's Multiple Tours Call Attention to War Strain," *New York Times*, March 17, 2012, www.nytimes.com/2012/03/18/us/suspects-deployments-put-focus-on-war-strains.html?pagewanted=all.

14. Jack Healy, "Apology, but No Explanation, for Massacre of Afghans," *New York Times*, August 22, 2013, www.nytimes.com/2013/08/23/us/an-apology-but-no-explanation-from-soldier-who-massacred-civilians.html; and Jack Healy, "Soldier Sentenced to Life Without Parole for Killing 16 Afghans," *New York Times*, August 23, 2013, www.nytimes.com/2013/08/24/us/soldier-gets-life-without-parole-in-deaths-of-afghan-civilians.html.

15. "Army Reviews Notorious Drug after Afghan Massacre," RT.com, March 26, 2012, http://rt.com/usa/army-drug-mefloquine-bales-500/.

16. Healy, "Apology, but No Explanation, for Massacre of Afghans."

17. "Army Reviews Notorious Drug after Afghan Massacre."

18. Mark Benjamin, "Robert Bales Charged: Military Works To Limit Malaria Drug in Midst of Afghanistan Massacre," Huffington Post, March 25, 2012, www.huffingtonpost.com/2012/03/25/robert-bales-malaria-drug_n_1378671.html.

19. Healy, "Soldier Sentenced to Life Without Parole for Killing 16 Afghans."

20. David Wood, "Moral Injury: The Recruits," *Huffington Post*, August 14, 2014, http://projects.huffingtonpost.com/moral-injury/the-recruits.

21. Wood, "Moral Injury: The Grunts."

22. *The Unknown Known*, documentary film by Errol Morris (2013), www.imdb.com/title/tt2390962/.

23. Neville Symington, *Narcissism: A New Theory* (London: Karnac, 1993).

24. Stanley McChrystal, *My Share of the Task: A Memoir* (New York: Portfolio, 2013).

25. Michael Eric Dyson, conveying a saying from his pastor, on *ESPN First Take*, May 23, 2014.

26. "Democratic Senator Stands Up to White House on War Powers Act." Liberaland, October 6, 2014, available at www.alan.com/2014/10/06/democratic-senator-stands-up-to-white-house-on-war-powers-act/.

Chapter VI

1. "John McCrae," Wikipedia, http://en.wikipedia.org/wiki/John_McCrae.

2. Santayana Edition, http://iat.iupui.edu/santayana/content/santayana-quotations.

3.   "Mike Mullen Extended Interview," video, *Colbert Report*, October 1, 2014, http://thecolbertreport.cc.com/videos/8f6kuv/exclusive---mike-mullen-extended-interview.

4.   Ibid.

5.   *The Tempest*, Act 2, scene 2, 33–41, available at www.enotes.com/shakespeare-quotes/strange-bedfellows.

6.   "What Does Hamas Really Want? Israeli Journalist Gideon Levy on Ending the Crippling Blockade of Gaza," Democracy Now!, July 22, 2014, www.democracynow.org/2014/7/22/what_does_hamas_really_want_israeli.

7.   "Uri Avnery on Gaza Crisis," Democracy Now!, August 8, 2014, www.democracynow.org/2014/8/8/uri_avnery_on_gaza_crisis_his.

8.   David Vergun, "Desire to Be Resilient Can Sometimes Mask Underlying Depression," U.S. Army, September 22, 2014, http://www.army.mil/article/134002.

9.   Wood, "Moral Injury: The Grunts."

10.   Wood, "Moral Injury: Healing," *Huffington Post*, March 20, 2014, http://projects.huffingtonpost.com/moral-injury/healing.

11.   Malcolm Gladwell, *David and Goliath* (New York: Little, Brown and Company, 2013).

12.   "Former U.N. Special Rapporteur Richard Falk on the Legitimacy of Hope in the Palestinian Struggle," Democracy Now!, October 21, 2014, www.democracynow.org/2014/10/21/former_un_special_rapporteur_richard_falk#.

13.   Scott Shane, "In Din Over Iran, Rattling Sabers Echo. S. Shane," *New York Times*, February 21, 2012, www.nytimes.com/2012/02/22/world/middleeast/in-din-over-iran-echoes-of-iraq-war-news-analysis.html.

14.   Much of this discussion comes from my *Huffington Post* piece, "Dosey Doe to War: It Never Gets Old," *Huffington Post*, January 14, 2015, www.huffingtonpost.com/joseph-bobrow/dosey-doe-to-war-it-never-gets-old_b_6161286.html.

Coda

1.   Greg Friccione, *Compassion and Healing in Medicine and Society: On the Nature and Use of Attachment Solutions to Separation Challenges* (Baltimore: Johns Hopkins University Press, 2011).

Acknowledgments

There are many people I want to thank:

All the veterans, service members, their families, children, and care providers with whom I've had the honor of "living a bit of life together."

The Coming Home Project team, comrades-in-arms (of peace), without whom none of this would have been possible: Chad Peterson, Steve Torgerson, Mary Dudum, David Rabb, Therese Garrett, Beth Olengerber, Sandy Peters, Jerri Lee Young, Nathan Johnson, Carrie Knowles, Lisa Cruse, Wanda Garner, Sandy Peters, Sally Broder, Mark Pinto, Catherine Morris, Bob Bradley, Ed and Kathy Dieden, Dave Walker, Nancy Saum, Ilene Serlin, Susan Strouse, and others. With logistical support from Libby White, Amanda Schoeneman, Jim Hatzapolous, Eric Torgerson, and our invaluable retreat planner Nicolette Oliaro.

Loren Krane, for the quality and education of our psychotherapist cohort. Maureen Devine, for her administrative support. Coming Home Project psychotherapists who volunteer their professional services.

Dan Lowenstein and University of California TV San Diego, for their support of the "Invisible Wounds of War" live video-teleconference series. John Briere, Robyn Walser, Keith Armstrong, Erica Curran, Mai-Ling Garcia, Alicia Lieberman, Darrah Westrup, David Rabb, and Steve Torgerson, for their excellent presentations. Karl Marlantes, for a good weekend presenting together and for his interest and support.

Old friends Susan Kerman and Bill Barger, for reading the manuscript and providing feedback and encouragement. Joseph Caston, for his interest in my writing and for sharing his. Arnie Kotler and Noelle Oxenhandler, for their editorial suggestions.

Tom Rosbrow, for his interest and support. Vamık Volkan, for his interest and a lifetime of original clinical and psychopolitical contributions. Helen Marlo and Larry D'Arcangeles, for their support and encouragement. Keith Armstrong, Steve Xenakis, Mary Carstensen, and Paul Reickhoff, for their support.

Our donors and contributors, including David Gelbaum and the Iraq and Afghanistan Development Impact Fund, Bob Woodruff Foundation, McCormick Foundation, Kaliopeia Foundation, Frederick Lenz Foundation, Carrie Laureno and Google, Marin-San Francisco Jewish Teen Foundation, Shinnyo-en Foundation, Jerry and Paula Baker, Ed McClelland, Camp Newman, Presidio Riding Club, and many others.

Thich Nhat Hanh and Chan Không, for planting seeds that would grow. Robert Aitken-Roshi, for his love of peace and justice and for bearing witness with his life. Patricia Mushim Ikeda and Sharon Salzberg, for their interest and encouragement.

David Rabb and Steve Torgerson—brothers on the path. Tenzin Tethong, for his friendship and support. Tran Dinh Song, for his friendship and knowledge. Lawrence Wilkerson, for his interest.

My mother Helen and my father Robert, for fighting for social justice. My son Aaron, my sisters Rosy and Lucy, my brother-in-law Steven, my nieces Cassandra, Lauren, and Maria, and my nephews Demian and Jakob, for their support and love.

His Holiness the Dalai Lama, for his lifelong work of peace and for writing the foreword.

In memory of Steve Robinson.

About the Author

———•◦•———

Joseph Bobrow, PhD, is a psychoanalyst, Zen master, and author of *Zen and Psychotherapy: Partners in Liberation*. He is the founding director of Coming Home Project, whose evidence-based programs for Iraq and Afghanistan veterans, families, and care providers have served thousands nationwide. He teaches extensively and lives in Santa Barbara.